How to Run Your School Successfully

D1111883

Related titles:

Michael Marland and Rick Rogers: *How to be a Successful Form Tutor*
Jean Rudduck and Julia Flutter: *How to Improve Your School*
Chris Turner: *How to Run Your Department Successfully*
Helen Gunter: *Leading Teachers*

HOW TO RUN YOUR SCHOOL SUCCESSFULLY

Adrian Percival
and
Susan Tranter

continuum
LONDON • NEW YORK

Continuum International Publishing Group
The Tower Building   15 East 26th Street
11 York Road   New York
London SE1 7NX   NY 10010

British Library Cataloguing-in-Publication Data
A catalogue record for this book is available from the British Library.

ISBN 0 8264 7043 2 (hardback)   0 8264 7044 0 (paperback)

Designed and typeset by Ben Cracknell Studios
Printed and bound in Great Britain by Antony Rowe Ltd, Chippenham, Wiltshire

Contents

CHAPTER 1

The best job there is

An experience that many teachers have shared is the comment from friends and acquaintances that they 'wouldn't want your job'. This is normally accompanied by expressions of astonishment that anyone in their right mind would choose to teach, and that choosing to teach adolescents must surely be a symptom of some deep psychiatric condition. Sadly the reaction of some teachers is that they don't know why they do it either, but more commonly teachers will say that this is the best job there is, that there is a real reward in working with young people, they are funny and kind and interesting and that helping them learn and giving them life chances is something that cannot be traded.

Interestingly though many of these self-same teachers react towards their headteachers in just the same way. How many heads have had the experience of colleagues saying to them that they 'wouldn't want your job'. So why do people do it? And furthermore, how is it that those who do (for the most part) enjoy it so much.

Perhaps it is first worth unpacking why headship seems to others to be such a bad deal. To judge from the public face of school leadership it would appear that heads are pawns in the game of education. They are set targets by – well practically everyone – there is a constant stream of bureaucracy landing almost daily on the desks of heads from local and national government, there is apparently increasing indiscipline within schools and decreasing parental support; and whatever powers heads did have to deal with both of these are being gradually removed. Heads have to manage everything with no money, are generally held responsible for all the ills of society and preside over declining standards as evidenced by improving or worsening results. On the face of it there doesn't seem to be much going for the job of secondary headteacher.

While the catalogue of unpleasantness above will ring true to many headteachers there must be something else which makes this the best job there is. What is it?

For many of us drawn into school leadership the attraction can be summed up very simply. It is the opportunity to make a difference. A classroom teacher has the privilege of making a difference to many hundreds of young people that they teach. They make a difference to these individuals through the personal interaction they have and as a result of their passion and skill for teaching their subject. Teaching offers a unique sense of satisfaction. The opportunity to make a difference to the lives of so many young people is a privilege. Our pupils only get one chance at their school education, which is why it is so important to ensure that the experience is a valuable one. Teachers have the responsibility not only of helping each of our pupils to make the most of their education; we also have the responsibility of helping to shape the society of tomorrow.

If teachers can make this much difference, how much more difference can a headteacher make? People are attracted to headship because they passionately believe this is where the biggest difference can be made. Secondary heads occupy a unique position in education, backed by their governors they are in a position to set out their preferred future for the school and to set about achieving this. They do this with a large amount of money behind them and a considerable number of expert staff. The people who want to do this want to do it because they have a vision for education of young people and wish to make it happen. This vision is most powerful when it is based in a clear set of values that form the framework within which young people can be helped to grow. For this is what it is really about. Any parent would wish their children to achieve their very best exam results and for this reason target setting and its associated systems are important, but this isn't what schools are for. Schools and school leadership are about establishing a set of values within which young people learn, where they learn to become productive and mature members of their community and of society at large. School leadership therefore has an enormous responsibility to make a difference to the world in which we live. This is the challenge and this is the privilege.

So where does the gloomy list above fit into all of this. These are the challenges that we face and form part of the reason for this book. School leadership is the best job there is, but it is by no means the easiest. The starting-off point for any leader is their preferred future; in order to arrive at the destination then it is clearly important to know what the destination is. But it is perhaps better to think of the journey to the destination not so much as a route map along clearly signposted roads, but rather as trek through occasional high hard places surrounded by low swampy ground. To arrive at the destination requires resolve and spirit, and it requires a good strong machete for cutting through the undergrowth. The undergrowth in question is the plethora of initiatives that land almost daily on our desks from central and local governments.

The key question about any initiative presented from outside the school is 'does this fit our school and our priorities?' If the answer is 'no' then it must be discarded. This is sometimes difficult and sometimes means that the letter of the law isn't followed, but the maxim is that the school must follow its own priorities.

A particular example is the introduction of the key stage 3 literacy strategy. At a previous school pupils' literacy difficulties were causing problems with accessing the curriculum and therefore depressing attainment. We put in place a series of measures strikingly like the literacy strategy that surfaced some years later. Having moved schools when the literacy strategy was launched our first reaction was to welcome it, and indeed the focus on teaching styles in the English curriculum is beneficial. But the element of the strategy that focused upon literacy across the curriculum that had been so important at this previous school did not seem nearly so relevant at this school. There were other issues that were more important priorities, for example schemes of work, assessment and quality of teaching. Consequently the decision was made that we would not adopt this aspect of the strategy as, to be done properly, it would require large amounts of time and energy for the whole school which would be bought at the expense of our key priorities. The lesson here is twofold: first it is important to focus on a small number of priorities but make sure they are done well; secondly that external change should be adopted where it is good and aligned with school priorities, but school leadership must have the courage to adapt or even reject external initiatives where they dilute the energy of the school from its main goal. As Ronnie Woods (2002) found from his *Enchanted Heads* research, 'imposed change is to be taken, adapted and made to work in their schools'.

Establishing the vision

Naturally enough in order to establish what fits in with the school's priorities clarity about these priorities is essential. In this section we will explore how the framework of values, aims and vision leads to the planning priorities and ultimately the action that results in school improvement.

Before embarking upon this it is worth spending some time considering the purpose of schools. The response to this depends upon who is asked. The Labour government elected in 2001, for example, saw education in terms of economics.

> In the twenty-first century, to be prosperous, the economy will depend heavily on the creativity and skills of its people. In a knowledge economy it is vital that we tap the potential of every one of our citizens
>
> *The Secretary of State for Education (DfES, 2002)*

It can be deduced from this that the function of education is economic competitiveness. Now this may be a tactic for liberating finance from the Treasury, but the straightforward utilitarian viewpoint that a more skilled workforce results in greater economic competitiveness clearly has considerable force behind it. Education can simply be seen in terms of the acquisition of a set of skills that are necessary to get a good job and become a functioning economic unit. Many of us will have had conversations with employers who take a very similar standpoint – there is much discussion about the skills that employers need and how, for the most part, young people are found wanting.

However, a high-profile rejection of such a utilitarian view is made by such luminaries as Chris Woodhead who concentrates much more upon the liberation of the human spirit and the transference of the cultural capital of our society for example in this celebrated piece where he describes education as:

> a conversation between the generations in which the young learn what they can about the cultural inheritance upon which our humanity depends.

> … I believe our government has a primary responsibility to foster education for its own sake.

> C. *Woodhead*, Daily Telegraph, *1 March 2001*

The notion of the required skill-set for productive economic performance has dominated much recent thinking, hence the introduction of 'key skills', initially as part of General National Vocational

Qualifications in 1992 and latterly the extension of these key skills as stand-alone qualifications and the expectation in the Dearing Report (1996) that they should form a component of all post-16 programmes. There is a fundamental difficulty with skills-based education. Proponents have long argued that, with the introduction of new technology and the fast-changing nature of the modern world, anything that is learned at school is redundant. Most people, they argue, will not keep the same job for more than a few years, and in any event, who knows what skills and knowledge are required for the future. What is required, the argument goes, is that young people learn the skills to learn in future. They need to be taught thinking skills, problem-solving skills, skills in being aware of their own learning and how to improve it, teamwork skills and (lest we think content has no place at all) skills in maths, English and ICT.

This prescription is scorned by the Woodhead contingent. This is all liberal, woolly-minded nonsense, they say. What young people need is to acquire a body of knowledge, to understand the history and culture of our country, to appreciate the beauty of the ideas expressed through arts, literature and philosophy. And the way to do this is through academic study of these subjects. Skills are nothing without this context, and are impossible to teach.

There is much to commend both of these viewpoints, but perhaps they both miss the point as they focus upon the principal purpose of schooling as learning. Secondary schools are placed in a unique position in people's lives. They stand at the crossroads between childhood and adulthood. In our school we see the principal function of schools as to provide a bridge between these two stages of life. Schools have many functions, and it is undoubtedly the case that one of them is to enable young people to become qualified and to gain a good job. Another function is undoubtedly to act as guides to the beauty and depth of our culture. But above all else, schools are moral organizations. They have the function of helping to turn children who enter at eleven years old into mature adults who are ready and able to take their place as good citizens in their community and in their society. How do schools achieve this? They do it by fulfilling both of the functions described above, but they also do it by operating as moral organizations within the clear framework of values that make the ethos of the school.

It would follow, therefore, that establishing a clear framework of values is the first and key task of school leadership. Having some statement of the values of the organization serves to set the tone of what goes on, it serves as the cornerstone that anchors the school, or the yardstick by which many of the judgements that have to be made can be measured. If such a statement is well constructed it more or less precludes the need for a set of 'school rules'. For example, it is possible to envisage a school that has a set of rules about the way people should behave towards one another – readers may well work in such schools. The rules may be that pupils must not use foul language, that they must follow their teachers' directions, that they must not bully one another; they must not be rude to each other or their teachers. This set of prescriptions rapidly turns into the feeling of an organization hidebound by rules, where the rule-book must be consulted before any action is taken, it can also lead to a complex series of punishments for those who break the rules. On the other hand if the school has a value statement which says that the school regards mutual respect as its most important value then this encompasses all of the rules above – furthermore it has the advantage of being readily understood by all. Another example would be a statement that the school values the individual's right to learn, this would clearly imply that any disruption of a class is unacceptable because of the impact this has on the learning of others.

Having established the values it is then possible to move on to consider the aims of the school. Frequently this forms the second half of the couplet of 'aims and values' which are frequently referred to. This implies the similarity of the two concepts, but it is important to remember that they form two distinct ideas. Aims are more operational, where values describe the climate of the school, aims describe its purpose. It is instructive to read through the aims listed in a school prospectus (as indeed they must be according to the law). Two sets of aims are extracted below:

SCHOOL 1

We wish to do all we can to foster a love of learning and to encourage pupils to see education as a lifelong process. We will do this by:

1 providing a stable, ordered environment
2 helping all members of the school to find courses best suited to their interests/abilities
3 organizing the school in such a way that all students, regardless of gender, background or special needs, have full access to the curriculum and life of the school
4 furthering links between school, parents, community, industry and continuing education
5 improving the standard of work and public examination results

6 encouraging students to participate in the life of the school and community and initiate ways of improving the quality of life for themselves and others
7 preparing students for flexible learning, the world of work and further and higher education

SCHOOL 2

Our high expectations of achievement and behaviour; of openness, honesty, trust and mutual respect, lead to the well-ordered and purposeful environment that are the prerequisites for effective learning.

We encourage our students to work hard and to be enthusiastic in all they do. We want them to attain the highest standards of which they are capable so that they can face the challenging world ahead with confidence and assurance. We value right attitudes and strength of character and by encouraging these in our students we will help them become good citizens in their future walks of life.

We aim to ensure our students:

- are happy and safe within a rich learning environment
- succeed and achieve their full potential academically, socially, physically and personally; have the skills, knowledge and understanding to take their place as mature adults in society
- value education as a lifelong experience that will continue into the world of work and of leisure
- develop a sense of citizenship and responsibility to the community and to society as a whole

Consider the aims for school 1. To what extent do they provide clarity about what the school is hoping to achieve? To put this another way, how easy would it be for this school first to demonstrate how it is going about achieving its aims, and secondly to know whether it has achieved them? We would venture to suggest that in both cases these tasks would prove a considerable challenge. Indeed, despite the lengthy list of how the school would go about achieving its aim, there really is only one aim which is to 'foster a love of learning and see education as a lifelong process'. You may say 'So what?' – after all this aims business is just about aspiration and can never be seriously analysed. The response to this would be to ask the questioner to look at the aims of school 2. The first thing that distinguishes this piece is the clear value statement prior to the aims. But looking at the aims it would be possible to go to that school and establish the extent to which it is meeting its aims and to establish the extent to which it has procedures to secure those aims in the future. For example, the school aims for all its pupils to achieve their full academic potential. Visiting this school you may expect to find that there is a system of baseline testing where academic potential is assessed, the academic outcomes of the school – i.e. its external examination results – can be measured against this potential for each pupil and so it can be established whether the school is meeting this aim. In order to meet this aim you might expect to see that pupils have individual targets set in each subject and that there are teaching, learning and assessment strategies in place to ensure that these targets are met. Although this is, perhaps, one of the easier aims to carry out, we would contend that it is possible with all the others that are listed. To take this a step further, because these aims are operational they can be shared meaningfully with the pupils of the school, in this way they go to reinforce the ethos of the school. For example, the first aim that sets out to 'ensure pupils feel safe and happy in a constructive learning environment' can be used to ensure that pupils understand that they have a right to expect to feel happy and safe at school and also that they have a responsibility to help others to feel happy and safe in school.

Aims and values together encapsulate the vision for the school. Vision is rapidly becoming a hackneyed term. 'What is leadership?' is a question often asked; the standard answer is 'vision'. This term is losing its meaning, but while it still has one we can think of it as the preferred future for the school. And how can this preferred future be described other than in terms of the climate we aspire to and which we wish to achieve for the school. To put this another way – the aims and values of the school. Therein lies a tension. This talk of leadership vision would seem to imply that the vision resides with the school leader, or the head. This conjures up images of the charismatic speaker standing in front of the school staff setting out the vision of the school and rousing everyone to follow. There are images of great oratory from an inspiring hero figure. But what place is there for the staff of the school in all this, they become relegated to the role of meek followers, indeed this analysis of leadership would imply that one of the most important components of leadership by the hero leader is the followership of the followers he or she creates. This does not sit easily with the view of an inclusive organization where everyone makes a valid and valued contribution. An alternative view of leadership is provided by Ralph Nader:

> I start with the premise that the function of leadership is to produce more leaders, not more followers.

The function of the leader by this analysis is not so much to persuade others of the rightness of their vision, but rather to create that vision within them. Consider this, the hero head is leading a wonderful organization. The power of his or her personality and charisma sweeps all before them, everyone knows what to do and when to do it and they know that if this doesn't happen they are letting down their leader, which is something that they don't want to happen. All is well with the world, but then the leader leaves, or worse takes long-term sick leave. Suddenly the flock lose their sheepdog and they have no idea what to do, everything goes to pieces in short order leaving only a disintegrated group of people without direction.

Compare this with the inclusive leader who has created leadership in each person in the school. Each member of staff has their own vision for what should happen and how to achieve their vision. The potential recipe for fragmentation is avoided because the leader of the organization has ensured that each colleague's vision is aligned with the organizational goals and their own vision (you may ask how is this accomplished? This will be answered in a later chapter in this book). As above, everyone knows what to do and how and when to do it, but this time they know that if it doesn't happen they are letting themselves down. So far, so much the same in terms of the outcomes. Now consider the scenario described above, the leader is absent for a long period of time. How does the organization cope with this loss? As people are working as a self-sufficient units within the organization they are able to continue working towards their internalized goals without constant direction from their leader. One particularly famous leadership quote is from Lao-tzu who says:

> The good leader is he who the people revere. The great leader is he who the people say, 'We did it ourselves'.

It is for this reason that creating the vision, aims and values of the school must be a shared enterprise. All those who work in the organization (staff, governors and pupils? This is a question that can be explored later) must have the opportunity to contribute to the creation of this fundamental statement for the school and all must be able to recognize that at least some of what they have contributed is reflected in the final statement. This is the first part of creating leadership in all and the first step away from relying upon followership.

Perhaps at this point it would be appropriate to come clean about the aims of the two schools listed above. These are in fact the aims of our school, the second set resulting from a review of the aims in 1999. Before appointment to this post it seemed that, although reviewing the aims of the school might be a good exercise for a staff discussion, such an activity would be likely to prove to be a distraction from whatever more important tasks were at hand. But as it turned out we reviewed the aims of the school more as a pragmatic exercise because those that existed were unsatisfactory.

The review did indeed consist of a staff meeting where all of the staff worked in groups and recorded the things they felt were important about what, as a school, we should stand for (our values) and what we should be trying to achieve (our aims). This feedback was summarized by the senior management team, each member of which took away the written feedback from the staff and wrote up a statement of aims and values, from which were ultimately distilled the statement above. Governors then agreed this. The aims are, of course, the governors' aims for the school, as it is the governors who should set the strategic direction of the school. The governors' discussion was lengthy on the aims and largely rotated around the grammar of the statement rather than its content, which may sound a familiar scenario for those readers familiar with the workings of governing bodies.

This was, as has already been mentioned, a pragmatic response to the difficulty of having a set of aims that had no resonance for those of us working in the school. As it turned out, creating this new set of aims in the way we did has been fundamental, we believe, to the success of the school. It was the first step in forming a shared vision. Colleagues who contributed to the staff meeting could see how their contribution had been included in the final statement, and the final statement was inclusive of all the views expressed. It is interesting that they form almost no relationship whatsoever with the aims they replaced. This is indicative of the extent to which those aims did not represent any sort of shared vision. It may be argued that the opportunity was taken to change for change's sake; it would be our contention (untested admittedly) that a repeat exercise to re-establish the aims of the school would not produce any significant change. And this is because our aims and values are shared, as is our vision for the future of the school. Every day that goes by reaffirms the view of the importance of having this shared vision. It is the cornerstone of the organization and does inform all decisions and judgements that are taken.

A postscript to the visioning process. Many people ask whether pupils took part in the creation of this new direction for the school. You will observe from the account above that they did not. Was this an oversight? No. Does this indicate that the views of pupils are not regarded as important? No. This apparent omission represents part of the value system in which we operate. Pupils and their parents choose the school they join (or at least they do in our part of the country. It is clear that this is not the case for many parents and their children). In this sense they are customers choosing to 'buy' a service. It seems clear to us from this analogy that it is for the school to 'set out its stall'. In our prospectus our aims and values are reproduced inside the front cover, this is the first thing that the reader encounters, here we are saying that this is the service we provide. If you like what you see here, then we are the school for you. What we are not saying is that this is the sort of school the current population of pupils wants, but if you don't like it then we can change it. As indicated above, the statement of aims and values is the cornerstone of the organization; it is appropriate therefore to have it fixed and not dependent upon the approval of the current set of 'customers'.

The personal aspect of leadership

The survey by PWC (2001) revealed that headteachers spend a good deal more time at work when measured against comparable workers. The debate over workload that has ensued from this survey looks set to increase. There are, of course, a number of aspects to workload – and no discussion of the issues above would be complete without some analysis of the personal aspect of school leadership.

The paradigm of principle-centred leadership is fundamental to this discussion and it is this that makes the enterprise sustainable and enables us to spend that additional hour in order to achieve the desired result.

The context for the following discussion is the seven 'habits' that Covey (1996) espouses:

1   Be proactive
2   Begin with the end in mind
3   Put first things first
4   Think win-win
5   Seek first to understand before being understood
6   Synergize
7   Sharpen the saw

That being the leader is about being proactive is the first habit. The act of setting out a vision statement that underpins and indeed regulates the organization's work is vital. The headteacher is responsible for determining the agenda – this is a proactive model. For example, by exerting control over the target-setting agenda the school leader ensures that the demands are realistic and challenging. It is, in our case, a matter of some pride – the targets for each cohort that enters the school are calculated, this is then adjusted for challenge and progression – but overall, we know the capabilities of our school. And so when it comes to meeting with the LEA, we are in the position of putting forward a categorical position on our targets. This might mean in fallow years arguing for a lower target than the LEA might suggest, but in more prosperous times (to continue the metaphor) this will result in more challenging targets that might be required of us. It is about us being confident in the analysis and knowing the capacity our school has for realizing that potential.

But, moreover, this proactive characteristic is about understanding and interpreting the future. Looking forward to the school of the future, determining what is needed for our school, for our community and for our staff – this is the stuff of leadership – but it is also what makes the job exciting and never dull. More importantly, however, it is about acknowledging responsibility for the school and the organization.

The second habit acknowledges the need to think about the 'end'. School leaders should never feel victimized – although there are many who feel that their agenda is always being compromised by a circular from the DfES. Aims that reflect social need by acknowledging the educative process (in that schooling is a means to prepare people to take their place in the adult world) and also represent the ideals of potential and personal fulfilment will always have a currency whatever the political or particular pedagogical debate. School leadership is too important to be left to the maelstrom of political sway; it has to be prepared to have that sense of hope and purpose even where it is lacking in others. The school leader has to be able to see the future in their own mind and imagine what it will be like; one way to do this is to see yourself in the school, as you want it to be. See yourself talking to that student; think about the conversation you would like to have with that teacher, think about the kind of talk you want to hear at Open Evening. Responding to that situation will be a very pleasant time; and by using the imagination in this way we are able to see our future as we want it to be and by responding to the pictures we create we can think about the way we want it to look.

There is of course this personal dimension to the school leader. Put simply it is about the individual who goes to work and makes something wonderful happen. Work is what we all do (unless we win Lotto or have a personal fortune); it is very much about us going to a place, doing a job in return for a salary. And indeed this aspect of the job is no different to managing a baked bean factory. The factory manager is responsible for the number of cans of beans produced and fulfilling a quota. The school leader is responsible for taking in the students and ensuring that the product (whatever that is) is produced to time. But the school leader's task is so much more than the baked bean factory manager's – it isn't about processing inanimate objects until they taste good; it is about creating life chances for the children entrusted to us. Running a school is more than placing teachers on a production line of lessons and examinations – it is about creating an organizational culture that empowers and is sustainable. But there is the business dimension to school leadership and this will be the subject of sections where financial planning and monitoring are undertaken – we have to account for the use made of public money and demonstrate value.

How do we deal with this? Well, Cohen and Greenfield (1998) – AKA 'Ben and Jerry' said:

> When we started making ice cream in 1978 we had simple goals. We wanted to have fun, we wanted to earn a living, and we wanted to give something back to the community.

Not bad, for a pair of ice-cream sellers! Now we think that this is really important and these three things underpin the business of school leadership.

Having fun. Enjoying what you do makes so many things possible. It means that when one sits down on a Saturday night or a Sunday afternoon to work on that piece ready for Monday morning, you don't mind (or, at best, you want to do the piece) because you understand that, as school leader, if you don't do it, then the organization will not move forward in the way you want. But the headteacher needs to inject that enthusiasm and that purpose into the management or leadership team (and these terms are used, without explanation – although they are problematic in themselves). So how does the headteacher do this? By enacting this 'visioning' activity with the leadership team and by developing in them those same visions. By constantly referring to this values' framework then the vision is sustainable. And so the burden of school leadership is shared.

Secondly, the earning a living bit. Clearly the fortunes of the school leaders are inextricably linked to those of the school; headteachers rarely survive a poor Ofsted report, deputies who don't do what headteachers require of them will last a very short time! But moreover, this earning a living business really does emphasize that while we should have the aims of education and schooling firmly to the fore as we organize the teaching process – it is a job and if we don't do it well we are in trouble. Or more, positively – do it well and the rewards are not only altruistic.

Thirdly, giving something back to the community. There is in many teachers a sense of wanting to give something back. Many teachers teach because they want to tell others about their subject. They want children to enjoy the pleasures of scientific understanding and mathematical discovery (the authors are a physicist and a mathematician!). But also want others to enjoy the prosperity and life chances that they have been able to enjoy as a result of their education. Moreover it is not just about giving something back to the community, it is about being a cultural architect of that community. The school plays such a dominant part in the majority of children's experience that the school leader has the opportunity to build something that makes a real difference, that realizes society's aims in a particular manner and ensures that the education system leaves that lasting mark on the life of the individual.

School leadership is, severally, about being the chief executive, the leading professional and the cultural architect. The chief executive role is very much about allocating resources, ensuring that the 'business' of the school is carried out, and presenting and interpreting to the governing body and the LEA (where appropriate) information concerning the school's achievements. In this sense, the job of the chief executive is bound up in that of the cost management accountant, the management consultant and the role of managing the business. To do so would be to undermine the processes that are concomitant with this role. For to allocate resources means making value judgements; does the chief executive follow the parable of the talents (Holy Bible: Matthew 25: 14-30) where each is given resources according to his ability? Or do we invest heavily in those failing areas in the hope that money will help to address the issues? Again, this will be addressed later in the book.

Is it the job of the school leadership to be leading professionals? Certainly leading a team of highly qualified people demands particular strengths. But professional leadership is concerned with task achievement, with group maintenance and development and with the external representative aspect of the role. In addition, the rise of the 'strategy' and the instructive nature of school leadership – in that there is the 'way' of teaching mathematics, literacy and science – means that the school leadership has to be expert in understanding how the learning paradigms operate in order to assess the effectiveness of the model. This pressure is not a new one – the famous Ruskin speech by Callaghan (1976) sets out the position:

> On another aspect there is the unease felt by parents and others about the new informal methods of teaching which seem to produce excellent results when they are in well-qualified hands but are much more dubious when they are not . . . the goals of our education, from nursery school through to adult education, are clear enough. They are to equip children to the best of their ability for a lively constructive place in society and also to fit them to do a job of work.

Written over twenty-five years ago, there is a rejection of that 'chance' aspect – the strategies with their prescription for the lesson set out the way in which the curriculum should be delivered – this is a move on from the 'what'. The headteacher is the leading professional in the school. Working with the governing body the headteacher provides vision, leadership and direction for the school and ensures that it is managed and organized to meet its aims and targets. This is the dominant discourse of the National Standards for Headteacher's (TTA, 1998) where their professional knowledge is seen as a key attribute necessary to carry out effectively the key tasks of that role.

Indeed the role of school leader as some sort of resident inspector – in that the headteacher lives out the role of a permanent Ofsted inspector means that they have to have a deep understanding of what it is to teach to a Very Good (Grade 2) or Excellent (Grade 1) standard – and know the difference. Because the leader inevitably will be involved in a critical appraisal of the contributions of others and in the use of professional and political judgement in coordinating and reconciling and integrating these contributions. Informal contacts with staff – such as over a cup of coffee in the staff room, are highly political occasions providing opportunities for collegial influence to be exerted in both directions through 'dropping hints', 'sowing the seeds' and 'making suggestions' and that most manipulative of all activities 'making one's own idea look as though it came from someone else'.

But more so is the idea of the cultural architect. The person who builds the framework – the ethos and the values of the organization. In this context the school leaders are the core of the organization; they represent as 'persons' what it is to be part of the organization. This is manifested in the way they dress, the standards they uphold in their professional lives (such as punctuality, neatness, conduct at meetings, behaviour at social occasions and so on) and the way they deal with staff, parents and students. Is the leadership paradigm one of collegiality or one of hierarchy or one of instruction?

Increasingly the dominant discourse is that of instruction. Simply because there is aversion to risk and a concomitant desire to get it right because of the associated difficulties when it is wrong. So-called 'trendy' or 'progressive' methods have been pilloried but there has also been a rise in research that has validated particular methods. The Numeracy Strategy specifies what is to be taught and how it is to be taught – the questions and exercises are set down for the teacher. One aim is to provide a guarantee – it doesn't matter if your child's teacher is not a mathematician, if they deliver this programme then children will learn the material or possibly your child's teacher may be a mathematician but this document sets out how it is to be delivered. Such schemes have their strengths – they remove the need for lesson planning and the painstaking preparation of huge amounts of resources, they enable the teacher to concentrate on teaching the class. The size of the task and the higher expectation that are made of us all should mean that such schemes are welcomed. Life in the twenty-first century is complex and complicated and, for most, is fraught with difficulty. The issues that arise emerge so much from time and frustration; so much is possible because of technological advances but less is realized because of human frailty. We may have the means to create that perfect word-processed document but the constraints that the pursuit of perfection will place on our busy lives are prohibitive. The author Iris Murdoch wrote out her work by hand – other authors could not conceive of such a thing. To write places enormous constraints and the act of writing is made possible by the commonplace word processor – and such is the case for teachers. But the possibilities that computers suggest are only realized by the expenditure of effort and sacrifice.

Leadership paradigms are only satisfactory up to a point. Teachers need to feel part of the school organization; but with that comes a price. All those who participate in the organization's work need to have a vision for what it is they are about – that is how they sustain themselves over the days that make up the years. But also, there has to be a process that is, indeed, instructive. Because without instruction the leadership paradigm is doomed to failure; simply because of responsibility and the size of the task that lies ahead. The responsibility for the future lives of the thousand or so children that pass through the average secondary school is huge and this is no less diminished for the head of subject in charge of English and the class teacher of History who teaches 85 per cent of the week with the responsibility for the progress of some 400 children in their subject. There has to be a balance.

This book is about how to run a school. It is about how to manage this huge task in a way that enables the individual and the group to 'have fun'. It is about earning a living, in that it sets out what needs to be done to make the organization run efficiently. But it is about making sure that there is something given back to the community and to the individuals who do the giving.

This book is a practical guide to how to run a school. It is about what to do – its rationale derives from the aims and values that are set out in this chapter. Moreover, it is about a leadership paradigm that is based on fundamental and inviolate value system. There are common threads throughout the chapters and these derive from the premise that much can be achieved, that high standards of presentation are important and that systems provide data. Managing the systems and the resulting data is one thing; acting and interacting with the data to analyse and produce conclusions is another.

The next chapters will address topics including working with governors (Chapter 2), managing finance (Chapter 4) and how to market the school (Chapter 10). The themes presented in Chapter 5 move into development planning and the curriculum as well as managing the student experience. School leaders exert control over their environment and the agenda by understanding target setting and performance management (Chapter 3 and 7). No book on school leadership and management would be complete without advice on what to do when things go wrong and this will be interjected at appropriate points.

Running a school and making it happen are the outcomes that will acknowledge the work that school leaders do – ensuring that the system works, that it is sustainable and is a job that the leaders themselves want to do is where the book ends.

Bibliography and References

Covey, S. (1996) *The Seven Habits of Highly Effective People*. London: Simon & Schuster.

Cohen, B. and Greenfield, J. (1998) 'Lead with your values' in *The Book of Leadership Wisdom* ed. Peter Krass. New York: John Wiley.

Callaghan, J. (1976) Speech at Ruskin College, Oxford.

Dearing, R. (1996) *Review of Qualifications for 16–19 year olds*. London: School Curriculum and Assessment Authority. SCAA ref: COM/96/460.

DfES (2002) *14 – 19: extending opportunities, raising standards*. London: TSO.

Holy Bible

PWC (2001) *Study into Teacher Workload*. London: DfES.

Teacher Training Agency (1998) *National Standards of Headteachers*. London: TSO.
Woodhead, C. (2001) *The Daily Telegraph*, 1 March.
Woods, R. (2002) *Enchanted Heads*. Nottingham: National College of School
    Leadership.

CHAPTER 2

Getting started
On effective governance

Consider this, you have just been appointed as head of a school. What do you find around you? Well of course schools exist in many different contexts. Some are highly successful when they are taken on, some have the 'privilege' of a particular focus on their work as a result of an Ofsted category (special measures or serious weaknesses), some are just OK. Whatever the scenario it is likely that as new head you will have a view about what needs to happen in the school, and this view will almost inevitably represent a contrast with what has gone before. The major question you will face is how to get started on your campaign. This chapter aims to examine how to get started with the key players in the school, i.e. the leadership group and the governors. The leadership group is the vital tool in the head's toolkit as it must be able to take the lead on the various aspects of the school's functions. The next chapter will examine how such responsibilities might be structured and how the team can be led and managed to maximum effect. Before that some consideration must be given to the role of governors in the school. The governors are an aspect of the work of the head that cannot feasibly be carried out by anyone else and are an extremely important and potentially time-consuming part of the job. The importance of ensuring the governors work well and effectively cannot be overestimated, without this the school, and more particularly the head, will not be able to function well and effectively either.

Type	Fraction (rounded to nearest whole number)	Constituency
Parent	One third or more	Directly elected by all the parents of children at the school. Must be a parent at the time of election, but the term of office is four years whether or not the child(ren) leave the school in that time.
LEA	One fifth	As a community school we have governors directly appointed by the county council. They are political appointees and will often be elected local government members.
Staff	At least two but no more than one third	Directly elected by all the staff directly employed by the school, but excluding those who work in the school under contract to another employer. Again a four-year term of office, but this is foreshortened if the governor leaves the employment of the school.
Community	One fifth or more	These are governors who are invited by the non-community members of the governing body to serve in order to bring a particular perspective or expertise to the governing body. Typically a community governor might be someone drawn from the local business community. They might have an interest in education in general and an interest in the school concerned in particular as a result of employing its leavers. Community governors have a term of office of four years.
Sponsor	Up to two	This category would include governors appointed, for example, by sponsors of a school's specialist school application.
Head	1	As head you have the option to be a governor in an ex officio capacity. Your term of office is as long as you are head.

Table 2.1 *Constitution of community schools*

Governors

Who are the governors?

It is not the purpose of this book to explore the legal status of governors in any great depth. For such a treatment the reader is referred to *A Guide to the Law for School Governors* (DfES, 2003) or the excellent and highly comprehensive *Croner's Guides to the Law*. Rather it is a treatment of a more pragmatic nature. However, a brief overview of legalities is necessary before going further.

The regulations for governors that came into effect in 2003 opened up considerably more flexibility for governors to choose their constitution, which hitherto had been very rigid. Briefly the constitution is as follows: the governing body of a secondary school should be made up of no fewer than 9 and no more than 20 governors. The membership of the governing body are people who are broadly 'stakeholders' in the school community. The exact constitution depends upon the type of school (community, foundation, aided, etc.). For community schools the constitution is summarized in table 2.1.

Some variations are as follows:

Foundation schools

- one third or more must be parent governors
- at least two but no more than one third must be staff governors
- at least one but no more than one fifth must be LEA governors
- one tenth or more must be community governors, and
- at least two but no more than one quarter must be foundation governors or, where the school does not have a foundation, partnership governors
- the governing body may in addition appoint up to two sponsor governors

Voluntary aided schools

- at least one but no more than one tenth must be LEA governors
- at least two but no more than one third must be staff governors
- at least one must be a parent governor
- such number of foundation governors as outnumber all the other governors listed in above by two, and
- such number of foundation governors as, when they are counted with the parent governors, comprise one third or more of the total membership of the governing body

In addition

- the governing body may appoint up to two sponsor governors, and
- the person who is entitled to appoint foundation governors may appoint such number of additional foundation governors (up to two) as are required to preserve their majority

Voluntary controlled schools

- one third or more must be parent governors
- at least two but no more than one third must be staff governors
- at least one but no more than one fifth must be LEA governors
- one tenth or more must be community governors, and
- at least two but no more than one quarter must be foundation governors
- the governing body may in addition appoint up to two sponsor governors

The governing body having determined its constitution will have decided upon the maximum number of each type of governor. The reality for many governing bodies is that they are rarely fully constituted; so ensuring that vacancies are filled becomes one of the aspects of working with governors with which the head must be engaged for most of the time!

What are they for?

Legally the governors are the school. They are responsible for its conduct, for the way it serves its community, for its mission, ethos, strategy and policies. As well as being accountable to parents for all of these matters they are also accountable to the school's funding authority (in our case the county council) for the finances of the school. Significantly, the governing body are responsible for appointing the headteacher and any deputy headteachers the school may employ. In law the headteacher is responsible for the day-to-day management of the school and is accountable to the governors for the execution of this responsibility.

One of the immediate tensions that arises here is the extent to which it is reasonable to give all of these responsibilities to a group of 20 or so people who are all volunteers and who may not have any specialist expertise; but, even if they did, this would not form part of the reason for their being on the governing body. There are many analogies for the relationship between head and governors. Most typically it may be described as that of chief executive and board of directors in a commercial company, or possibly that of politicians and their civil servants. Indeed that latter analogy famously led to John Patten, Secretary of State for Education (1992–4) communicating only with chairs of governors on the assumption, it must be presumed, that this was the school-level equivalent of the minister of state in a government department. These analogies do not really help, nor do they form a useful discussion – school governors are what they are and it is up to headteachers to make that work.

It is in making it work that the relationship between the head and the governors must be found. And it is as a body that governors must be worked with for it is as a body that they hold the powers they do. Frequently the relationship with the chair of governors is emphasized. Heads talk of their weekly meetings with the chair and so forth. It is undoubtedly the case that this is a key relationship and that the chair is a significant governor. But in terms of power, with the exception of the ability to take a 'chairman's action' (i.e. to act on behalf of the governing body if an emergency arises, a power to be used sparingly if at all we would suggest), the chair has no special status in comparison with any other governor.

To explore the functions of governors a little more you will see from the list of roles and responsibilities above that governors have matters for which they are accountable to the outside world and they have a function in making the head accountable to them for what goes on within.

The accountability of governors

As already indicated governors have the responsibility for determining the strategy and vision for the school, for determining its policies and as a result its ethos. Of course, and to be quite candid about this, the ability of governors to seriously determine all of these things is significantly compromised by their constitution. They are not experts and so have to draw upon the expert knowledge in the school to determine policies and they are volunteers who can only spend a small amount of time with the school. The net result of this is that although they have the responsibility for ensuring, for example, that the National Curriculum is taught in the school there are very few practical methods by which they can exercise this responsibility other than charging the headteacher with the same responsibility. Indeed it will generally be the case that the head is considerably more aware of the things for which governors are responsible than most governors are themselves. So in this case it is most likely that the head will inform the governors that they have responsibility for ensuring that the National Curriculum is taught and then will go on to make suggestions about how that should be done. Anyone familiar with the workings of governing bodies will, we are sure, recognize that this is how it goes. Typically the work that goes into the governors exercising their responsibilities is done by the school staff and most likely the leadership team. And this is of course how it should be. Thus the responsibility to ensure certain things happen, rapidly turns into the second aspect of the role of the governors, that is to be the body to whom the head is accountable for the conduct of the school.

Accountability to the governors
It is in this capacity that the governors' role is particularly important. The head of a school is in the unusual position for someone in paid employment of not really having a boss. This is something that is frequently misunderstood by many stakeholders in the school. Parents frequently believe that they can go over the head of the head (so to speak) by contacting the local education authority (LEA), who in turn often seem to believe that the chair of governors should be the one a parent contacts as they are the ones who are in charge of the school. Of course neither of these is correct. To the extent that the head has a boss it is the whole governing body. Without the governing body then the choice would either be that the head would genuinely have no one to answer to, or they would have to be replaced by the LEA (or in the absence of an LEA, some similar body created for the purpose). There are few people with knowledge of the days before schools were locally managed who would choose to go back to those days, certainly it would not be unacceptable for heads to become completely unaccountable despots (as opposed, a cynic might say, to the accountable despots we currently have), so in the absence of a better alternative governors seem pretty good to us.

The head must present governors with the means to fulfil their responsibilities, and this means presenting them with policies that are well thought through, with alternatives and with a clear briefing on the advantages and disadvantages of any course of action. Providing this sort of information is an important discipline in school improvement. The fact that governors are responsible for strategy and policy and that they must make decisions on these matters means that policies must be clearly thought through in order that the case can be made to the (by and large) lay people who have to make the decision. The intervals between governors' meetings means that decisions of significance cannot be made hastily as governors are required to make these decisions and not the head. Although this can at times seem tedious, it is an essential part of the checks and balances of school leadership. (Of course an unscrupulous head can blame the governors for unpopular decisions – not that the authors would ever condone such behaviour in a principal-centred leader!)

The head must also provide governors with the information to hold him or her to account. This will consist of a whole range of information, definitely any performance information that is going to be published, certainly any information that looks beneath the surface of that – a good example is that we are required to publish the percentage of pupils gaining five higher grade passes – but this is a crude measure of performance. Governors will also need to know about the subject results and any value-added analysis that has been carried out and at the end of this they need to have a view about the standard of the performance. This is a good example of an occasion when the head is accountable because there are many temptations towards economy with the truth, or spin. We never cease to be amazed how each August a string of quotes from headteachers appear in the local press that indicate the results this year were completely fabulous – rather in the manner of politicians in the wake of an election, there is always something to celebrate. This is all good stuff for the local press, but a headteacher should beware of trying the same thing with governors. It would perhaps be overstating it to say they should always be given the completely unvarnished version of events – but spin with governors is a hostage to fortune which, when the relationship is long-term, is a risk that can't be taken.

Organization for effective governance
A theme to which we will return is creating structure to support school improvement, and more particularly to support the priorities of the school. Governing bodies, as a result of their size, can be unwieldy. To avoid this it is essential to consider very carefully the structure and working practices of the governors. Of course such matters are for governors to decide for themselves, and this is the art of working with governors. They must be guided and managed by the head, which they will expect. Things can go wrong where the head becomes presumptuous and tries to take decisions away from governors. An example of this might be in the thorny area of the school development plan. Now this is firmly the responsibility of governors as it determines the future direction and strategy of the school. The difficulty arises in that it is also

very much a professional document produced by the professionals within the school who have the knowledge and expertise of the school and its business to produce the strategic plan the school needs. Balancing the need for governor ownership with the production of a plan which meets the needs of the school and is produced in a timely fashion can be somewhat taxing. Give governors the impression that they are just expected to 'rubber-stamp' the plan by, for example, tabling the plan at the meeting where it is to be discussed and a governor revolt might be predicted. Readers will judge for themselves how far and how fast they can take their governing body, but some of the strategies below may be useful for consideration.

Delegation of powers

In effect this is about streamlining the decision-making process. As a general rule, throughout the school, it is better that decision-making is delegated to the lowest possible level. This is never more true than with governors' decisions. As implied in the list of governors' responsibilities above, governors could make themselves directly responsible for a great deal that goes on in the school. For example the governors could determine that their responsibility for finance means that their approval must be sought before any expenditure is made. Naturally enough this would make the school unmanageable, so it is more likely that governors will seek approval of all contracts over a certain minimum level, perhaps £3000. Approval for expenditure below this level is delegated to the head, who in turn will delegate responsibility for, say, science expenditure to the head of science. This is the essence of delegation. There are certain decisions that only the full governing body can make, for example approval of the budget submitted to the relevant authority, approval of the school prospectus, variation of the school day and, perhaps more quirkily, the sex education policy for the school (please refer to *A Guide to the Law for School Governors* (DfES, 2003) for a comprehensive list). Further there are decisions that governors must take, but it is possible (indeed in some cases essential) to delegate these decisions to committees of the governing body. Examples of this might be decisions relating to staffing structure, or pay, or choosing successful contract tenders. Then there are governors' responsibilities that may be delegated to the head, for example many governors will delegate responsibility for appointment of junior staff to the head, expecting governor involvement only for more senior posts. There must be clarity about roles and responsibilities for effective governance, each party must know what decisions are to be taken where and, for greatest effect, everything that can be delegated should be delegated.

Committees

There can be confusion among governors over committees. Firstly a committee has fully delegated authority to make decisions, in contrast to a sub-committee that makes recommendations to the full governing body, who will then make the decisions based upon this advice (in our view a hopeless waste of time as frequently the whole issue will be debated again, at length, by the full governing body thus making the subcommittee deliberations quite pointless). There are two statutory committees, these are a pupil discipline committee (3 or 5 members) and a staff discipline committee (constituted according the governing body's choosing, but requiring a second similar committee to hear appeals). These are specified in law and have their functioning specified similarly. Contrary to popular belief there is no statutory obligation to have any other committees at all. Mostly through delegation of powers and the need to have the issues of governance discussed more fully than is possible with a full board meeting of 20 governors leads to the creation of a range of committees.

Which committees?

There is a range of different practice here. Very often governors will have a curriculum committee, a pastoral committee, possibly a staffing or staffing and finance committee, a premises committee or premises and finance committee and, if finance isn't subsumed into another committee, then there will be a finance committee, and there may be a range of others created for a variety of purposes. Frequently governing bodies will have a general purposes committee comprising the chairs of the other committees. What is often not particularly clear is why these committees exist as they do. Our chosen approach was to create a range of committees to support the improvements we needed to make in our school:

- the school had a history of financial uncertainty; it is also the case that finances are a significant responsibility for the governors, so they would need a finance committee. Many schools choose, as indicated above, to couple finance to staffing or to premises, as these are major areas of expenditure. On the separation of powers principle we decided that this was inappropriate. Financial control should be separated from spending. In addition to setting the budget, there are responsibilities relating to approval of virement and adjustments to the budget within the year that must be made. More importantly this is the committee that will monitor the budget, and so its principal duty will be holding the leadership of the school to account for its management of the budget.

- the key priority for the school was to raise the achievement of its pupils from a position of under-achievement. Considering what issues governors would need to consider and the changes we would be asking them to make meant that the traditional divide of curriculum committee and pastoral committee seemed sterile and would be rather missing the point. While it may be the case that governors enjoy discussing 'the curriculum', it is our contention that this is just one factor that affects achievement. For governors to spend a lot of time on making decisions on subjects offered and syllabuses used did not seem particularly appropriate. In short these sort of curriculum decisions are, by and large, professional matters of means not ends and therefore not within the remit of the governing body. We would rather have governors discussing pupils' achievement and the barriers to it, rather than spending hours discussing whether to use the AQA or the OCR syllabus for A level psychology! The remit of the committee is to consider all aspects of the school that affect pupils' achievement and to take a much more holistic and integrated approach than would be possible with the curriculum/pastoral divide. So the committee has considered attendance, uniform and its implementation, statutory target setting, examination results analysis, the key stage 3 strategy and many more items across the range of the work of the school with its pupils.
- any visitor to our school could not fail to be struck by how appalling our buildings were. Indeed in the asset management plan survey of 2001 it appeared that our building stock was the worst in the county. This made another committee focus. A large part of our budget was to be devoted to this priority improvement area and so a governors' committee was necessary, and we created our premises and community committee.
- finally we did, of course, require a staffing committee. A principal function of the governing body is to determine the staffing structure of the school and to act as the employer of those staff. This committee is responsible for decisions relating to these matters, but in addition the annual review of staff salaries is carried out here, the headteacher's

performance management and remuneration committee are drawn from this group, and it is responsible for all matters relating to personnel policy and performance management.

The key thing about these committees is not so much that they are radically different from those listed as the 'traditional' above – they clearly aren't – rather it is the emphasis upon how the committees link to our school priorities and the rationale that underpins them that is important. The logic is also that committees can come and go. While it is unlikely that pupil achievement will ever cease to be a priority in a school, it is certainly the case that the emphasis could change and as a consequence either the title of the committee, or its terms of reference, or both could change. This is a theme to which we will return under management structure later in this chapter.

On the subject of committees, a final point about the 'general purposes' committee. Many governing bodies have such a committee – its title will vary from school to school, but it will normally consist of key governors, the chairs of the other committees for example. On the face of it perhaps it seems entirely reasonable to establish such a grouping, a tightly focused group that can maintain an overview of the business of the school; pragmatically, it may be argued that it is very difficult for the whole governing body to fulfil this function. Conversely, it is our view that one of the potentially most debilitating aspects of the workings of some governing bodies is their propensity to form cliques, those in the know (the A team) and the rest. It would appear that if this is what is desired then the creation of a general purposes committee would be a very good way to go about it, if governors wish to operate democratically and in an inclusive manner then the correct place for the overview to be maintained, however difficult, is the full governing body.

Working groups

As has already been indicated, many of the policies of the school are very deeply in the realm of professional matters – assessment policy has been cited as one example, teaching and learning policy might be another. It is clearly the governors' responsibility to set policy in all circumstances, and so in these cases the most appropriate approach is for the professionals in school to draft a policy and for this to be discussed and approved by the governors. There are other areas of policy that are not specifically professional matters. Here it is appropriate to ask for governors to take part in drafting the policy. Of course trying to accomplish this, generally, lengthy process at a committee meeting is likely to mean that the other business of that committee is going to be seriously knocked off schedule; a more appropriate means is to create a working group. We have done this on a number of occasions, most recently for our equal opportunities policy and our substance misuse policy, both of which drew together a range of school stakeholders including governors, staff, students and other members of the community (for example our community police officer on the substance misuse group); and our staff emergency and special leave policy where governors and a range of staff, including the union representatives, drafted the policy. Typically a working group should aim for three meetings:

- the first to discuss the issues and consider the response to each one; after this meeting the group leader should draft the policy and circulate it in advance of the next meeting
- the second to discuss the draft policy; after this meeting the group leader should rewrite the policy, given the comments at the meeting, and again circulate it in advance of the final meeting
- the final meeting to ratify the completed draft and approve it for submission to the governors' committee to whom the working group reports

This is a highly effective approach to developing inclusive policies that are transparent both in their creation and implementation and which use governors in an appropriate and effective way.

Running the meetings
The essence of working with governors is the meetings. Before we go any further on this a really obvious point but one which is not universally adhered to, governors' meetings for the year should be calendared and agreed to in the last full governors' meeting of the previous year. Without this we end up with the frustration of diary flipping at the end of each committee meeting while a date suitable for all 7 or 8 (or 20 in the case of full governors) is found.

There is a deep level of contradiction in many governing bodies. Frequently governors will profess a dislike of meetings and urge that meetings should be concluded as speedily as possible. Indications that the meeting will be very short are greeted with approval. But given that these are people who have volunteered to be governors and that being a governor consists almost exclusively of taking part in meetings, one is forced to the view that despite protestations to the contrary, governors like meetings. Indeed typically the person who wants the meeting to be over quickest is usually the head (with the possible exception of the clerk), on the grounds that he or she will often attend all the governors' meetings with no possibility of parole. Left to themselves governors will not generally run meetings very efficiently, neither will agendas be prepared nor will minutes be written with any degree of reliability. This sounds critical but it is not meant to be, the people with the greatest interest in the school and who are, after all, paid to make everything work, are the staff of the school and, in particular, the leadership team. It is for this reason that these are the people who need to make everything happen.

Clerking

Part of the legal constitution of the full governing body and its statutory committees is a clerk. The purpose of the clerk is to manage the committee that he or she serves, to write the agenda, to provide advice to governors on the legal framework of governance and to write the minutes. There are some very good clerks to governors around the country, many LEAs provide clerking services and there are some professional clerks (perhaps retired heads or local authority officers) who serve a number of governing bodies as their full-time employment. If you have the services of such a clerk then you are very fortunate, but even if you do it is unlikely that you will choose to pay for these services for your non-statutory committees, so it is necessary to think about how this is to be accomplished. In our case a member of the leadership team clerks each committee other than finance which is clerked by our bursar. The function of this role is, as identified above, to make sure that the meetings have agendas, that these agendas are circulated with all the required paperwork seven days in advance of the meeting and that minutes are taken and written up.

A brief word on circulation of the papers. This is absolutely essential. As a member of a committee it is intensely annoying to arrive and be confronted with large numbers of lengthy documents over which one is required to make comment. It gives the impression of disarray and that the committee is being taken for granted. Of course it is also the case that many governors turn up at the meeting and open their document packs for the first time then and there – this is annoying for whoever has lovingly assembled the documents, but the point is no one can say they have not been given the opportunity. The relationship between head and governors is vital and above all must rest upon governors having confidence in their head. Tabling documents (i.e. presenting documents at the meeting) is one quick way to ensure that governors lose that essential confidence.

Drawing up agendas

An area which sometimes does not manage to attract the attention it deserves is that of drawing up the agenda. At one level the agenda is an aide memoire for the chair to ensure that the correct matters are discussed. But it can and should be much more than this. The agenda should not only contain the title of the item to be discussed, it should also contain a brief description of the nature of the discussion required, and crucially it should indicate the purpose of that discussion, does the agenda item require a decision, or is it just for information? Drawing up an agenda in this way ensures that everyone involved in the meeting is fully aware of the purpose of the discussion and has the overview of the issue on the agenda itself and is directed towards the relevant supporting papers. This leads to structured and effective meetings. The only thing missing from this agenda is the time allocation for the discussion. While textbook guidance on such matters would indicate this is an essential element of any agenda, and it probably is when dealing with the colleagues within the school, it can seem overly presumptuous to prescribe for governors how long they will spend discussing each item, and furthermore, pragmatically, it is our experience that frequently what is assumed to be the shortest item on the agenda turns out to be the longest and vice versa!

Box 2.1 contains a specimen agenda for a full governors' meeting.

Having dealt with all the basics of governors' meetings all that remains is to consider how best to make them productive and how governors can be led towards effective decision-making.

Making decisions with governors

We do require governors to make decisions on a whole range of matters. How can we ensure that governors make the best decisions? At one end of the scale headteachers may consider manipulating the governing body to ensure they get the decision they want – indeed such headteachers often pride themselves upon their ability to do just this. There are a whole range of manipulative strategies that can be used, perhaps squaring off a variety of key opinion formers beforehand, perhaps presenting the case for change with a considerable degree of spin, perhaps failing to mention the negative consequences of the change. This is all well and good but it is potentially a high-risk strategy. Manipulation can be very effective at getting the required ends, but it does require an exceptional degree of skill not to be found out and, given that frequently headteachers are suspected of manipulation even when it isn't happening, then the possibility of being found out is quite high. Generally people do not much favour being manipulated and so the consequences of being found out are severe.

MATTHEW ARNOLD SCHOOL
GOVERNORS' STAFFING COMMITTEE

AGENDA – 15 APRIL

Membership: GHE, HHD, LMM, TES, AJP, RPC

1. Apologies
2. Minutes of the last meeting (document 1)
3. Matters arising
4. Staffing update – please see the enclosed summary of recent staffing changes and comments (document 2)

For information

5. Achievement award outcome – we were notified that Matthew Arnold School was to be the recipient of an Achievement Award from the DfES on 22 March. The total award was £19,760 and has been divided up according to the policy determined at the last meeting of this committee. A copy of the policy is enclosed (document 3) as well as a list of staff recipients and the amount each member of staff received (document 4).

For information

6. Performance management – the assistant head (staff development) will present his report on performance management procedures (document 5).

For information

7. Assessment administrator – the current holder of the post of assessment coordinator has resigned (he will be taking up a post as key stage 3 consultant for ICT in another LEA). It is proposed to replace this position with that of an administrator. Please see the attached paper outlining the rationale for this proposal (document 6).

For decision

8. Cover – attached are the cover statistics for the first two terms of the year (document 7).

For information

9. Proposal to create the post of deputy head of sixth form/key skills coordinator on 2 points – please see the attached paper outlining the rationale for this proposal (document 8).

For decision

Box 2.1

Perhaps the way to go is just to present the decision required and ask the governors to get on with it. The author once observed a governors' meeting where the issue under discussion was increasing the number of science technician hours requested by the science department. The information provided to the governors was the number of hours requested, how much this would cost and a calculation of technician hours required according to the Association for Science Education formula (which some would say provides very generously for technician hours!). What wasn't provided was any indication as to why this was being raised at that particular time, no indication of the benchmark technician hours in other schools in the same county and, most importantly, no indication of where this expansion in expenditure fitted into school priorities and what the consequences of spending the money on this rather than other things might be. Naturally enough, given that all that was presented was the reasons why this should happen and none of the reasons why it shouldn't the governors agreed to the request. At the same meeting the committee agreed to several other requests of the same nature. Now of course it may have been the head's intention to get these decisions through in the easiest way possible, and presenting the case for without any indication that there may be a case against is certainly an easy way of doing this, but there is no quality to the decision-making process, governors are not given a choice or even the opportunity to engage in the process of reaching a sensible decision, they were simply agreeing to things that would be nice for those who requested them.

So how should decisions be arrived at? In part this depends upon the nature of the decision, the following three examples illustrate how some different sorts of decisions might be approached.

A Policy for the distribution of the School Achievement Award

From 2001 the government introduced the idea of School Achievement Awards: this is a policy by which 'successful' schools are rewarded with a cash lump sum to distribute among the staff of the school. The distribution of the lump sum was to be determined by the governors of the school. It seems under these circumstances that the normal ways of developing policy, to prepare a draft policy for governors to consider or to set up a working party of stakeholders, would be inappropriate as any members of school staff involved in the policy-making process would have a direct financial interest in the outcome. But to request the governors to consider the issue cold, without any guidance at all would also seem ill-advised. It appeared likely that our school would receive such an award in 2002 and so it seemed wise to create a policy for its distribution in advance.

ACHIEVEMENT AWARDS

A briefing for governors

For the first time last year the government introduced achievement awards for schools. The achievement recognized is sustained high performance or significant improvement. Improvement can be in terms of value added or simply improvement in raw GCSE results. The award is a cash sum to be divided up between employees of the school; the award cannot be used for any other purpose. For an average-size secondary school the total award to the school is likely to be between £20,000 and £30,000.

Where a school receives such an award it is for the governors to determine the basis upon which it should be disbursed to the staff. Governors will therefore need a policy on this matter should the occasion arise.

In developing such a policy governors are recommended to consider the following questions:

1   Who should receive the money?
   a)   All teachers, admin staff, technicians, teaching assistants, site staff, caterers and cleaners?
   b)   Staff 'on roll' during the year to which the results relate only?
   c)   Staff currently on roll only?
   d)   Staff currently on roll who were on roll in the year in question?
   e)   Only those staff who worked with the pupils who obtained the relevant results in the year in question?

2   How much money should they receive?
   a)   Equal shares for everyone who is to receive the money?
   b)   Shares in proportion to full-time equivalent (e.g. a full-time term-time's only member of the admin team is on a 0.88 fte contract, therefore would receive 0.88 times the allocation to a full-time teacher)?
   c)   Shares in proportion to salary (e.g. a teacher earning £20,000 pa would receive two thirds the share of a teacher earning £30,000)?

d) Where a member of staff is absent for a significant part of the year (e.g. more than four working weeks) should the share be reduced?

e) If the award relates to GCSE performance should a teacher who has worked with a group for both years 10 and 11 receive more than one who has just worked with the group in year 11 (or just year 10)?

3 Should account be taken of performance? Where a class or department has done particularly poorly should this be recognized? If so how can this be applied to non-teachers if they are to receive a share of the award?

Box 2.2

In order to assist governors in arriving at a decision they would be happy with they were presented with the discussion document in Box 2.2.

The intention was to provide a framework within which governors could make their decision, and to provide them with the full range of questions that they would need to consider in order to frame their policy. The headteacher was a member of the committee considering the policy but did not take part in the discussion at all (neither did other members of staff who were members of this committee), but having heard the full discussion was able to frame a policy that was genuinely the governors' intention. This was then presented to the committee at its next meeting for final approval.

Of course the accusation could be levelled that by asking the right questions the desired outcome was arrived at, and that by turning the discussion into the final written policy then the desired 'spin' could be put upon the wording. This is undoubtedly true, but would risk the charge of manipulation with all the risks to the trusting relationship between head and governors referred to above – in short it would not be worth it.

The Behaviour Support Service

In common with many schools we are faced with pupils exhibiting very challenging behaviour in a climate of social inclusion. The ability of the LEA to provide support to schools is limited in many ways, not least the enormous cost of providing such support. It is increasingly clear that schools must make such provision for themselves. This is the position we reached and our chosen solution was to employ a teacher experienced in behaviour management to establish and manage our on-site referral unit.

Costing such provision is dealt with fully in chapter 3, but in short our costings showed a capital start-up cost of £10,000 (for resources, furniture and a small amount of building work), with a revenue cost of £50,000 for the teacher. Previous experience with governors showed that this is the sort of initiative that would meet with warm approval and that it would undoubtedly be very easy to gain a positive governors' decision by simply presenting them with the costs and the advantages of the initiative. While this would have been expedient, there were several reasons for not pursuing this course of action:

a) it would not be a genuine decision with out a fully informed discussion
b) it is difficult for governors to put the finances required into context, i.e. they needed to have the opportunity to consider what else the money could pay for
c) in an environment of financial uncertainty the consequences of a positive decision could be very severe on other aspects of the functioning of the school. Unless governors are aware of this then the head must carry responsibility for any resulting downside decisions on his or her own

The end result is that it is necessary to create a debate that puts the finances and the possible consequences of the decision in context. What should that context be? There are only so many aspects of the functioning of the school that could be offset against this cost – clearly energy costs, rates, cleaning, grounds maintenance and so on will cost what they cost. The context could have been to set the costs off against premises investment, for example if there is a planned project to re-furbish the pupils' toilets for £50,000, then governors could consider which they would prefer; capitation is another area, but there is a sense in which these are easy targets and in any event to offset capital projects against revenue expenditure in this way would, as the Chancellor would say, break the golden rule. It so happened that at the time we had some large classes in one year group, so the question was put 'Would you prefer average class sizes of 31 in this year group or the behaviour support service?' This seemed to encapsulate the debate and provided a good context for a good decision.

Oh, and did they decide to go for it? They certainly did, but in the full knowledge that a significant sum was being committed and that the consequences could prove difficult to support in other areas of our function.

Using permanent exclusion

An area of school life that can be a source of friction is that of permanent exclusion. It is often the practice of headteachers to report the numbers of fixed-term and permanent exclusions in their report to governors. It became apparent that there was some unease being expressed by at least one governor whenever this subject came up. This is the sort of thing that can become difficult if not addressed, but the question of how to address it is problematic. It hardly seems appropriate simply to ask for governors' support for the use of this sanction; few governors would deny that there are occasions when the use of this sanction is the correct course. The crux is under what circumstances it is the correct course. It may be that the approach is to strictly define the circumstances under the governors' policy on behaviour, but again it is hard to avoid using phrases that require judgement to be used, and in any event surely the role of the head-teacher is, in many respects above all else, to exercise judgement.

Our chosen approach was to consider a case study. This case study was lengthy and cannot be reproduced here but the guidance to governors is in Box 2.3.

PERMANENT EXCLUSION CASE STUDY

Attached are summary notes from a recent permanent exclusion case. These were presented to a pupil and his parents in preparation for a meeting to consider the pupil's future at the school. Our procedure is to hold such a meeting where a pupil has had a fixed-term exclusion for a serious offence, or has reached a point where the accumulated discipline record for the pupil provides evidence to show the pupil is on course for permanent exclusion. The agenda for the meeting is to consider:

1   the incident that led to the fixed-term exclusion
2   the wider context of the pupil's record at school
3   to consider whether or not the school can provide additional support for the pupil upon their return to school

At the end of the meeting the participants adjourn and the headteacher and the invited governor consider what should happen next. The outcome may be one of the following:

1   return to school with a support strategy in place
2   an extension of the fixed-term exclusion to investigate

further options, for example trying to enlist the support of
a pupil referral unit

3   permanent exclusion

Governors are invited to read the attached case study notes and
judge whether the pupil has been:

1   dealt with correctly
2   maintained too long in school before permanent exclusion,
     or
3   permanently excluded when further strategies could have
     been tried to adjust the pupil's behaviour

It should be noted that accompanying this summary were 27
supporting documents including copies of letters home, pastoral
support plans, special needs documents, records of involvement
with the educational psychologist and exclusion letters.

Box 2.3

Although this discussion did not end in a decision in the normal
sense of the word, it did provide an opportunity for governors to
consider in some detail the way their discipline and behaviour policy
was being implemented by the head. It provided them with the
opportunity to either affirm their support for the conduct of this policy
or to indicate that an adjustment was required.

In the end no governors felt the pupil had been excluded when
further strategies could have been tried, there was a narrow majority
in favour of regarding the incident as having been dealt with correctly,
and the remainder felt the pupil had been maintained in the school
too long.

Involving governors in the school
The final area we would like to consider in the work of governors is their
duty to monitor the work of the school. Clearly much of what has gone
before relates to this duty, but how much can governors monitor through
governors' meetings and just through contact with the leadership team
and the staff governors? Governors need to have a greater interface with
the work of the school than can be provided through these means alone.
Without wishing to imply that the leadership team are necessarily
attempting to put a gloss on matters, it is true to say that the interpreta-
tion of events simply through this one point of contact is limiting. How
do governors gain an understanding of how the school functions, what

the teachers are like, what the everyday experience of pupils in the school is and an appreciation for the climate for teaching and learning in the school?

A relatively common approach is that of governors linking with departments. Here each governor has a particular responsibility to gain an understanding of a specific subject area. The notion is that the linked governor will spend time with the teachers of the department, will perhaps observe some lessons, will gain an understanding of the issues the department faces, their strengths and weaknesses and their plans for improvement. This approach has the considerable strength that it necessitates governor involvement with an aspect of the work of the school, thus creating a range of expertise across the governing body; it should also provide an opportunity for governors to carry out their monitoring function. But here is the rub, it is our contention that link governor arrangements provide confusion for both staff and governors about the role of the governors. They are supposed to monitor, but they are not inspectors and have no expertise in teaching and learning. If a governor believes that their link work is part of their monitoring function then there is a risk that they will begin to make judgements of the teacher concerned. This is where relationships between staff and governors can break down and a lack of trust can begin to develop. Furthermore, it is our experience that as common as these arrangements are, equally common is the fact of their failure. Born as they are out of good intentions, it is also the case that governors do not have the time to make it work correctly and teachers in departments rarely have the desire to push for it from their end. All told, the notion of link governors is not an enterprise to be commended.

Naturally enough, if the concept of link governors is rejected then there needs to be something to take its place. In determining an approach it is worth reminding ourselves of the purpose:

1   that governors should feel confident that they are gaining an overview of the work of the school from those in the school other than the leadership team or staff governors
2   that they should have the opportunity to experience the school from first-hand experience

To address the first of these points one approach is to involve a wider group of staff in the work of committees, so typically a head of department might be asked to brief a committee on the implementation of an aspect of the work of the school. An example might be the head of mathematics providing governors with a briefing on the key stage 3 numeracy strategy, or, in a specialist school, the director of the particular specialism briefing governors on implementation of the community plan. An approach we have found particularly successful with governors is to begin each full governors' meeting with a 30-minute seminar on an aspect of the work of the school. Over a period of time seminars we have offered have been:

- implications of circular 10/99 'Social Inclusion: Pupil Support'
- the work of the school counsellor
- the work of the professional tutor with initial teacher training students
- the work of the PE department

And a whole range of others. All told this seminar series has given governors a far better feeling of understanding how the school works than many years of supposed link governors.

Of course this does not provide governors with a sense of the experience in the school. In order to tackle this aspect then a governors' 'Open afternoon' might be considered. The purpose here is straightforward, it is to give governors the opportunity to learn about the experience of pupils. Typically the agenda for an individual governor might be as follows:

1.30 arrive for lunch with the head

1.55 attend assembly

2.15 observe first half of a technology lesson

2.45 observe second half of a history lesson

3.15 take part in bus duty

3.30 tea and debrief with the leadership team

4.00 break

5.30 full governors' seminar

6.00 full governors' meeting

This fulfils the need for governors to have some direct experience of the school, it allows them to undertake a monitoring function guided through the debrief at the end of the afternoon, it offers a specific opportunity when governors are expected to be in school and finally it provides a non-threatening occasion for staff to be observed by governors.

Summary

In this chapter we have considered a range of ways that might be considered to ensure the smooth running of the governing body. There are a whole range of matters that have been left out, the headteacher's report to governors, the function and operation of the statutory committees, headteacher performance management and a range of other matters. In the final analysis there is no substitute for knowing the law and, as headteacher, unless you are very fortunate and have a clerk who can fulfil the role envisaged by legislation, there will be no one else to do this but you. As has already been indicated, there are a variety of sources for finding out what the law is, the DfES website and associated 'governornet' service are a mine of useful information, *Croner's Guide* similarly. But, having satisfied yourself that you do know the law, then the guidance in this chapter, we hope, will provide a useful set of ideas to think about in arriving at your own method of organizing your governing body. We have focused upon the areas we have because it seems that these issues form the heart of that which is most essential, the creation of a trusting and effective relationship between governors and head. If this is right then the other things are either much better covered by legal texts or are matters that will follow naturally given the correct relationship.

To summarize:

- Governors need to be managed, they need to feel they are in the safe hands of the professional who they appointed, and they need to feel that if they follow the advice of their head then they will not go far wrong.
- They need to be informed of what is going on in the school; if there is a potential downside to a decision, they must know what it is, and are thus enabled to make an informed decision.
- Governing bodies are about procedure, the procedures must be followed in order for them to feel confident about what is going on.
- The committees and structures of the governors need to be focused upon the priorities for the school if they are to be effective.
- Managing the governing body is time-consuming and a fact of life for a headteacher – so just get on with it.
- Tabling documents (i.e. presenting them at the meeting for the first time), is one sure way to make governors feel they are taken for granted – don't do it.

By paying attention to these brief points in dealings with governing bodies, then this can be one of the most rewarding aspects of the job. It is a relationship that can validate so much of the work of the leadership team and as such can be intensely rewarding and positive. So while for much of the time many headteachers find themselves spending a disproportionate amount of time looking after their governors, it is our contention that this time is worthwhile, because a governing body working well and taking part in the work of the school can genuinely add value.

CHAPTER 3

Where the buck stops
On leadership, the leadership team and distributing leadership throughout the school

Certainly a leader needs a clear vision of the organization and where it is going, but a vision is of little value unless it is shared in a way so as to generate enthusiasm and commitment. Leadership and communication are inseparable.
Claude Taylor

Hay-McBer, in their research for the National College of School Leadership's Leadership Programme for Serving Headteachers, identify three key dimensions that provide the setting for school improvement. These are standards, rewards and clarity. In brief, Standards refers to the extent to which high standards are set and attained by the leadership of the school. Rewards are the extent to which those whose work is of a good quality are recognized; this can either be in the obvious form of financial rewards and promotion, or in the more subtle sense of praise and encouragement. Clarity is the focus of this chapter and refers to the extent to which staff in the school are clear about the mission of the school, its systems, policies and procedures and the lines of accountability within the school.

To some extent this exhortation for clarity represents the shifting paradigm of the secondary school over the last twenty years. The traditional view of the school teacher as professional is that of the relationship of a consultant with their hospital. It is widely regarded in hospitals that the consultant has the final say on the clinical judgements regarding their patient, they have no accountability to the hospital for their judgement, their accountability is to their patient and the General Medical Council. That consultants work together in a hospital means they have to have due regard to one another, but this is a collegial and professional regard not one of accountability, the consultant has no 'line manager' in relation to his or her clinical judgements. By analogy, the view of teacher professionalism taken by many in the profession some time ago and still held by some today is that of the professional who has the supreme authority to make educational judgements in relation to their pupils. Under this model the school would be seen as a collegiate of professionals all pursuing their diagnosis of the needs of their pupils to the best of their ability. As they are professionals exercising professional judgement then there is no need for a wider accountability beyond that of the teacher to their client (pupil, parent?). This position is somewhat exaggerated, but the point is that under such an analysis all teachers can be relied upon to act in the full interests of all pupils in their care and therefore there is no need for line-management arrangements, there is no need for monitoring, indeed there is no need for school leadership. This analysis will be familiar to anyone who has taken part in meetings with union representatives who can sometimes appear to inhabit an *Alice in Wonderland* world where such teachers are the norm.

Of course the reality is that such collegiality is false and, where all teachers are accountable to their 'clients', then this is much the same as no one being accountable. The analysis also ignores the reality of the pupils' experience at school, that is that they move from one teacher to the next and so have a legitimate expectation that there is going to be consistency of procedure and expectations in each class they visit. Again, exaggerating to make the point, it would be difficult for pupils if during their first lesson of the day they were expected to wear a school uniform, and during the second lesson they were required not to wear the uniform. It is clear that the collegiate has to be more of a team than this. Hence the importance of clarity. All those who work in the school must have a shared understanding of what matters to the school, the highest priority must be placed upon gaining this shared understanding.

This must be an understanding of the long-term aims of the school and the values that underpin those aims, it must also be an understanding of the medium and short-term goals. Saying all this is one thing, achieving it is quite another. This is where the structure of the school must be carefully crafted to support the aims and priorities of the school. Structure means the leadership and management structure and the lines of accountability contained therein, it also means the policies, systems and procedures that the school adopts. Everything about the school must support these aims and priorities.

Structure

In order to produce clarity then the starting point is clarity of structure. This means everyone must know who is accountable to them and to whom they are accountable. Where roles and structures have grown by evolution rather than design it is not uncommon to find people with significant responsibility who do not believe they are accountable to anyone; examples we found were the examinations officer, the staff who produced the timetable, all of the admin staff, the SENCo. Of course, these people were all accountable to someone, but it wasn't determined in their job description or the management structure of the school; by default then the line manager becomes the headteacher – the end result of this sort of haphazard evolution is that the head becomes operational line manager for more people than can possibly be handled, and the organization becomes bogged down in the bottleneck of the head's desk. Our approach has been to ensure that every aspect of the work of the school is managed by a member of the leadership team thus creating a series of teams that can be led by the leadership team and ensuring a clear line of accountability to the head. Critical in this is the role of the leadership team.

The leadership team

The key team for effecting change in the school is the leadership team. Or at least it can be if properly used and well directed. Of course upon taking up appointment as a new head you will inherit a leadership team which will almost inevitably not be to your liking. But before going any further it is worth pointing out that the essential quality of a leadership team is not so much the jobs they do, but rather the leadership they bring to the school. At one level we believe that anyone of calibre can do any of the jobs needed by the leadership team – the essential quality that team members must have is that of leadership.

The purpose of this section is to consider what structures you might consider and the principles underlying the choice. As with governors' committees the function of the leadership team structure is to achieve the school aims and goals; therefore it is essential that the aims and goals are clearly defined and put at the heart of the structure. So, for example, it may be that the securing the future viability of the sixth form is a key strategic priority – if so then it would be sensible for the head of sixth form to be part of the leadership team. This achieves a number of objectives:

1   the salary for a leadership team member is generally higher and the status represents a promotion so it should be possible to appoint a better candidate than for just a management allowance

2 leadership team status identifies this as a key priority for the school both to the staff and to the governors

3 as a member of the leadership team then the role will be line-managed by the headteacher, therefore making the post 'closer to the action'. Although it is clearly the case that the head can manage those not on the leadership team, that does muddy the waters – this relationship creates clarity about the importance of the sixth form as a priority

Given the overarching requirement to have all aspects of the work of the school line-managed by a member of the leadership team then it becomes a case of establishing how those responsibilities are to be divided among the team. One of the most thorny issues here is the how to lead the heads of year (or house) and the heads of department.

Vertical or horizontal

The traditional arrangement in leadership teams has always been the two-way split of deputy head (curriculum) and deputy head (pastoral). More recently, and for a variety of reasons, it has become the norm to split these roles horizontally, so one team member may line-manage heads of year 7, 8 and 9 and another heads of year 10, 11 and the sixth form. Departments may be split across the entire team and, rather than being described as line managers, they might be called link managers.

There are undoubtedly advantages to this system, and even more are claimed; the following list is of both of these in no particular order:

1 preparation for headship requires experience across the range of the work of the school

2 there are too many heads of department for one person to line-manage (this is sometimes addressed through the creation of faculties wherein some heads of department are line-managed by heads of faculty; this structure will be explored later in this section)

3 it requires members of the team to work together on pastoral and discipline matters, thus ensuring a more cohesive team

4 it ensures that all members of the team who have link responsibility for departments are focused upon teaching and learning and it encourages discourse on these

5 the tasks and responsibilities are shared out more evenly across the leadership team

6 the structure recognizes the continuum of the work of the school and does not create curriculum and pastoral silos

This does appear to be a prodigious set of advantages, but on further consideration perhaps the underlying values that create this arrangement are somewhat suspect. It appears that the list focuses principally upon the needs and wants of the senior leaders in the team rather than upon the outcomes. For example, point 1 is certainly not to do with anything other than the development needs of the individuals concerned which, while important, should not form the principal reason behind the structure – it is hard to envisage this as a key aim of the school over and above providing for the pupils for example. Point 2 relates to a, perhaps pragmatic, desire not to overload one person on the team, but again this is weak and would be better achieved by ensuring that the other responsibilities of the HoD line manager take into account the size of this task. Point 3 plays to the desire for human interaction, where it is regarded that working with others is a good thing in itself. If the starting point was clarity, consistency, efficiency and effectiveness then it is hard to see how this structure would fit the bill.

How does this compare to what has been described above as the traditional arrangement where heads of year are line-managed by one team member and heads of department by another? Clarity and consistency – these middle leaders know they are part of a team with one leader, there are no mixed messages and no potential for issues falling between two stools. Where difficulties arise then the referring point for department issues is always the same, pupil welfare and discipline issues are always referred to the same person too. This gives a consistency of message to pupils and their parents that cannot be achieved where the responsibility is split. Efficiency – not only is it more efficient for a leader to be dealing with a relatively confined area of responsibility – they are not spread too thinly – the supposed advantage of splitting responsibilities to ensure that team members have to communicate with one another appears to be another way of describing a very inefficient system where people are always having to check with one another to ensure consistency before acting. Effectiveness – clearly providing clarity, consistency and efficiency are all likely to improve effectiveness within themselves, but consider the matter of curriculum leadership. Where management of heads of department is split across the entire team then a variety of things happen:

1   This area of responsibility becomes a marginal part of the activity for most leadership team members (think of the person who is dealing with years 7, 8 and 9 and also looks after the humanities departments; a moment's reflection

will indicate that little time is left over for curriculum matters once the year groups are dealt with!). Rather than everyone having a focus upon teaching and learning the danger is that no one does.

2   There is a great variety of curriculum expertise in most leadership teams, if one person is to provide leadership then a teaching and learning expert can be appointed.

3   There is no overview, no consistent message on, for example, schemes of work, the use of learning outcomes to plan lessons, indeed as a result of 2 above, it is possible that some leadership team members are on distinctly shaky ground themselves in terms of their understanding of these issues.

4   As a result of all of the above, performance management becomes a bolt-on rather than central to the management of this key group – how can it be otherwise with so many involved in the process?

5   In the end, by trying to make everyone in the team responsible for curriculum leadership the result is no one is.

It is for these reasons that our strong recommendation is to locate responsibility for discipline and welfare of pupils with one member of the leadership team and curriculum leadership with another. It may appear old-fashioned, but it does work.

Table 3.1 shows an example of the structure of a school whose priorities are teaching and learning, making good use of assessment information, robust approaches to discipline and welfare, securing a successful sixth form, ensuring ICT is effective and securing value for money and continued improvement of a very tired building stock. It is clear that the headline and key responsibilities are associated solely with specific senior leaders. There are also a range of other responsibilities that do not naturally fit within those broad headings, for example public relations, prospectus, careers and so on. To ensure coverage of all these areas these are shared out across the team. It is also worth noting the inclusion of a business manager to carry out all the functions that are not focused upon teaching and learning. The business manager has a salary commensurate with an assistant head, but works according to administrator conditions of service (i.e. 44 weeks per year rather than 39).

A brief word about anomalies. The principle behind the illustrated structure is that the team manages each area of the school and the head manages the team. You will notice that the head also manages the

Headteacher

Leadership and management of the school, recruitment of staff, personnel, marketing, school development plan, financial planning, curriculum planning, pupil exclusions, performance management, oversight of learning support

Line manager to: Leadership team, bursar, director of learning support

Chairs: Leadership team meetings, academic board, staff meetings, science college management team

Attends: All governors' meetings, HSA, HoDs' and HoYs' as appropriate, senior prefects' meetings

Deputy Headteacher	Assistant Head	Assistant Head	Head of Sixth Form	Business Manager
• Deputize for Headteacher	• Discipline and welfare	• Strategic oversight of ICT including curriculum and administration	• Leadership of sixth form	• Asset management plan
• Quality of teaching – monitoring the work of departments	• Pupil induction	• Academic monitoring of pupils throughout the school	• Sixth form marketing, recruitment & induction	• Premises management
• Science college development	• In year admissions	• Pupil target setting and tracking	• Sixth form options	• Coordination of events – including open evening
• Options at KS4	• Assemblies	• Oversight of baseline assessment	• Sixth form activities	• Administration
• Set lists	• Uniform	• Assessment monitoring and reporting	• UCAS process	• Health and safety
• Primary liaison	• Duties	• Parents' consultation evenings	• Management of sixth form resources	• Fire and emergency procedures
• Cover arrangements	• School prospectus	• Oversight of examinations' arrangements	• Prefect responsibilities	• School transport
• Exams analysis and dept target setting	• School photographs	• Yearbooks	• School council	• Contract supervision
• Department development plans	• Tutorial programme	• Oversight of public relations	• Careers	• Calendar
• Timetable construction	• Student planners	• Oversight of library	• Staff handbook	• PLASC and September count
• Professional development of all staff	• Equal opportunities		• Curriculum enhancement and offsite learning opportunity coordinator including health & safety/risk assessment	
• Investors In People	• Oversight of Connexions			
• Oversight of NQT supervision and induction of new staff				

Line Manager to:	Line Manager to:	Line Manager to:	Line manager to:	Line Manager to:
• Heads of Department • Professional tutor • INSET coordinator • Curriculum manager	• Heads of Year • Connexions team • CPLO	• Press officer • Head of ICT	• Deputy Head of Sixth Form • Sixth Form tutors • Careers administrator • Librarian	• Administration staff • Caretaker and site staff • Exams officer/system manager • Assessment administrator
Assisted by Admin 1	**Assisted by Admin 2**	**Assisted by Admin 1**	**Assisted by Admin 2**	**Assisted by Admin 3**
Chairs: • Heads of Department meeting • Learning to Learn Group Attends: • Leadership team • Science college management team • Full governors (Advisor) • Pupil achievement committee (Clerk) • Academic board • Primary link group • IT strategy group	Chairs: • Heads of Year meetings • Connexions team meetings Attends: • Leadership team • Learning to Learn Group • HSA • Pupil achievement committee (as required)	Chairs: • ICT strategy group Attends: • Leadership team • Science college management team • Learning to Learn Group • Curriculum reporting and assessment group • Pupil achievement committee (as required)	Chairs: • Sixth form tutors' meetings • Senior prefect meetings Attends: • Leadership team • School council • Heads of Year meeting	Attends: • Leadership team • Premises committee meetings (Clerk) • Community education management committee • IT strategy group

Table 3.1 *A leadership team structure*

director of learning support, this was a compromise arrived at out of pragmatism; given that the SEN role involves considerable liaison with the education authority (on such matters as statements, inclusion and so forth) then decisions made by this post holder are often going to have to be cleared by the head. An example would be if the LEA are pressing for the school to provide home tuition for a pupil. It is appropriate for this commitment to be agreed by the head and therefore to introduce another layer in between the director of learning support and the head is likely to introduce inefficiency, hence the apparent anomaly. There are often likely to be specific cases such as this which require particular and, on the face of it, anomalous treatment. Where this makes sense then it should not be shied away from, but it is important to be clear about the rationale for all such decisions.

Other structural considerations

There are of course many ways of organizing the rest of the structure of the school. For example, should pupils be organized by year, by house, by key stage? Is there a necessity for an intermediary (middle) leader between form tutors and the leadership team? What about the organization of teaching? This could be (though rarely is) organized by key stage; more usually it is organized by subject, or clusters of clearly similar subjects into departments, and sometimes departments are organized into faculties. Now the fashionable view on all of this is that it is standards not structures that matter (to coin a phrase). Although this is a truism it is undoubtedly the case that standards can be supported by the right structure, and further, it can be difficult to secure standards where there is an inappropriate structure.

Pupil organization

Firstly is there a need for a middle leader in between form tutors and the leadership team? There is a superficial attraction to flattening the structure by the removal of the head of year/house layer in school. The attractions are:

1. empowerment of the tutors to take appropriate action
2. the supposed closeness of tutor to the pupil
3. it is undoubtedly cheaper as the middle layer is frequently rewarded with management allowance points and some timetable remission

However, our experience (although admittedly not rigorously researched) suggests that where the pastoral structure is delayered it rapidly becomes layered again, usually with new titles (year coordinator for example) to cover the embarrassment of the policy reversal. So why is this? Is there a fundamental requirement for middle leaders in the pastoral structure? Fundamental may be putting it too strongly, but some of the reasons may be as follows:

1   pastoral leaders have usually applied for the post and have a commitment to the work – the same can be said of some form tutors, but by no means all

2   there is an economy of scale in the role of pastoral leader: significant problems may only be presented by a relatively small number of pupils; the pastoral leader has the time to deal with these, tutors do not

3   pastoral leaders will usually be a relatively small team (5 or 6), tutors a much larger group (30? 40? 50?) and not one that can readily be described as a team. There is no capacity for a senior leader to manage such a large group at all, never mind doing so effectively

4   there is a wide range of skills among the teaching staff, some of whom do exceptional work as tutors, some of whom are dreadful. The experience of the child in each group is bound to be influenced by this variability, but at least a middle pastoral leader can provide some leadership, some management, some development for the tutor thus mitigating the worst impacts of weak tutors

Having acknowledged the need for pastoral leaders, then the pastoral structure needs to be decided. Perhaps year structure provides a more manageable task for the member of staff concerned and also provides consistency across the year group. There are common concerns associated with each year group. Pragmatically it seems better to have one person (and their tutors) focusing upon these concerns rather than having the whole middle team focusing upon all at once. On the other hand there are advantages to the house system, perhaps a greater sense of belonging for pupils: a house creates a subsidiary identity and esprit de corps for pupils. On balance we prefer the year system for its efficiency; however there are strong arguments both ways for effectiveness.

Curriculum organization
The challenge faced here is the number of different subjects taught in the average secondary school. Although it is perfectly standard to group some subjects into one department (for example physics, chemistry and biology are rarely identified as separate departments), for most

they really do stand alone. Typically then there are 14 or so different departments in an average secondary school. This does cause some difficulties. The heads of department meeting becomes a rather large affair not conducive to good discussion; where there is one identified person who leads the head of department team then this is a big task as there are so many people to monitor and performance manage. The expedient often adopted is to structure into faculties, so for example a humanities faculty might include history, RE, geography, business studies, government and politics and sociology. The head of faculty would then become the line manager of all the other heads of department in the faculty and represent them at the curriculum leaders' meeting. While the idea of leading a team of around 7 heads of faculty is attractive for the senior leader, there are some significant downsides to this approach, in particular the difficulty of the accountability between heads of department and head of faculty, and the communication onwards to the leadership team. This interaction is important in all sorts of ways. Each subject should be given a voice at the curriculum managers' team meeting; this is not replicated by faculty heads speaking on their behalf. The accountability for the performance of the department cannot be transferred through the heads of faculty and the heads of faculty themselves cannot perform this function in a meaningful way. In short, the interaction between a head of department and their leadership team line manager is of a significance that should not be readily sacrificed just to provide an expedient solution to an over-large curriculum managers' meeting. In contrast to the argument presented for pastoral leadership, flat management here is of critical importance.

Summary

So we now have a position where members of the leadership team are accountable for every dimension of the school; where there is a leader of the pastoral team, a leader of the curriculum team and a number of other leadership team members that have responsibility for strategic priorities for the school. Pastoral leadership is organized preferably in year teams, although houses can work; curriculum leadership is through a flat structure of heads of department reporting directly to their leadership team line manager. Within this structure the head's key role is to lead and manage the leadership team.

Of course, having a structure written down and having job descriptions and policies for operation are all well and good, the next step is to consider how to make the structure work. The purpose of the structure is to aid the fulfilment of the school vision and aims. There are many obstacles that can potentially lie in the way of the success of this purpose. Systems need to be in place to ensure that the vision is communicated and shared throughout the organization, that staff gain the necessary skills to implement the improvement plans and that the whole enterprise is kept on target through an appropriate system of monitoring, evaluation and review. This will be the purpose of the next section.

Running the team

In the discussion above much emphasis has been placed on efficiency and effectiveness and the part clarity plays in securing both of these. We hope it is self-evident why such efficiency and effectiveness are desirable, but for some these words speak of an approach wedded to managerialism and lacking in the creative spark and the human touch that are so important in education. It is important not to see efficiency and effectiveness as at odds with humanity and creativity. Schools are, above all else, human organizations. They deal in the human condition, however messy that can sometimes be. But one thing is also true, there is precious little time to deal with issues if they are not dealt with efficiently. Efficiency is a prize worth winning, and at a time when we have to consider the workload on our staff more than ever, efficiency should be a watchword for the way we run our organization. While efficiency is about doing things right, about reaching the desired goals in the best, most time-efficient way, essentially it is about management, effectiveness is about leadership, it is about doing the right thing. As Stephen Covey (1989) puts it:

> Envision a group of producers cutting their way through the jungles with machetes. They're the producers, the problem solvers. They're cutting through the undergrowth, clearing it out.
>
> The managers are behind them, sharpening their machetes, writing policy and procedure manuals, holding muscle development programmes, bringing in improved technologies and setting up working schedules and compensation programmes for machete wielders.
>
> The leader is the one who climbs up the tallest tree, surveys the entire situation, and yells 'Wrong jungle'. (p.101)

In this example the managers are being highly efficient at completing the task. They have everything in hand and it is all going really well. But they are completely ineffective because they are tackling the wrong task! Efficiency is only worth having if there is also effectiveness, that is the ability to ensure the right job is being done. So part of the right job being done is about all those things that some in schools shy away from as the increasing business-ization of education. So we are completely unapologetic about wanting effectiveness and efficiency for our school.

Having set up a structure that is efficient in terms of management, accountability and communication then we need to consider how to ensure our efficient structure is effective.

One answer to this is coaching. This is the most intensive form of staff development. It is heavily dependent upon one-to-one meetings. In our school the structure is designed to support this coaching approach. We have a leadership group comprising a head, deputy head and four assistant heads. Each member of the team has a team of colleagues that reports to them, for example the deputy head line-manages all the heads of department, one of the assistant heads manages the heads of year. In turn these team members are in charge of their own teams. To support the coaching paradigm there is an absolute expectation that each team leader will meet with each team member individually on a regular basis. The frequency depends upon the size of the team and (in the case of heads of department, for example) the time available to carry out these meetings. The headteacher meets with each of the leadership team once per week, the assistant head meets with heads of year every two weeks, the deputy meets with heads of department every four weeks. Each teacher has an entitlement to an individual meeting of 30 minutes with their head of department each half term.

Now this lengthy description of meetings above sounds like a prescription for endless meetings-bloody-meetings. How does this system, which on the face of it is the antithesis of 'modern management' with its delayering principles and empowerment models, deliver school improvement? Surely all it delivers is staff weighed down by bureaucracy? This would be a risk if the system was not based upon the school development plan and action-focused. To put this more clearly, if the heads of department team are required by their development plans to work upon improving attainment at GCSE, to improve schemes of work and to improve assessment in their departments, then these items form a clear agenda for a sequence of meetings. For example, at an initial meeting a head of department might be asked to produce a commentary upon their most recent GCSE results. This commentary will illuminate some issues that doubtless will include matters relating to schemes of work and assessment. Having discussed this a series of action points will emerge which can be minuted and become actions for the next meeting. At the next meeting progress can be reviewed and new action points will emerge.

Aha, I hear you say, but why is there a need for the meeting, could this not all be done on paper? Progress could be recorded, action points and deadlines set, new progress recorded and so on. This is where we come to the crux of the matter. The purpose of the meeting series with a head of department is not simply a monitoring exercise (as has been described above), rather it is a coaching meeting. The key purpose of the meeting is, in fact, staff development. In the example it may not be evident to the head of department where the issues in their department lie; it is only through skilled questioning and probing that these issues can be teased out. Perhaps the HoD has not considered schemes of work, or may indeed actively disagree with the whole concept of schemes of work (it does happen), then the meeting is an opportunity for the team leader to work through this and make the case. Again this will rely upon skilled questioning and probing, but over a relatively short period of time dramatic changes can result from this approach. Running throughout all these discussion is the alignment of culture and thinking referred to above. The outcome when this system is performed well is a cohesive team with a deep shared understanding of the expectations they should have of themselves, their team and their pupils and also an understanding of what is expected of them.

At leadership group level it is common practice for there to be a weekly leadership group meeting. What place do one-to-ones have here? The answer to this depends very much upon the nature of the leadership group. It is our view that it is more efficient and leads to greater consistency for senior colleagues to have complete responsibility for aspects of the school, hence our somewhat traditional pastoral/curriculum divide. Accepting this to be the case then the place of the leadership group meeting becomes discussion of items that have already been thought through previously. Bringing problems without suggested answers to the leadership group is wasteful of time and leads to shoddy decision-making. In this structure those with responsibility for an area have the responsibility of doing the thinking on that area, preparing discussion papers for the team as appropriate. Of course the thinking has to take place some time and this is one of the reasons for the weekly bilateral meeting between a team member and the head. The school development plan forms the agenda for the meeting where the issues relating to implementation are thought through. Perhaps this will include rehearsing a particularly difficult meeting, going through a lesson observation note to arrive at a judgement, considering what steps need to be taken with a member of staff who is under-performing. It is important that these things are gone through not only because the team member may not know what to do or how to go about achieving the desired ends, but also because this provides an opportunity for *the* way as opposed to *a* way to be determined. By discussing these issues the team member knows not only that they are pursuing the correct procedure, but also that they are doing so in a way that is congruent with the culture of the organization and vision the head has for its future development. Again as well as providing an opportunity for coaching and development, the meeting allows an opportunity for alignment.

When a new team member joins then the mode of this coaching meeting will be very different. The new colleague will be learning the ropes, trying to make sense of the school and their new role. The purpose of the meeting will be about induction, but also a large degree of direction; there are things that need to be done and they need to be done in a particular way. As time goes on though the mode changes rather in the manner of Figure 3.1, which is a familiar representation of situational leadership. Progress through the diagram though is not, as sometimes is indicated, a straightforward journey; where new activities are demanded then the mode may well return from delegating to directing. This is entirely appropriate.

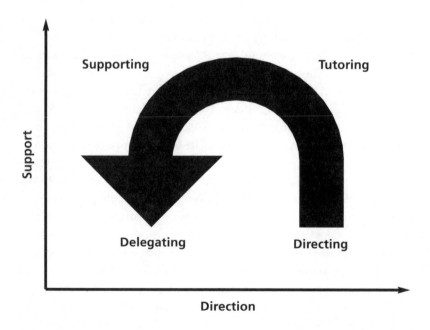

Figure 3.1 *The coaching paradigm*

Mark was a head of science in a secondary school. In his first year in the school it happened that he was scheduled for one period more than his proper allocation. Under the circumstances his line manager, the headteacher in this case, decided that the fortnightly meeting he had planned with Mark would be lapsed for the year so as not to overburden this new colleague in his first year.

As it turned out Mark did not make good progress through the first year. There were a range of difficulties in the department relating to schemes of work and development planning. Mark's annual department review was late, as were his reports on a number of occasions. There were always a range of plausible excuses. However, once Mark's exam classes left, then the head decided to schedule the fortnightly meeting that had been lapsed for the first two and a half terms. The meetings began with a performance review for the year (as it was that time in the cycle). Mark's teaching was found to be of an at least satisfactory standard and he was able to talk convincingly about his plans for the future of the department. With the head he worked out a schedule for the use of planning time released from year 11 classes for the remainder of the term. This was noted and progress awaited. When he came for the next meeting Mark had carried out a small number of fairly inconsequential tasks, but the planning time had not been used. Again with a range of reasons that sounded plausible.

The new term started and Mark had to present himself for his fortnightly meeting with the head. It turned out that none of the planned work had happened at the end of the last term. New goals were set and the agreed short-term targets were recorded as a minute of the meeting. Progress was reviewed each meeting, and usually there was none. The plausible reasons kept coming, but while individually they were convincing, collectively they were less so. Over the course of the first ten weeks of the term, through this process of fortnightly meetings it became apparent that Mark was not capable of doing the job for which he was employed. A capability procedure was initiated, leading, on the advice of the area union representative, to Mark's resignation.

Box 3.1

This does sound all a little top–down, but the best thing about the process is the extent to which it encourages bottom–up thinking. Where the system is working well then the team leader lets go of the agenda and allows the team member to bring their issues to the meeting. Each team member grows to value their meetings as it is time allowed for them to develop their thinking about areas that they wish to develop. If the team member's agenda is not quite aligned then the team leader has a regular opportunity to re-focus the work of the colleague concerned. Under these circumstances the regular meeting performs two functions, first, it provides an opportunity to expose lack of progress on an area of development, i.e. the team leader can find out that progress has not been made. Secondly, it allows an opportunity to address the lack of progress in a forum that is considerably less threatening than a meeting specifically set up for that purpose.

At the harder end of things, if a team member is a cause for concern then having a regular time where they are held to account for their work means there really is no hiding place. Box 3.1 is an example.

This example provides a number of learning points:

1   The first half of Mark's time at the school, when he wasn't having regular meetings with his team leader, allowed him to carry on in the way that he had been used to in previous schools. The phrase 'Talks a good game' is often used to mean that the person sounds plausible but there is rarely evidence of what they say they can do. By saying the right things at the right moment Mark was able to avoid any unpleasant reckoning through the normal course of events.

2   Mark's life became a lot more difficult when the head started his meetings. Every two weeks he had to face the reckoning. What had been achieved, what had not? There was no hiding place.

3   As the meetings were part of the normal procedure of the school there was no threat implied. It was not a 'monitoring meeting', where the progress of someone who was failing to meet the standards required was going to be reviewed, it did however fulfil this purpose given the circumstances where this was required.

4   As time went by matters built their own momentum. The mere fact of having a meeting provided an imperative for action. That there was no action became more and more obvious.

5   In the end it was clear to both the head and to Mark that there was only one conclusion to this case: Mark would have to go. This outcome was achieved without animosity and with a degree of shared understanding that this was the only natural conclusion. In a sense the process provided no hiding place for the head either, the performance of this team member required action to be taken; with integrity it was not possible to avoid this conclusion.

It would be a great mistake to think that this system of performance management should only apply where the team leader is unhappy with the work of one of their colleagues. And an even greater mistake to think that it is in some way an extension of the capability procedure described in Chapter 7. That it can fulfil these purposes is important, but at its best this system provides for clear and empowering leadership, for the creation of a shared vision, aims, values and goals, and provides for a supportive, trusting and valuing relationship between team members.

Conclusion

Looking at different models of leadership team structure can be quite a diverting pastime. It certainly appears as though there are plenty of ways to skin that particular cat, as it is unlikely that any two schools have an identical structure. Heads and leadership teams up and down the country will advocate strongly their own particular approach, given the purposes that they want their structure to achieve. When considering your approach, remember that its purpose is to achieve the school goals, and use that as your marker for its efficacy, remembering that it is easy to persuade yourself that whatever you want to do is rational, even when sometimes it isn't!

School finances are a bit of a roller-coaster at the best of times. Frequently schools find themselves in lean times. In times of such financial difficulty it is tempting to see the leadership team as an expensive luxury. After all there are all these highly paid people who don't do much teaching. Why not just get rid of them and save the money? In fact it is even possible to appear really forward-thinking and modern if this is presented as 'flattening the structure'. But it is our contention that school leadership is the last thing that should be starved of resources: without school leaders where does the vision emanate from, without a leader who sets the standards and provides the clarity necessary for a successful school? The leadership team is vital and should be provided with the tools to do the job. Don't think that it is possible to squeeze the non-contact time and still get a job done and, after all, your leadership team are very expensive classroom teachers. Don't think that just loading a small number of team members with vastly lengthy job descriptions means that those jobs are happening. The reality is that each team member is likely to put their heart and soul into their work but they can only do what is possible and what isn't possible will get pushed out. And, as a very important part of this, think about when you will have your leadership team meetings, both the full team and the bilaterals. Does your team meeting take place during the school day, or, as at one school we know of, at 6 pm on a Friday. When is the best time to get high-quality thinking happening? If the leadership team meeting is important and, given the cost of such a meeting (given the hourly rate of the participants), then surely it should be scheduled at a time to gain maximum effectiveness which will be during the school day. Ours is at 11.30 on a Monday; we think this is the best time to get the most from our team. It also has the merit of having a clear finishing time at 1.05 when team members have to be elsewhere thus concluding business rather than drifting on into the evening.

Finally, a brief word about the performance management meetings' system we have described. In discussion with colleagues from other schools we find a common reaction is 'where do you find the time?' The response to this is that we don't think we can afford not to find the time. As in so many areas of school life the leader has to prioritize scarce resources. We describe prioritization of finances at length in Chapter 4. But time is one of our most valuable resources and its use must be prioritized in the same way as, in fact even more carefully than, any other resource. Time is a tricky chap, it evaporates if you let it. Build your bilateral meetings into your schedule and give them the priority that your team give them. If you aren't already doing this, give it a try, we think you'll be surprised at how much you and your team get out if it.

Bibliography
Covey, S. (1989) *The 7 Habits of Highly Effective People*. New York: Simon & Schuster.

CHAPTER 4

What do we do with all this money? On prudence and getting the most from the school's resources

The introduction of Local Management of Schools (LMS) after the 1988 Education Reform Act produced a sea change in the role of the headteacher, the leadership team and the governors in the conduct of schools. Prior to this much of the responsibility for the management of schools lay with the Local Education Authorities (LEAs). The LEA would determine how many teachers and other staff each school would have, and their pay scales, they would decide upon such matters as improvement to premises (decoration, refurbishment and the like), provide cleaners and catering staff for the school and administer all purchases. The local financial responsibility for the school was limited to an amount of capitation from which curriculum materials and resources would be purchased. Even then, the LEA would retain an amount for special bidding by schools which covered what was considered to be larger items of furniture, apparatus and equipment (FA & E). Naturally enough the bureaucracy required to administer all of this was formidable and, as one would expect, led to some spectacular examples of bureaucratic nonsense. For example at one school the head of physics made an application under FA & E for some data-logging equipment. The value of the two items requested was approximately £50 each – one can imagine the delight when the news was released that this application had been granted. Though the joy was short-lived as it turned out that the LEA provided only one of the two essential pieces of equipment, an item useless on its own and £50 wasted.

Contrast this with the scene today where secondary school governors are responsible for multi-million pound budgets, where they are responsible for employing all the staff of the school and making decisions about numbers of staff, their salaries and the leadership structure of the school. In essence the governors of a 1000-pupil school are given around £3.5m per annum and a building, and must then get on with providing an education for those 1000 pupils. There are some checks and balances, there are audits (to ensure financial probity) every so often, there are Ofsted inspections every six years or so (to ensure that children are getting a good education), and there is the LEA who does have some power over schools in that, *in extremis*, they can remove the governing body (how often has anyone heard of that happening?), but otherwise must rely largely upon influence rather than direct power. This is a formidable responsibility and given, in large part, most of the running of a school rests with the headteacher, it is a formidable responsibility to be carried largely by one person.

Of course one cannot help but notice that headteachers are almost exclusively drawn from the ranks of teachers, a role that does little to prepare a person for the discharge of this responsibility. Of course, in a well-regulated world, aspirational headteachers would be able to call upon the newly established National College for School Leaders to provide training in all the aspects of financial and personnel management for which their own careers as classroom practitioners have done little to prepare them. Indeed one of the elements of the National Professional Qualification for Headteachers (NPQH) is on just this topic. The reality, though, is that this does little to actively prepare senior staff for what is to come; headteachers of the future must rely upon finding their own preparation through their work in the leadership team prior to assuming the role of head. Here lies an important matter of principle. To what extent is it reasonable to expect those who have gained their leadership positions as a result of their expertise in teaching and learning to have the business skills of finance directors and managers of personnel departments of medium-sized businesses. There is a strong body of opinion that believes that none of these matters should reside with the head, that headteachers should 'stick to the knitting' of being the leader of learning rather than being distracted by all these rather prosaic matters of paying the bills and so forth. And there is certainly merit in this idea. Any headteacher who has spent inordinate amounts of time worrying about the cleaning contract, having meetings with the contractor and generally getting very irritated by the complete lack of cleanliness in the school may well yearn for the days when they could simply be the leader of learning and not worry about all of those more distasteful matters. But notwithstanding such moments we do not believe there are many heads who would wish for a return to the days pre-LMS where all such matters were dealt with by others.

And here is an illustration of why this is. Each year, just after the mock GCSE examinations the headteacher of our school spends a short time having a meeting with each year 11 student. We discuss their performance in the mock exams, we look at their target grades, we decide what needs to be done in order to meet, or preferably exceed those targets. We then move on to their future plans, are they staying in the sixth form (if not why not?!), then we end up by them saying what they like most about the school and what they would change or improve. On this last pair of questions there is a great consistency in their responses. What they like best is (mainly) the friendly atmosphere and the helpful/friendly/relaxed teachers (there are also some minority opinions about the canteen food and the like), what they would change or improve has an even greater uniformity to it, most likely they will identify the toilets and where opinion strays from this then it will still mainly be premises or facilities-related (or the canteen food).

The 'Leader of Learning' contingent decries the result of local management of school as resulting in headteachers being only concerned with budgets, repairs and transportation. But I wonder what those young people in year 11 would make of it if, when they raised their concerns with the head, all he could say was 'Sorry, I'm the Leader of Learning, toilets really have nothing to do with me'. We suspect they might be less than impressed and really begin to wonder what the head was for.

Why is school leadership much more than being the 'Leader of Learning'? Perhaps it is more accurate to ask 'Where does learning take place?' It is a truism that we are always learning, most schools have it as a stated aim that they wish to develop the whole child. Thus learning takes place in lessons where children learn about science, geography, French and the rest. But it also takes place as a result of the environment within which the child functions and as a result of their interactions with other pupils – hence the answers from year 11 students about what matters to them. So questions such as 'Is the school clean and well looked after?', 'Do the toilets smell or are they clean and bright with plenty of paper?', 'What are the arrangements for eating, do they encourage civilized behaviour or mindless troughing?' are all issues that should concern the school leader.

But surely others could deal with all this leaving the head to get on with the important business of leading learning in the school. What about managing the budget? Is this just accounting? How much money have we got at any particular time is certainly an important question, the answer to which is probably best left to an expert. But does this mean that the entire budget should be left in the hands of the accountant? What is it that allows the head to secure good teaching and effective learning? Well it is a matter of having the correct teachers doing the correct job with the correct pupils and, where these things are not entirely possible, making the correct judgements about how to allocate resources to achieve the outcomes. What about refurbishing those wretched toilets? This might cost £50,000; perhaps this can only be afforded by increasing class sizes in a year group. How is the judgement arrived at? It is simply not good enough to ask the accountant because inevitably the choice is not as simple as that presented here.

The vision for the school is all-encompassing. To reduce this to the head as leader of learning ignores the reality that school is a complete experience for young people and so every aspect of the school is the concern of the head. Local management of schools liberated school leaders to function in the best interest of their pupils and their communities, but only if they use the power for the best interests of those pupils and communities. That is the purpose of this chapter, to consider how to go about running the business aspects of the school for the best interests of the pupils and how to ensure that that all-encompassing vision is achieved and to ensure that the complete experience for pupils is as good as it can be.

Where to begin?

We first need to gain an understanding of the sources of funding for schools. Although it is well understood that schools gain the majority of their funding based on the number of pupils they have, there is still a significant amount of further funding that comes in for other reasons. Indeed at the Secondary Heads Association (SHA) conference of 2003 John Dunford identified 63 different funding streams into schools. It is also said, apocryphally one must suspect, that only two people have ever understood school finances, and one of them is dead! A typical county comprehensive school may receive funding under the following headings within the individual school's budget:

- Total pupil funding
- Special educational needs non-statemented
- Special educational needs' statements
- Fixed costs
- Work experience insurance

- Free meals provision
- Grounds' area allowance
- Floor area
- Repairs and maintenance allowance
- Building insurance
- Rent and rates
- Pupil numbers' adjustment (rising rolls)
- Learning and skills council (LSC) funding
- LSC Pupil Retention
- School standards grant
- National Insurance Additional Allocation

In addition there are a variety of sources of funding supposedly hypothecated (more on this later) for particular purposes, all of which are known as Standards Fund. In 2003 the government took a variety of (rather controversial) actions relating to school funding, one of these was to reduce the number of standards funds available. At Matthew Arnold in that year we received the following:

- Specialist School Grant
- Study Support
- ks3 strategy
- Support Staff Training
- Teaching assistants
- ks3 behaviour
- National Grid for Learning infrastructure
- ks3 ICT
- NQTs
- e-Learning

Finally, funding is received outside both of these headings. Again in 2003, these included:

- Threshold supplement
- Upper pay spine advancement
- Leadership pay progression
- Seed challenge (a grant for capital projects disbursed by the LEA that provides matched funding for external fund-raising efforts)

In addition to this income there is any income the school manages to generate itself, possibly including:

- Lettings income
- Bank interest

- Mobile phone base station rental (probably more trouble than it's worth!)
- Catering income, and
- Balance brought forward from the previous financial year

All told, in our case, pupil income amounted to only 62 per cent of our total income for the year. So while it is undeniably true that the per capita income from pupils is very important (and indeed standards fund in particular can be largely dependent upon pupil numbers), other sources of income provide a very large proportion of the effective school budget. A key message here is that those responsible for the finances of the school must ensure that, first, they maximize the income from other sources, which will inevitably involve lettings and maximizing interest on unspent portions of the budget, but it will also involve ensuring that correct attention is paid to the various funding streams that can be accessed but are not automatically allocated to every school (frequently dispersed through bids).

Secondly, it is one thing to be promised funds for various reasons, it is quite another to end up with it in the bank. There can be a significant gap between being promised funds through, for example, the standards fund, or repayment for supply costs when a member of staff is released from school, or, perhaps most importantly, overpayments to members of staff, but the bureaucracy of LEAs or any of the other funding bodies that we deal with can quite easily lead to such transfers being lost. It is a crucial element of financial monitoring to ensure that all these items are tracked and accounted for – here very good communication systems with the school bursar are essential.

Benchmarking

Having received all this money, then it is time for some decisions to be made. We indicated earlier that the governors may receive around £3.5m and a building and then must get on with it. The question is how to begin making decisions. And it is certainly the case that there is never a problem finding things to spend this money on. Some of the decisions are made for you, for example there are rates to pay, energy to provide, water must be supplied, the buildings must be insured, some pupils are entitled to free meals, examinations must be paid for, bins collected and so on. But a very large proportion of the budget is subject to discretionary decision-making. For example:

1   how many teachers should the school employ? This decision is contingent upon:
    a) the size of classes

b) what options should be offered at GCSE and A level
c) the amount of non-contact time teachers should have on average and for different responsibilities
d) the provision that might be made for those pupils with special educational needs or behavioural difficulties

2   how many curriculum support staff should be employed?
a) learning support assistants
b) other teaching assistants
c) technicians

3   How much administrative support should there be?
a) is admin support provided for
   i)   the leadership team?
   ii) heads of department?
   iii) heads of year?
b) Will there be reprographics assistance?
c) What hours is reception covered for? Just when the pupils are at school or for longer periods?
d) What about admin support in the school vacations, does the school open all year round or is it term times only?

4   How much should be spent on site staff?
a) caretakers
b) cleaning staff

All of these decisions just affect the staffing. Then of course there are a whole range of decisions to be taken regarding curriculum resources and, that well-known money pit, ICT facilities. What about premises improvement, decorating, repairs and maintenance? Clearly all of this represents a prodigious number of decisions to be taken.

Now as a new head in an existing school (few of us have the luxury of starting from scratch) there will be a certain number of overhanging commitments and the gathered experience of 'the way things are done here'. While this will give you some grace – in other words things can carry on as they are, at least for the time being – it really is vital that decisions are taken with all of these matters and the many others not listed in order to ensure that the available, and always limited, resources are directed at fulfilling the vision and aims of the school. Far too often the historical evolution of funding decisions leads cumulatively to some apparently bizarre situations which result from a series of decisions, all of which seemed entirely rational on their own and at the time.

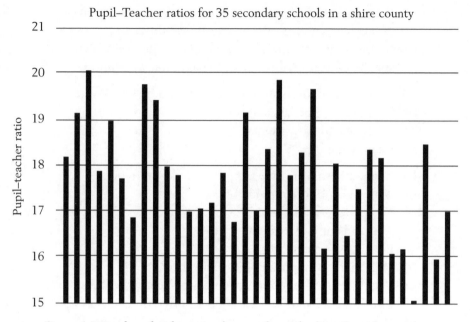

Figure 4.1 *Benchmark information for secondary school pupil–teacher ratios*

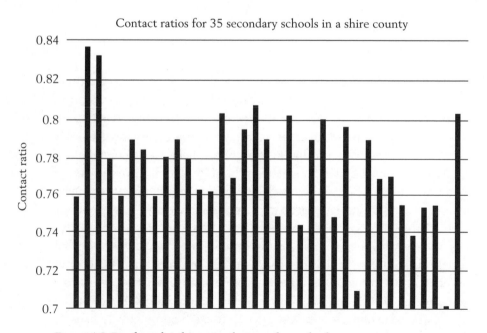

Figure 4.2 *Benchmark information for secondary school contact ratios*

The question is how do you come to a view of what is reasonable to spend? The answer to this is benchmarking.

Benchmarking is the process of comparing expenditure in your school to that of others. The LEA should provide you with financial and curriculum information about all of the schools in the LEA so that you can compare all aspects of your work with that of others – in particular this allows you to compare yourself to the average of the other schools. If your LEA does not provide this information as a matter of course, then they can so make sure you get it from them!

Figures 4.1 and 4.2 show two examples of benchmarking information. Figure 4.1 is the pupil–teacher ratios (PTRs) in one LEA and you can see the wide variation of PTR from school to school. Figure 4.2 shows contact ratios (i.e. the average amount of time each teacher spends teaching each week) for the same schools and again there is a wide variation. It may well be that PTR impacts upon contact ratio and that schools with low contact ratios pay for this with high PTRs. It may well be that your school is one such school. Now, as long as this is a matter of strategic choice, you have made a conscious decision to pay for high non-contact with bigger class sizes, then others may take issue with you, but you have made that choice which is yours to make. However, if this was a historical situation that you have inherited, then you may well see a strong case for changing the balance.

There are two specific points to make about benchmark information:

1   That little can be gleaned from only one piece of information; they all impact upon one another and it is the whole that is important rather than the individual elements that make up that whole.

2   It is very easy to become a slave to the tyranny of the average. In other words, wherever your school compares adversely to the average then it is easy to feel a strong pressure to move the indicator back to the average. If you have made a strategic decision to have larger than average class sizes so that income can be spent elsewhere on capital projects perhaps, then, as indicated above, others may disagree, but the decision is yours (and of course your governors') to make. Benchmarks are vital to the process of financial management, but remember they are there to help you make decisions, not to make the decisions for you.

Different types of expenditure

Before going on to look in more detail at financial decision-making and monitoring it is worth spending a small amount of time thinking about revenue and capital expenditure. This is important because, while spending decisions must be affordable within the financial year in question, there is also the consequences for future years. Briefly, revenue expenditure is that which is required to sustain the operation of the school, and capital expenditure is that which increases the value of the stock of buildings or resources within the school.

Example

A particular comprehensive school was in some difficulty with a poor reputation and a declining roll. The head and governors were very exercised about the condition of the buildings and the very poor impression this made on visitors to the school. Fortuitously, there was a certain amount of underspend on the previous year's budget and so the head and governors decided that this windfall should be spent on refurbishing the reception area of the school. The existing reception area was very cold and unwelcoming with a 1950s terrazzo floor, a reception desk in a small office to one side of the entrance hall that visitors would frequently not be able to find. Similarly, the door screen was the original 1950s steel-framed single-glazed affair.

The work was agreed at a premises' committee meeting and then reported to the full governors.

The following day a teacher governor present at the meeting discussed the issue with a variety of colleagues in the staff room. This was the first anyone had heard of the plan (an undoubted error on the part of the headteacher), and it caused some uproar among the staff. Why was money being spent so frivolously when everyone knew that class sizes were too big in year 7? What about employing more support staff or increasing the contact time in the sixth form?

In this example the staff making these alternative propositions were making a basic error of not understanding the difference between capital and revenues expenditure. In this school the work did go ahead and the entrance area was renovated. The final cost was around £40,000. Now this is undoubtedly a lot of money and could have been used to decrease class sizes, increase support, or increase contact time in the sixth form, but it could have done so for that year only. All of these other suggested improvements were revenue costs, i.e. increasing class size in the sixth form would cost, say, £30,000 in the year in question and would continue doing so for ever after. Employing more support staff would be a cost every year that they were employed. By contrast a building refurbishment is a capital cost – while this project cost £40,000 one year, the following year it cost nothing at all, and would cost nothing until the work needed to be done again. Say, for example, the entrance area needed to be refurbished again 8 years later (which I am sure most people would hope was a very conservative estimate) then the annual cost of the capital project would be £40,000/8 years or £5000 per annum. In revenue terms this is a very small amount indeed.

So this is why it is most important to be very careful about committing to revenue expenditure, and the most important part of revenue expenditure, because it accounts for such a huge proportion of the total costs, is salaries, and in particular teachers' salaries. Where schools find themselves in financial difficulties the first place to look for the reason is the teaching staff. For this reason the next section is devoted to planning teacher numbers and monitoring expenditure.

Teacher costs

Cost of teacher time

How much does a period of teacher time cost? Of course this quantity more than any other over recent years is subject to inflation, so each year the cost must be recalculated. But, for example, take a school of 900 pupils with 51 teaching staff, a total number of periods taught of 1895 and a total cost of teaching staff of £1.95m.

A very straightforward calculation provides a cost per taught period of:

$$\frac{\text{Total cost of teachers}}{\text{Total number of taught periods}} = \frac{£1,950,000}{1895}$$

$$= \quad £1029 \text{ per taught period}$$

Which means the average cost of a teacher who teaches an 86 per cent timetable (e.g. 43 periods out of a cycle of 50) is £44,247. Now at this point any newly qualified teachers will be saying 'Hang on a minute – I only get £18,500 so who gets the rest?' Well here are some of the items that go to raise the average:

1 employers' national insurance contributions are about 9 per cent
2 employers' pension contributions towards the teachers' final salary pension scheme 12 per cent
    • (both of these together are referred to as 'oncosts')
3 non-contact time – of course we have only costed the taught periods, not the teacher periods. Matters would be

much cheaper without non-contact time, though with the new contract for teachers the flexibility available to school managers in this respect is much circumscribed

4   management allowances – in most secondary schools around 65 per cent of the staff are on promoted scales for various leadership and management functions

5   the headteacher – a very expensive item!

6   increased non-contact time for those with leadership and management responsibilities

There is, of course, little that can be done about 1, 2 and 5 (as schools are required to have a headteacher), but the other three items in the list are all at least to some extent discretionary expenditure. But even these pale into insignificance when it comes to curriculum decisions regarding class sizes.

Just a comment on the methodology. Some may argue that a good deal of what is included in the total teachers' pay budget amounts to fixed costs, the head's salary, management allowances and so on, and that the marginal increase in staffing budget is what should count when costing taught periods. So if a new A level course is proposed the key issue is not the average cost, but the actual cost of employing an extra teacher for that time, which if they were a main-scale teacher low down the pay spine would be about half as much as our calculation here. There is a certain merit in this argument – however it rapidly becomes complicated. What if the new course was taught by the head? Should we account for the much higher costs of teaching the course under these circumstances? It generally seems simpler all around to consider that each taught period must bear its share of the fixed costs on the staff rather than go in for more complicated calculation procedures.

Class sizes

Many readers will have the luxury of working in oversubscribed schools where class-size management is not problematic. If each year has an intake of, say, 210 then this will probably be organized into 8 classes of 26 or 27. Where pupil populations are more variable from year to year, and particularly when there is a steady stream of non-normal age of transfer pupils joining year groups then matters are more complex.

For example, year 8 is running with 148 pupils, and the standard number for the year group is 172. Should this be 5 classes of average 29.6, which is a little tight especially in old-fashioned classrooms not designed for groups of 30, or should it be 6 classes of average 24.6? Well, the latter certainly sounds better. Let's consider how much this will cost. Given the average teacher cost above, then the calculation is:

cost per taught period × periods in a timetable cycle = cost of one class

so in this case, say there are 50 periods in a cycle and the cost per period is £1029 then:

£1029 × 50 periods = £51,540

and given that some subjects may be split more ways, e.g. technology, then the total costs will be even more. Also this cost will not only be for year 8, but for year 9 too, and then what happens to class sizes in years 10 and 11? So over two years the cost of reducing class sizes in this year group by 5 is over £103,000. Now consider what that could buy in capital projects – how about a major expansion of ICT facilities, perhaps a new classroom, possibly re-carpeting and refurnishing the entire school? All for the price of a reduction in class sizes by 5 in a year group for two years.

Of course, the matter is further complicated by the fact that, while it may be acceptable to teach 148 pupils in 5 groups, what if 10 more pupils join during the year? As the standard number is 172 it could certainly happen. What if those pupils are all permanently excluded from other schools? How would we feel about adding say 5 pupils with serious behaviour problems into 5 classes that are already averaging 30?

In the end the decision could go either way and will depend upon variables specific to the year group in question, particularly considerations of behaviour problems and special needs. There are undoubtedly other creative ways of mitigating matters, such as using teaching assistants, but the point is that such decisions must be made on the basis of the facts of the situation and that the cost of creating more teaching groups is huge. Keep control of teacher costs and in particular class sizes, and much of the rest of the budget will come right. Losing control of these costs means heading very rapidly for very large deficits.

Planning and monitoring

Keeping track of all of the variations of class sizes, option groups and non-contact time, practical considerations of being able to actually create a timetable, can be fraught. Here the technology of the spreadsheet comes to our aid. It is essential at all times to have a view on the curriculum requirements for the coming year. For a whole range of reasons, we must always ensure that we have enough teachers to teach the classes we have planned, but we also must make sure we don't have too many. Most schools have the need for some teachers to teach second subjects in order to provide coverage for smaller subjects (for example how many schools have a specialist PSHE team?) and so it is important to know how these teachers can be deployed to ensure the correct staffing balance. A relatively simple spreadsheet tool can provide all of this information and allow accurate predictions of the staffing need for the coming year on an ongoing basis (assuming, of course, that the spreadsheet is regularly updated). An example of such a spreadsheet is shown as Table 4.1.

Each year group is listed with the number of forms of entry for that year. These can then be transferred across to the subject columns throughout the spreadsheet using a formula. So in our example if year 7 is in 6 forms of entry then most subjects are taught in the same number of groups, but in technology we tend to reduce class sizes and so the number of groups = number of FE+2. Each year group is assembled in this way for each subject. Naturally option groups have to be manually entered and this is definitely something that it can be easy to miss when updating the records! The total curriculum need for each subject is then totalled, so in our example Science has a curriculum need of 256 periods per fortnight. Below each subject need calculation there is a list of all teaching staff with the numbers of periods of contribution to each subject listed. Now we have the number of periods required, and the number of periods supplied. If the difference between these is negative then we don't have enough teachers to cover the curriculum, if positive then we have too many. At the top of the spreadsheet we then have the balance for each subject which is totalled on the far right as the total deficit or surplus on staffing for the whole curriculum.

Having entered all the data it is possible to see where the gaps are and where there is overstaffing. It is also relatively easy now to model various scenarios, for example, what is the total effect on staffing of adding another group into the core in year 10? A simple adjustment to the spreadsheet and you can see that this increases staffing need by 36 periods overall. Now we know from our previous work on staffing costs that this will cost us £1029 per period so the question is, can we afford it? Or perhaps the question is more how do we afford it? Which question is being asked depends upon the local circumstances and the priority placed upon the reduction of class sizes. The important point is that by planning in this way the costs become transparent – decisions can be made on the basis of correct information.

Of course, one of the general inconveniences of staffing the curriculum, is the tendency for there to be inconvenient bits and pieces of time that need filling. Broadly if, for example, an English teacher leaves then you will replace them with another English teacher, but what if that teacher was a head of year with a greater than average non-contact time, or someone who also happened to contribute to teaching A level sociology, then matters become more complex. Added to this are any changes in curriculum structure or patterns of options and before you know it you find yourself short of 5 periods in this subject and 4 periods in another. Again the staffing planner comes into its own here: first, if you have a staff shortfall then this is indicated in the net negative figure in the top right of the spreadsheet. If this is showing, say, −120 periods (on a fifty-period timetable), then you know you are looking for around 3 fte teachers, which if they are all mainscale teachers on 43 periods per cycle would provide 129 periods giving a (very) small amount of timetable flexibility. But it is unlikely that all of these three people will neatly fit into three subjects. Teacher commitments can be moved around across subjects with the objective of creating suitable shortfalls of around 43 periods in three subjects. The trick, always, is to know what your existing teachers are happy to teach (experience indicates that requiring teachers to teach in areas they are not comfortable with, while providing the short-term benefit of balancing the staffing planner, has the longer term impact of creating significant dissatisfaction and therefore should be avoided). So in the English department in Table 4.1 we can see a shortfall of 15 periods, but an overall shortfall of 120 periods. Ideally it would be nice to employ a full-time English teacher and the overall staffing deficit indicates that we need three teachers, so one could be English. We know that J. B. Bloggs is happy to teach PSHE and S. Smith is good at drama, we also know that J. Jones wants more A level work and will be keen to develop her expertise in sociology and politics. Therefore by moving those staff out of English we create a shortfall of 38 periods, which is close enough to make the full-time appointment possible. Add to this the suspicion that A. M. Bishus is keen to move on for promotion and is likely to get it, then making the appointment can easily be justified. All of this becomes possible with your staffing planner.

			English			Maths			Science		
Total REQ			214			190			274		
Balance	NoR	FE	-15			2			0		
			groups	periods	req.	groups	periods	req.	groups	periods	req.
Y7	165	6	6	6	36	6	6	36	6	6	36
Y8	157	6	6	6	36	6	6	36	6	6	36
Y9	146	5	5	6	30	5	6	30	5	6	30
Y10	150	6	6	7	42	6	6	36	6	9	54
Options					0				1	5	5
Y11	172	6	6	7	42	6	6	36	6	9	54
Options					0				1	5	5
Y12	70		1	8	8	1	8	8	3	8	24
GS			3	2	6				3	1	3
Y13	70		1	8	8	1	8	8	3	8	24
GS			3	2	6				3	1	3
Total REQ					214			190			274
	930										
					199			192			274

	English	Maths	Science
J Jones	43		
A Linton			
D Hart			32
J Wilkinson	8	6	
K Smith		38	
L Crouch	20		
F Fleming			39
S Carpenter			18
L Wheeler			20
H Cooper		24	
N Appleby	7		
M Cross		38	
R Brook			
T Blair			43
J B Bloggs	43		
G White			
Z Havering		43	
Y Miller			38
A M Bishus	43		
U Hutchinson		43	
J Evans			
H Williams			42
S Smith	35		
G Rhys			
J Jay			42
P McPherson			
Q Arnold			
L Pert			

Table 4.1 *A staff planning tool*

Psychology			Design & Technology			MFL			
	32			171			132		1013
	0			-9			16		120
groups	periods	req.	groups	periods	req.	groups	periods	req.	0
			8	5	40	6	5	30	178
			8	4	32	4	6	24	164
			7	4	28	4	6	24	142
									132
			5	5	25	4	5	20	50
									132
			6	5	30	4	5	20	55
2	8	16	1	8	8	1	8	8	72
									9
2	8	16	1	8	8	1	6	6	70
									9
	32			171			132		1013
	32			162			148		
									43
	4			36					40
	8								40
							28		42
									38
									20
									39
	12								30
									20
	8								32
									7
									38
				40					40
									43
									43
							40		40
									43
									38
									43
									43
							42		42
									42
									35
				43					43
									42
							18		18
							20		20
				43					43

One small word of caution. It is very easy to base all your decisions on a set of numbers from your planner, but these are only any good if your planner is right. It is all too easy to miss out the bottom few rows in a calculation and end up showing a large deficit in staff where there is none. We have never yet got as far as appointing someone we didn't need, but it has been close on occasion!

Managing the staffing budget

If you are new to financial management then the scale of staffing costs can be daunting, but it is easy to assume that they are largely fixed throughout the year. After all, you need the staff you have and, if people leave, well it's not going to be that often and in any event you will replace them with someone else to do the same job anyway, so what's the difference? I think this was certainly our operating principle for the first year or two. How wrong we were. In an organization of around 100 employees (including cleaning and catering staff) there can be frequent changes of staffing, and even when the staff do not change then hours and grades can change. Given that on a budget of £3.5m over £2.5m might be spent on staff, then small errors can lead to big difficulties. A 1 per cent variation in planned staffing costs would be difference of £25,000 over the year – a lot of money for a small variation.

So what changes do happen after you have set the staffing budget for the year? Here are some examples with their consequences:

- An experienced teacher on upper pay spine two who has responsibility for exams on two management points retires. You replace this colleague with a newly qualified teacher (NQT).

• Original salary costs:	UPS 2	£28,000
	management 2	£3500
	oncosts	£6615
	total	£38,115
• New salary costs:	MPS 1	£18,500
	oncosts	£3885
	total	£22,385
• difference in a full year:		£15,370

Clearly a few of these will make a very big difference to the planned staffing budget, although not as much as appears above as, crucially, the financial year begins in April, but the older colleague retires in August, so in planning terms you still have 5/12 of the year carrying the old high salary with 7/12 of the new. The total cost for this post for the financial year in question in therefore:

$$£38,115 \times 5/12 + £22,385 \times 7/12 = £28,939$$

A financial year saving of just under £10,000.

- A teaching assistant leaves in June, you decide not to replace them until September.
  - If the teaching assistant gets paid £700 per month, then this would be a saving on the planned budget of 2 months × £700 = £1400.

- You are unable to appoint a 0.8 NQT for September and have to employ an experienced teacher on upper pay spine 1 on a full time salary.
  - planned costs were:
    0.8 (fte) × £22,385 (full year salary including oncosts) × 7/12 = £10,446
  - actual costs are:
    1 (fte) × £32,670 (full year on UPS 1 + oncosts) × 7/12 = £19,057

Here there has been an unplanned-for additional cost of nearly £9000.

And of course there are many other scenarios. All of which goes to make the point that planning and setting the budget is one thing but what you actually end up doing is quite another.

There is a further complication, and that is what people end up being paid. The amounts allowed for oncosts above are 21 per cent (NI + superannuation), but this is an average amount of oncost. Each member of staff may well have a different actual oncost, depending upon whether they are on contracted-out National Insurance and whether or not they are contributing to the pension scheme. For this reason not only must you ensure that you adjust your planned expenditure as things change throughout the year, but you must also ensure you monitor your actual expenditure against your plan.

Table 4.2 shows how we monitor our teaching costs (non-teaching costs are basically monitored in the same way but are on different scales so are handled separately).

	Contract	CPS pt	CPS	UPSpt	UPS	Term 1 LG, AST, UQ	Management point	Management allowance	Salary inc. oncost
J Jones	1		0	2	£29,730		3	5688	£43,068
A Linton	1	1	18,105		0			0	£22,016
D Hart	1		0	2	£29,730		2	3312	£40,179
J Wilkinson									£ –
K Smith	1		0	2	£29,730		3	5688	£43,068
L Crouch	1		0		0	41,208		0	£50,109
F Fleming	1		0			42,240		0	£51,364
S Carpenter	1	2	19,536					0	£23,756
L Wheeler	1		0		0	41,208		0	£50,109
H Cooper	1		0		0			0	£ –
N Appleby	1		0	2	£29,730		5	10,572	£49,007
M Cross	1	4	22,734		0			0	£27,645
R Brook	1		0	2	£29,730		3	5688	£43,068
T Blair	1		0	2	£29,730		2	3312	£40,179
J B Bloggs									£ –
G White	1	1	18,105		0		1	1638	£24,007
Z Havering	1		0	2	£29,730		4	7833	£45,677
Y Miller	1	4	22,734		0			0	£27,645
A M Bishus	1	3	21,108		0			0	£15,400
U Hutchinson									£ –
J Evans	1		0	2	£29,730			0	£36,152
H Williams	1		0		0			0	£ –
S Smith	1		0	2	£29,730		2	3312	£38,572
G Rhys	1	1	18,105		0			0	£11,008
J Jay	1		0	2	£29,730			0	£21,691
P McPherson	1		0	2	£29,730		4	7833	£45,677
Q Arnold	1	6	26,460		0		3	5688	£39,092
L Pert									£ –

Term 2

	Contract	CPS pt	CPS	UPSpt	UPS	LG, AST, UQ	Management point	Management allowance	Salary inc. oncost
J Jones	1		0	2	£29,730		3	5688	£43,068
A Linton	1	2	19,536		£ –		1	1638	£25,748
D Hart	1		0	2	£29,730		2	3312	£40,179
J Wilkinson	1		0	1	£28,668		4	7833	£44,385
K Smith	1		0	2	£29,730		3	5688	£43,068
L Crouch	1		0		£ –	41208		0	£50,109
F Fleming	1		0		£ –	43290		0	£52,641
S Carpenter	1	3	21,108		£ –			0	£ –
L Wheeler	1		0		£ –	41208		0	£50,109
H Cooper	1	1	18,105		£ –			0	£22,016
N Appleby	1		0	2	£29,730		5	10,572	£49,007
M Cross	1	5	24,525		£ –		1	1638	£31,814
R Brook	1		0	2	£29,730		3	5688	£43,068
T Blair	1		0	2	£29,730		2	3312	£40,179
J B Bloggs	1	1	18,105		£ –			0	£22,016
G White	1	2	19,536		£ –		1	1638	£25,748
Z Havering			0	2	£29,730		4	7833	£ –
Y Miller		4	22,734		£ –			0	£ –
A M Bishus		4	22,734		£ –			0	£ –
U Hutchinson	0	6	26,460		£ –			0	£12,870
J Evans	1		0	2	£29,730			0	£36,152
H Williams	1	6	26,460		£ –		3	5688	£39,092
S Smith	1		0	2	£29,730		2	3312	£40,179
G Rhys	1	2	19,536		£ –			0	£14,253
J Jay	1		0	2	£29,730			0	£21,691
P McPherson	1		0	2	£29,730		4	7833	£45,677
Q Arnold	0	6	26,460		£ –		3	5688	£ –
L Pert	1	1	18,105					5688	£22,016

Table 4.2 *A staffing salary planner*

You can see that each term is treated separately and that each element of each teacher's pay is calculated. This gives a total per member of staff including oncosts. Table 4.3 shows how monitoring is carried out. Each month's planned expenditure for each member of staff is calculated from the planner then this is compared with the actual amount of money paid. This allows for several things. First, we see whether our plan is on target – any omissions will show up very clearly. Secondly, any anomalies shown up as the variances between the plan and the actual are significant. Now it may well be that your LEA has a system in place to provide you with all of this information, in which case this will all be completely unnecessary. This is not always the case, as it wasn't in ours. You may find you have a bursar who is completely on top of all of this information and is able to provide you with very good financial information whenever you need it (though it is always as well to satisfy yourself that you are as confident in your bursar as they are in themselves) – you may not be so lucky. Whatever the situation you find yourself in it is absolutely critical to do two things with your staffing budget, first adjust the plan to new circumstances, second monitor what is actually going on. What we have presented here is one way of accomplishing those two priority activities.

Managing the premises

Naturally enough sorting out the buildings can be a very time-consuming exercise. Indeed some headteachers can easily be labelled as very expensive site managers, as all they seem to do is worry about the premises. Of course this is a very important part of the job, as indicated at the beginning of this chapter; the state of the buildings and their cleanliness can be uppermost in the minds of those using them and so as a headteacher they must be very important to you too.

There are two aspects to managing the site. First, maintenance, in its broadest sense means cleaning, grounds maintenance, as well as fixing things that are broken. Secondly, there is renewal and replacement, of minor items such as furniture right up to whole buildings.

Take the first: if respect is an important tenet in your aims and values as it is in ours, then a basic way to show respect is by providing a suitable, well-maintained and clean environment to work within. Of course, schools have to put up with a lot of hard wear and tear and, perhaps rather too often in many schools, there is an element of the users who positively go out of their way to damage the school. Given this tendency of, thankfully a small proportion of, our clients then all too

	Apr-03	Budget	Variance	May-03	Budget	Variance	Jun-03	Budget	Variance
J Jones	£3648	£3589	£59	£3548.95	£3589	-£40	£3606	£3589	£17
A Linton	£1859	£1835	£24	£1815.16	£1835	-£19	£1817	£1835	-£17
D Hart	£3392	£3348	£43	£3349.82	£3348	£2	£3350	£3348	£2
J Wilkinson		£0	£0		£0	£0		£0	£0
K Smith	£3642	£3589	£53	£3603.89	£3589	£15	£3603	£3589	£14
L Crouch		£0	£0		£0	£0	£4065	£4176	-£111
F Fleming	£4274	£4280	-£6	£4317.91	£4280	£38	£4335	£4280	£54
S Carpenter	£2002	£1980	£22	£1961.60	£1980	-£18	£1962	£1980	-£18
L Wheeler		£0	£0		£0	£0	£4069	£4176	-£107
H Cooper		£0	£0		£0	£0		£0	£0
N Appleby	£3776	£4084	-£308	£3739.11	£4084	-£345	£4868	£4084	£784
M Cross	£2329	£2304	£26	£2288.86	£2304	-£15	£2289	£2304	-£15
R Brook	£3505	£3589	-£84	£2872.01	£3589	-£717	£3822	£3589	£233
T Blair	£3392	£3348	£43	£3349.82	£3348	£2	£3010	£3348	-£338
J B Bloggs		£0	£0		£0	£0		£0	£0
G White	£2023	£2001	£23	£1982.78	£2001	-£18	£1983	£2001	-£18
Z Havering	£3867	£3806	£61	£3825.65	£3806	£19	£3826	£3806	£19
Y Miller	£2125	£2304	-£179	£2192.77	£2304	-£111	£2092	£2304	-£212
A M Bishus	£1827	£1283	£543	£1013.63	£1283	-£270	£914	£0	£914
U Hutchinson								£0	£0
J Evans	£3045	£3013	£33	£3004.78	£3013	-£8	£3005	£3013	-£8
H Williams		£0	£0		£0	£0		£0	£0
S Smith	£3252	£3214	£38	£3213.26	£3214	-£1	£3214	£3214	£0
G Rhys	£1090	£917	£172	£1052.55	£917	£135	£779	£917	-£139
J Jay	£1903	£1808	£96	£1787.84	£1808	-£20	£1797	£1808	-£11
P McPherson	£3864	£3806	£58	£3825.65	£3806	£19	£3826	£3806	£19
Q Arnold	£3297	£3258	£40	£2446.61	£3258	-£811	£3256	£3258	-£2
L Pert		£0	£0		£0	£0	£42	£0	£42

Table 4.3 Monthly salary monitoring

often site staff can develop something of a bunker mentality. They will try and only use the hardest-wearing most vandal-resistant items around the school, they will tend to want to paint things black so that they don't show graffiti, they will want to armour-plate the toilets and generally give the impression to the whole school population that they are all expected to smash everything up at the first opportunity. Of course, this then becomes something of a challenge to those so inclined and there develops a game of cat and mouse between site staff and the anti-social element. How much better it would be to provide an environment which, while suitably robust, does not give the impression of awaiting the next assault from the massed hordes. Alongside this, when there is damage (and there will be), it must be fixed as soon as possible, indeed as the next priority. This is what Rudolph Giuliani (2002) described as the 'Broken Windows' theory.

> The theory holds that a seemingly minor matter like broken windows in abandoned buildings leads directly to a more serious deterioration of neighbourhoods. Someone who wouldn't normally throw a rock at an intact building is less reluctant to break a second window in a building that already has one broken. And someone emboldened by all these second broken windows may do even worse damage if he senses there is no one around to prevent lawlessness. (p. 47)

Taking over at our current school this theory was closer to the mark than anyone would like. There was something of a fashion for breaking windows among some of our pupils. Indeed to the extent that the site team had rather given up. This could not happen, so we had all broken windows replaced (at a cost of some £4000!) and made the priority for the site team to replace any further broken windows. We have not had a problem with window breakers for many years now.

This, of course, forms part of the wider context of school ethos which is described in more detail in Chapter 6. But it does show the interrelationship between what might appear to be mundane matters of site maintenance and the bigger picture of school aims, values and ethos, and emphasizes why it is an essential part of the headteacher's role to concern him/herself with such matters.

Much of what passes for estate management in schools is little more than the collected wisdom of the ways things have accumulated over many years. Of course the job of the new head is to show that much of this is far from wisdom and a long way from how things have to be. Some examples:

- We can't afford to decorate, the only option is self-help, teachers coming in with the paint pots in the holidays. This is the public-service ethos. Well, no, it doesn't have to be. We had the entire school redecorated for £25,000, just one third of our repair and maintenance budget.
- Pupil toilets are always unpleasant, it's just a case of minimizing the problem, it can't be cured. Well what about providing pleasant modern facilities and providing someone to clean them during the school day. This has made a tremendous difference to this constant problem.
- Schools are just dirty places, nothing can be done. Well they well might be if you rely upon contract cleaners; why not employ your own, save money and get more cleaner time. You can then task them to anything you want without having to re-negotiate the contract every time.
- The furniture is all old and hopeless, but this is what school furniture is like. Not if you decide it should be otherwise. A classroom can be carpeted and fully furnished for around £1500. Why not decide to renovate five classrooms per year? Over six or seven years you will have done them all in a 1000-pupil school.

The change to fair funding in 1999 delegated much more of the repairs and maintenance budget from LEAs. This is now an appreciable amount of money that can be applied to any projects you wish. Make sure you make it work for you to support the ethos that you are trying to create. Make sure your cleaners, your site team, your grounds maintenance contractors all understand what you are trying to achieve, make sure they know how important their work is to the success of the school and make sure you show appreciation when the job is done well.

Getting new buildings

Some readers will have recently taken up post in shiny new buildings. The government has promised to replace the entire capital stock over the next 15 years. Well, time will tell. But for those of you who haven't the good fortune of brand-new buildings and haven't the patience to wait for 15 years, you will probably have some building needs. Particularly as someone new to this dimension of the work (and I suspect very few headteachers have much experience before taking up their headship), you will probably need to know how to go about getting money out of your funding authority.

A new head was appointed to a school with some very poor buildings. The lack of investment in the fabric of the school was extreme, the last investment by the LEA of any significance was an orchestra room some twenty years previously. The issue was not so much what the priorities for improvement were, it was what they weren't. There were a variety of actions that needed to be taken. First, according to the LEA records the school had over 300 surplus places. Now, while it was true that there were surplus places, no one was quite sure how an additional 10 or 12 classes would fit into the school. Furthermore, the school organization plan indicated that this situation would continue for many years hence. On the face of it there was not much hope of gaining funds for new facilities

Two key initial actions were to establish that the capacity calculation more accurately recorded the current status of the school and then to work through a set of reasonable expectations of the change in the size of the sixth form (operating at very uneconomic levels at that time) and the intake into year 7. A degree of persuasion was required for both of these, but after three years the situation had changed so that there was a forecast of a deficiency of over 200 places within six years. This was the result of having the capacity calculation downgraded to 810 and a forecast of a rising roll instead of a static one. The conditions had been established to provide for a more favourable reaction from premises officers when the subject of new build was broached.

The curriculum analysis revealed that the size of the science labs was too small to accommodate cost-effective groups. The DfES building bulletin prescribed labs of at least $85m^2$, whereas five of the seven labs were much smaller than this. A degree of lobbying of various key people then followed. LEA officers including the Chief Education Officer and the council chief executive were invited for a tour of the premises, naturally enough focusing upon the low points of the site, ensuring that the smallest science labs were visited. The science adviser was invited to comment upon the facilities. And then critically the LEA undertook a survey of all their capital stock for the asset management plan (AMP). This was critical as the AMP would form the basis for prioritization of coming capital expenditure under the suitability priority. As a result of the work with the science adviser and the preparation for the curriculum analysis it was possible to make a case for the five undersized labs (currently graded A) to receive the highest priority grade in the AMP – an A grade meaning that it was not possible to deliver the science curriculum in these facilities.

As a result of this the school had the highest number of such grades in the LEA. So, when the whole AMP process was complete, the school naturally rose to the surface as the highest priority for new facilities. The outcome was a major £1.5m project for a new-build science block and completely refurbished classrooms for use by the mathematics department.

Box 4.2

Every LEA will have a set of priorities for expenditure. The first priority is going to be basic need. The first strategic responsibility an LEA has is to provide sufficient school places. This is worked out with a straightforward calculation of the number of school places available compared to the number required. If there is a shortfall then there is a basic need. Clearly, this must be the highest priority for capital investment. After that will come a variety of further priorities. These may be related to condition, i.e. given that there are sufficient places, is the accommodation safe and worthy of use by school-children? In our LEA many old temporary buildings were condemned and replaced because their condition did not allow their use for children at anything like a satisfactory standard. Another priority might be sufficiency of specialist accommodation; then there might be suitability. So, given that, for example, a school has sufficient science labs in accommodation that is safe for use, is it actually suitable for its purpose.

To sort out all of these priorities the key LEA document now is the asset management plan. In order to lever funding for premises out of the LEA, then a good understanding of the asset management plan is required.

Some steps you might go through in order to start building a case:

- A premises vision. Any LEA officer will want to know how anything you propose fits into your big picture for your school. Of course you must beware of being fobbed off here. In our experience some premises officers are past masters at finding something to keep a headteacher occupied for a few months to put off any serious discussion about spending any ' LEA money.

- You must do a curriculum analysis if you are to demonstrate need.
- Have your subject advisers over to look at your facilities. If they are as bad as you think they are, then the adviser will support your case. Of course, if they are not, then you have no case – start thinking about something else!
- Do you have a case for basic need? As a result of your curriculum analysis you should be able to see whether you have enough workspaces for pupils. How are the demographics in the area shaping up in the years to come?
- Is the LEA record of the number of school places at your school accurate. On checking we had ours reduced from 1070 to 930.
- What about the school organization plan? Do the projections for your school numbers in the coming years match what you know about the numbers of pupils in the primary schools that feed you and the pattern of parental preference in your area? They are working from numbers and spreadsheets, you know your context.

It is difficult to be prescriptive about what you should do to obtain the building project you want as it all depends upon the context. Box 4.2 is a short case study about how a school got a new science block.

Now of course it is not possible to subvert the system, well not to any great extent anyway, and the case in this example fundamentally rested upon the fact that the science facilities were extremely poor. Who knows whether the outcome would have been the same if the groundwork had not been done by the school. We do know that a proactive stance on gaining an understanding of the AMP process and perhaps just as importantly ensuring that the case was made well and often to those who could influence events gave the school the best chance there could be of a successful outcome and, after all, there was a successful outcome. The same head has subsequently gone on to secure major projects to refurbish technology and art facilities and has, for the first time, secured the school a drama studio.

Conclusion

Many who arrive at headship have travelled the route through working with teachers on teaching and learning in the school. This is right because it is the core function of headship. We don't want heads who are site managers, who spend all their time worrying about budget, who build up reserves for a 'rainy day' in the interests of a false prudence. We don't want heads who see the buildings as their empire and who wish to see these grow for the imperial pleasure they get from this. We do want heads who understand the interrelationship between what may be termed the 'business functions' of the school and its wider purpose. In our school we see every aspect of what we do as an integrated whole, everything impacts upon everything else and when we get it right then the outcome is improved life chances for the young people we serve. New heads can be daunted or intimidated by the budget and by the responsibilities of estate management. This is natural. But those who are successful see beyond the problems of the lack of resources that we hear so much about, and see the opportunities there are and the genuine school improvement that can be won from careful and astute management of the priorities for expenditure, and from a clear understanding of the rules in which they operate.

Many new heads are so put off by these business aspects of their job that they are all too willing to delegate them to someone else. This seems to us to be a tragic missed opportunity. Don't be put off, get stuck in.

Bibliography
Giuliani, R. W. (2002) *Leadership*. New York: Hyperion.

CHAPTER 5

Isn't teaching and learning the most important thing? On development planning and the curriculum

The curriculum is the principal means whereby the school pursues its educational purposes and organizes and structures its time. While much of the content may be prescribed the ways in which the curriculum in a school is organized says much about the values and principles that are embodied.

The school day

For most schools the week consists of twenty-five or so taught hours – i.e. the amount of time that children spend in classes with a teacher. The school day has a legal basis; it is divided into two sessions separated by a break in the middle of the day, except in exceptional circumstances. With the exception of nursery schools, all maintained schools must meet for 380 sessions per school year. Teachers, of course, have to be available to work for another five days, usually but not always for training purposes.

The structure and length of the school day are often inherited but, of course, are not cast in stone. However, changing the structure of the school day and week will affect every member of the school community and the stakeholders. Parents will be affected by changes to the school day – existing timings may correspond with other schools, facilitating childcare arrangements – it is not unusual for children at secondary schools to be responsible for collecting younger siblings from primary school and taking care of them until parents return from work.

Changing the end of the school day so that it concludes beyond that of local primary schools may have a huge impact beyond the school. Also, staff will need to make their arrangements for childcare and other domestic matters. Within the school, language teachers sometimes like the shorter lesson that occurs daily; technology and PE, for example, often prefer the longer lesson to facilitate practicals and the like. Concerns over the timing of lessons and the length of the school day can be parochial but such is the effect on the whole school community that any change should emerge from a working group that includes staff and governors (including parent governors). Sufficient notice needs to be given about any change to give everyone the opportunity to raise any objections and make new arrangements – this is a process that cannot be hurried!

Changes to the timings of the start and finish of the school day can only take effect from the beginning of a school year. The procedures for changing timings are laid down in the *Changing the School Session Regulations 1999*. The school day is much more than this and some of the decisions that have to be taken reflect the range of opportunities and the discretion that the school can decide for itself.

First, the day itself. Is the school day to commence at 8.30am, or earlier or later? Is the registration system such that classes will register at the start of the first lesson? Or will there be a registration period with a teacher. In many secondary schools children are grouped horizontally (i.e. all year 7 children are regarded as being in one year group divided into tutor groups). The example below shows how the number of horizontal groups relates to the number of children in an average secondary school:

Year	Number of pupils	Number of groups	Average
7	190	7	27.1
8	167	6	27.8
9	165	6	27.5
10	169	6	28.2
11	172	6	28.7
12	84	3	28.0
13	69	3	23.0
Total	1016	37	

To manage the year groups so that there are roughly the same number in each tutor group will require 37 staff to be allocated to the tutor role.

The purpose of the tutor role can range from someone who formally registers children at school, collects absence notes, is a point of contact between the parent and school, undertakes some form of academic monitoring, adopts some pastoral role – the range of possibilities is great. Fundamentally, such decisions reflect the aims and values of the school. Broadly, a school that is aiming to maximize the potential of students will use all available resources to realize this aim; the frequency of contact between the group tutor and the child (in that it will happen at least twice daily, to cover the morning and afternoon registration times – unless of course, all registration takes place in lessons – made possible by technology) mean that some form of pastoral role is considered advantageous.

While the technology of registration systems makes it possible to do away with the registration by the group tutor and have classes registered only by their subject teachers, the benefits are considerable in maintaining contact with this one person. First, any correspondence for the student (letters to year groups, information to the individual) can be relayed efficiently – the alternative being a system where the administration team locate a student and then arrange for the correspondence to be conveyed. Secondly, registration provides an anchor point with a person whose task it is to focus on that small group of students – and can check uniform and deal with general welfare issues. If the group tutor remains with the group throughout the time from years 7 to 11 (or if necessary a shorter period) then a stronger relationship can develop. Registration and tutor periods also provide a buffer period of time between the breaks and lesson time – if managed properly they can have a calming effect – and the effect is noticeable in schools that do manage this time well.

The benefit of the horizontal grouping is that it provides an opportunity for the year group to meet together with a shared agenda and facilitates efficient and effective communication. There are a number of tasks and issues that affect year groups – induction in year 7 (for an 11–18 or 11–16 school), GCSE options for year 9, coursework for years 10 and 11, etc. The year-group structure makes the necessary effort of communication efficient as the comparison with the vertical grouping illustrates.

Rare, but by no means extinct is the concept of vertical division and so a few lines are devoted to a consideration of the year group divided for pastoral purposes into vertical groups.

Assuming the same number of staff are available then each year group would need to be divided thus:

Year	Number
7	5
8	5
9	4
10	5
11	5
12	2
13	2
	28

So this would mean each tutor group would have five children from year 7, five from year 8, four from year 9 and so on. The benefit of this system is to give opportunities for older students to take responsibility for younger ones, to distribute the leadership of the year groups across the staff (so, for example, all staff are involved in constructing UCAS references, because everyone is a sixth-form tutor). We would argue that locating the responsibility for the production of the UCAS references (for example) within a small group of 3 or 4 people means that the expertise is shared within a small group, the group is a manageable size and in-depth discussion and development can happen. Trying to train thirty-seven people (or more in the case of a school twice the size) to do one task would make the training a very difficult one to accomplish – multiply this by the range of important tasks that teachers have to undertake as part of their duties and the scale of the task becomes unmanageable and unrealistic.

To have a vertical grouping systems is an example of a school organized around the teachers' interests rather than the pupils' interests. Children will get the best from a system that is efficient (because the resources of time and money are not wasted on mass communication exercises) and effective because the expertise will be located within a small group that is manageable and sustainable.

Further, the horizontal grouping permits year issues to be located and delegated to one person who can reasonably be expected to manage these. The year head is someone who can be reasonably expected to have the interests of the cohort entirely to the fore. The enormous amount of information on pupils – much of which isn't recorded (often because it relates to interactions and individual perceptions of ourselves as people and as a community) can be shared within a tightly formed group who identify strongly with a group of children. While children will benefit from engaging with older children in the school and the vertical grouping is one way to facilitate this, children will also benefit from the communal aspect of working and interacting with a group of children who are at the same stage of their education.

We use the year structure to manage the student body; larger schools may combine the horizontal grouping with the vertical idea through a 'house' system. In this children are assigned to horizontal groups but in vertical houses. Thus some of the communal events – like assemblies – become house assemblies. A large school with a population of say 1600 creates four houses each with 400 children ranging from 11 to 18. House assemblies are the communal event and as such the school as a working community is sustained.

The point of having this discussion is that the pastoral structure has an impact on the way in which the curriculum is going to be planned through the structure of the school day. The unit by which children are organized for registration, administration and pastoral purposes is important because it will necessitate consideration as time will have to be set aside to facilitate it.

Length of the taught lesson

Schools vary considerably in the length of the lessons. In some cases each lesson is 30 minutes – the longest single unit we know is 75 minutes. Most range between these parameters – the 60-minute model being popular. Combining two 30-minute lessons of course produces the 60-minute lesson but it will still lead to some lessons remaining at 30 minutes and also introduce the notion of the 'double lesson' – this being different from the standard 30-minute stretch. How much food preparation, scientific experiment or PE can children do in 30 minutes? Indeed how much sustained and deep learning can be accomplished in such a short time? By having a standard unit of 60 minutes, lessons have the common denominator; children and teachers have a shared basis on which they will work. There will be none of the disadvantages of the double lesson (which require a different approach to planning, a tiresomeness of it being twice as long as the normal) and none of the inherent difficulties of the shortness of the 30-minute one (a site that requires movement, will quickly reduce a 30-minute session to one of 20).

The timing of breaks has been subjected to considerable change over the past twenty years and there are a number of possible models that schools adopt and adapt. A range of possible models is presented with some discussion on the merits and disadvantages of these.

1   A registration period of 15–20 minutes at the start of the day, with a shorter period in the afternoon. Schools operating such systems often will have a period of 15–20 minutes in the morning and 5 or 10 minutes in the

afternoon. The assembly will often take place during the morning period. The benefit of this system is that if children are late to school then lessons are not affected as much. This is a significant issue for schools where many children arrive by bus and are subject to the vicissitudes of public transport. Also the short registration in the afternoon minimizes the length of the afternoon session. The main disadvantage of this day is that some of the time when children are at their freshest is taken up with assembly and registration. With a 60-minute lesson unit the school day might look like this:

8.30am – Registration/assemblies
8.45am – Lesson 1
9.45am – Lesson 2
10.45am – Break
11.05am – Lesson 3
12.05pm – Lesson 4
1.05pm – Lunch
2.05pm – Registration
2.15pm – Lesson 5
3.15pm – End of the school day

Clearly these timings can be amended if the start is earlier or later than the 8.30am model presented here. Note that in this model the timing of lunch is such that the morning session is extended and therefore the afternoon session becomes very short indeed with only one movement of the school between registration/assembly and lesson 5.

2   A short registration at the start of the day with a longer period in the afternoon (a reverse of the previous model).

8.30 am – Registration/assemblies
8.40am – Lesson 1
9.40am – Lesson 2
10.40am – Break
11.00am – Lesson 3
12.00pm – Lunch
1.00pm – Registration and assemblies
1.15pm – Lesson 4
2.15pm – Lesson 5
3.15pm – End of the school day

Obviously this can be combined with the assembly in the morning model; the noteworthy issue is that of the timing of the lunch break. Here the model provides a balanced morning/afternoon session but there will be greater movement around the school in afternoon – the time when spirits are often higher and children and their teachers are a little less fresh for the rigours of the day.

3   Short breaks
The model presented below has two very short breaks:

8.30 am – Registration/assemblies
8.45am – Lesson 1
9.45am – Lesson 2
10.45am – Break
11.00am – Lesson 3
12.00pm – Lesson 4
1.00pm – Lunch
1.20pm – Registration
1.30pm – Lesson 5
2.30pm – End of the school day

Here of course, the school day ends very early. Schools operating this model find that the day is very rushed (but get used to it). Twenty minutes is a very short time for the mechanics of the lunch break (for students getting to the restaurant, queuing, eating, visiting the toilet) and ditto for the staff. It means that all meetings take place from 2.30pm onwards and therefore most are over by 4pm. However, it means that there is no time for extracurricular activity and this will inevitably take place in the period from 2.30pm and have an impact on meeting time.

4   Our preference is for a day like this:

8.40 am – Registration/assemblies
9.00 am – Lesson 1
10.00am – Lesson 2
11.00am – Break
11.15am – Lesson 3
12.15pm – Lesson 4
1.15 pm – Lunch
2.05 pm – Registration
2.15pm – Lesson 5
3.15pm – End of the school day

We hold some form of briefing meeting each day (whole staff, heads of year, year teams, and leadership team) and find that this is a good way to maintain effective communication during the school week. By starting the school day at 8.40am then these important communication meetings can start at 8.30am – a reasonable time compared with 8.15am, necessitated by a day commencing at 8.30am. By having four lessons in the morning it does make the session a long one but the benefit of the short afternoon does much to make up for this. Previously we had 40-minute lessons and a long registration in the afternoon. The last lesson of the school day could very easily be of 25 minutes or so, because of movement around the site being less reliable near the end of the school day.

Curriculum planning

Having determined the structure of the school day the curriculum needs to be organized and planned. In this sense we are describing the overall curriculum organization rather than the organization of each subject. Normally, children have to follow the national curriculum until the end of key stage 3 and only then can it be varied. There are no statutory percentages of time allocated to subjects but the Pre-Inspection School Context Indicator (PISCI) annex provided by Ofsted gives information on average allocations. However, like the structure of the school day, the curriculum plan is a school matter and is one that should be determined by the governors on advice from the headteacher.

Our curriculum balance is achieved via the model set out below:

The timetable is organized on a 50-lesson two-week cycle. Each lesson is 60 minutes in length and there are 5 lessons in each day.

Key Stage 3

Students study the full National Curriculum at key stage 3.

All students have 6 lessons of English, maths and science per cycle, throughout the key stage. Children start learning one foreign language (with five lessons per cycle) and in order to permit the study of an additional language, the amount of time allocated to D&T is reduced in year 8 and 9 from 10 per cent (i.e. 5 lessons per cycle) to 8 per cent (i.e. 4 lessons per cycle).

The allocations look like this:

Subject	Allocation			
	Y7	Y8	Y9	Ave
English	12%	12%	12%	12
Maths	12%	12%	12%	12
Science	12%	12%	12%	12
D&T	10%	8%	8%	8.7
Single Language				
French	10%	8%	8%	
Key Skills		4%	4%	11.3
Double Language				
French	10%	6%	6%	
Spanish		6%	6%	
Geography	6%	6%	6%	6
History	6%	6%	6%	6
RE	4%	4%	4%	4
IT	4%	4%	4%	4
PE	8%	8%	8%	8
Art	6%	6%	6%	6
Drama	4%	4%	4%	4
Music	4%	4%	4%	4
PSHE	2%	2%	2%	2

The allocations for history and geography are 6 per cent (i.e. three lessons per cycle) and the rest follow. The benefit of the two-week timetable is that it permits us to allocate more lessons to particular subjects – it means also that the smallest unit for the timetable is 2 per cent rather than 4 per cent. Having decided on a 5-lesson per day structure, then if we had a one-week timetable, the allocations for subjects would need to be the same for history as for drama (and this might be a good thing in another school). We decided to allocate one lesson per cycle to PSHE (Personal Social and Health education) – one lesson per week would be too much for our school.

Again these are decisions that need to be made at the local level. Schools that have specialisms in a particular curriculum area (in our case it is science) may choose to allocate additional time to particular curriculum areas. The key is to have full discussion of the issues and then communicate the decisions made widely in plenty of time before any changes are made.

The impact of this will be discussed later in the chapter when timetable construction is described.

Key stage 4

Our core curriculum at key stage 4 includes English, English literature, mathematics, science (all students do double science), ICT, RE, PSHE and PE. All students study a core curriculum with four options.

The structure is as follows:

Subject	% In year 10 and 11
English	14%
Mathematics	12%
Science	18%
PE	6%
RE	4%
ICT	4%
PSHE	2%
Options	4 x 10%=40%

We give a free choice for all students at key stage 4. Students choose all the remaining subjects – they can, for example, increase their science studies to do separate sciences, one or two foreign languages, technology together with the usual choices of history, geography, drama, music, art, PE, etc. The timetable blocks are constructed to maximize this free choice but it may involve students eventually studying a reserve subject.

Curriculum planning is something that does take a great deal of time. The decisions we take to amend the curriculum will often require additional or changes to staffing. For example, several years ago we decided to introduce A level psychology to the year 12 curriculum. Now the way in which this happened is a good example of the way in which a curriculum decision can be enabled.

Each year, around December, the headteacher interviews each member of year 11 to discuss individual progress and to talk about post-16 options. A number of students expressed an interest in psychology. In the previous academic year a member of the science team had said that she thought that there was interest in this subject and that she would be willing to set it up. Talking to more students, the interest in this new subject became increasingly evident and it appeared that if we were to run this subject it would be a very popular option. The curriculum decisions were as follows:

1 What was the interest in psychology? Were the students interested in this subject 'secure' students? – i.e. would the majority of those who expressed an interest qualify for a sixth-form place?

2 Who would teach it? Given that one member of staff was willing to set it up, what would be the impact on her home department (in this case science – if she taught 8 periods of psychology, who would teach the 8 periods of biology she left behind?)

3 What would be the impact on other subjects? Our research led us to believe that about half the sixth form would want to study the subject – this would mean not one but two groups. How would this affect the numbers and hence the viability of other subjects?

4 Was the interest sustainable? How many of these students would go on to A2? Would the recruitment levels be sustained the following year?

5 Costs – what would be the training costs for this subject, the costs of books and starting up a subject from nothing?

It turned out that there was considerable interest in the subject. We anticipated large groups and so needed to recruit some additional teaching capacity. Fortunately we were able to recruit a recently qualified DPhil student who, although an unqualified teacher, had some experience of teaching undergraduates and so with supervision was able to deliver some of the material. This was something of a stroke of luck because, although at the end of the year she was unable to continue, by then enough effort had been applied to the subject, the recruitment for the following year was secure and it was possible to make a substantive permanent appointment. We now have a head of psychology and three people teaching two groups in both year 12 and year 13.

This all sounds very good and readers may be thinking that it all sounds so easy. It is important at this juncture, we think, to analyse this evolving situation a little more closely.

First, the demand from the students was at a time when sixth-form marketing was something of an imperative. However, there was clearly a need to examine the motivation of the students and also to consider the sustainability of the curriculum offer. While the flexibility to offer new subjects and courses is obviously something that is vital if the curriculum is to progress, employing staff on the basis of only these new subjects is fraught with difficulty. Our experience with sociology serves as a good example of this.

Sociology had been taught by one teacher for a number of years – she also taught history. When she left the history offer had changed and so the only requirement was for someone to teach sociology. Now, efforts to recruit a part-time teacher in an area of very high housing costs proved difficult and we took the decision to try for a full-time teacher with a second subject. Having appointed such a teacher in order to, in the main, service the sociology department, when this teacher left suddenly (a bit of very bad luck!) we were left with a teacher's timetable that had been fitted to suit one person with a particular range of subjects. Trying to find a teacher who matched the other was impossible and this caused considerable disruption to the timetable for the school. Timetable construction has become for many schools a task that occupies us throughout the year, rather than the activity of June and July. It's very easy, when trying to solve one problem to end up in a situation where one teacher's timetable has been tailored to their offer but if they leave makes it very difficult to recruit another. In smaller schools where many teach a second (and even third) subject the potential for this is heightened.

Secondly, the potential of a staffing-led curriculum. This is where the staffing determines the curriculum. Like many schools we experienced considerable difficulty in recruiting technology teachers and modern foreign language teachers. We advertised for a head of technology on four responsibility points and received neither applications nor any enquiries. As a school we have always offered German as a second language; it became increasingly difficult and even impossible to recruit quality German teachers and so we made a change to our language offer. There is a balance to be struck between the teachers you have to deploy, those you might have reasonable chance of appointing and what the school needs in order to provide a suitable curriculum offer for the students it serves. We are in an area where housing is very expensive and this has a deleterious effect on recruitment – at all levels.

Thirdly, the decisions can be difficult and arouse considerable feeling. It is one thing to make a curriculum change – as described above by changing German to, in our case, Spanish. The appointment of a new head of languages was coincidental and timely to this decision. But for those German teachers who are left, the effect might be to hasten their departure to another school. With a curriculum decision of this nature, there will often be children who have commenced a course of study and, therefore, their programme needs to be run through until it reaches its conclusion. In our case changing the second language will take three years until there are no students following German courses. The need to plan in advance and still manage the existing programme is one of the more difficult aspects of curriculum planning. These decisions have to be taken in advance because of the recruitment cycle that schools are in. To employ a newly qualified teacher in September will often require advertisement in the previous January. To employ a teacher in post for September will mean a recruitment in the spring term, as the resignation date for a September start is 31 May of the previous academic year.

However, the decisions on these matters can be eased by planning out the curriculum, looking at the numbers in the year. This is covered more generally in Chapter 4 but the specifics relating to the curriculum are included here. A spreadsheet shows how this can be managed.

First, look at the year groups and the subjects they study. The following example in Table 5.1 illustrates how this is done in English, mathematics and science. The basis is year groups of the following sizes:

Year	Size
7	180
8	180
9	160
10	175
11	130
12	78
13	60

There are a number of decisions that have already been made before this spreadsheet can be constructed – these include the group sizes, the amount of contact time for a mainscale teacher and the consequent allowances for leadership and management time. By totalling the curriculum need and the staffing deployment it is possible to identify the shortfalls or overstaffing. Notice that in English the department is overstaffed by 5 periods and mathematics has a shortfall of 10 and science 64.

Having done these calculations the next decisions is what to do about the outcome. How is the overstaffing in English to be managed? – if one of the teachers can deliver another curriculum subject then the five periods can be transferred to another subject. However, if it is one of the mainscale English teachers then this would take their

Here decision is taken on class sizes to give the number of groups required

	English		236	Maths		236 Science			312
Balance			5			−10			−64
	Groups	Periods	Total	Groups	Periods	Total	Groups	Periods	Total
7	6	6	36	6	6	36	6	6	36
8	6	6	36	6	6	36	6	6	36
9	7	6	42	7	6	42	8	6	48
10	8	7	56	8	7	56	9	9	81
11	6	7	42	6	7	42	7	9	63
12	2	8	16	1	8	8	6	8	48
13	1	8	8	2	8	16	4	8	32
Total			241			226			280
Teachers									
HoD English			40						
2nd in English			42						
English teacher			43						
English teacher			43						
English teacher			43						
Assistant Head			30						
HoD Maths						40			
2nd in Maths						42			
Maths teacher						43			
Maths teacher						43			
Maths teacher						43			
Deputy Head						15			
Director of Science									25
Head of Biology									42
Head of Chemistry									42
Head of Physics									42
Biology teacher									43
Chemistry teacher									43
Physics teacher									43

Total curriculum need

Decisions on how much time each teacher should have – this includes time for leadership and management

Table 5.1 *Spreadsheet for curriculum planning*

English commitment to 38. To avoid split groups in the timetable this will commit the deployment of this teacher to something like this:

Year	Lessons
7	6
8	6
9	6
10	7
11	7
12	4
13	2
Total	38

Of course if this teacher cannot teach year 12 and 13 another model is needed:

7	12
8	6
9	6
10	7
11	7
12	0
13	0
Total	38

Here the teacher will have two groups in year 7. This will have an impact on the timetable construction process discussed later in this chapter.

While there is a need to consider the requirements of each department separately and each year group separately it is only when the information is combined that the full picture can be viewed and the effect of changes can be assessed.

Using a spreadsheet allows school leaders to experiment with a range of different ideas and assess the impact on the curriculum plan and the budget. The effect for example of adding an extra group to years 10 and 11 in the core subjects of English, mathematics and science is illustrated in Table 5.2.

Now the requirement in English is an additional nine periods – for mathematics 24 periods and science 82 periods. Based on a 50-period model, with 43 periods being the standard loading, the effect is to require 115 additional taught periods over the existing staffing. This is about 2.7 staff on the standard loading. By multiplying this by the salary for a teacher with approximately 23 per cent for oncosts, the true cost of the staffing budget can be worked out.

	English		250	Maths		250	Science		362
Balance			−9			−24			−82
	Groups	Periods	Total	Groups	Periods	Total	Groups	Periods	Total
7	6	6	36	6	6	36	6	6	36
8	6	6	36	6	6	36	6	6	36
9	7	6	42	7	6	42	8	6	48
10	9	7	63	9	7	63	10	9	90
11	7	7	49	7	7	49	8	9	72
12	2	8	16	1	8	8	6	8	48
13	1	8	8	2	8	16	4	8	32

Table 5.2 *The effect of adding extra groups to the core subjects in years 10 and 11*

Timetable construction

There are several timetable construction packages available – one of the most popular is the SIMS Nova timetable package. This section is not about the benefits of one system over another but is concerned with the methodology of timetable construction and the principles that underpin the process.

The timetable construction is carried out by the deputy head in some schools – sometimes by a senior member of staff, or alternatively by someone interested in the job. There are also schools where this task is contracted out to an external agency – occasionally this is a former member of staff. Although at first the timetable might appear a document that deploys staff to teach the classes and subjects that are designated, this is just part of the story. One question that emerges from this bald statement is: who decides the number of classes and who decides who will teach them? The curriculum need and staffing analysis have been covered extensively in Chapter 4 and some of the salient points included earlier in this section. The head needs to determine the number of classes and the deployment to the departments, with advice from the curriculum leaders in the school. Changes to this can only be made with the express permission of the headteacher.

We have a policy on the timetable construction that sets out the process and the principles of this important piece of work.

Timetable construction policy

RATIONALE

The school timetable is a major part of the school's strategic plan. It is set down for the whole school year and its quality is one factor that determines the educational experience of the students and the occupational experience of the teaching staff.

As such it must be constructed with the intention of producing the best timetable possible. However, it is subject to a short time-frame for its construction and is subject to factors that include late resignations and other random events.

Comment

The school timetable is a highly significant piece of work. First, the effect on students – having a poorly constructed timetable can lead to behavioural difficulties and issues for the school. In addition the timetable can have an effect on the results. The generally held view is that mornings lessons are better than afternoon ones and that lessons at the beginning of the week are better than, for example, Friday afternoon. There are a number of decisions that can flow from these premises. Firstly do we accept that learning is better on Monday morning than on Friday afternoon? Consider the effect of this: for year 11, we programme core subjects to morning lessons and PE or PSHE on Friday afternoon. Now what does this say to the PE and PSHE staff about their subject? And does the scheduling of these subjects to Friday afternoon improve pupil motivation or might it be responsible for increased truancy and behavioural problems at this time. Alternatively, scheduling optional subjects to Friday afternoon might be better – or indeed, scheduling core subjects to this point in the school week could be tactical. These are decisions that can only be taken at the local level.

It is important to appreciate the effect of the timetable on the staff. Using our model of 43 periods out of a potential 50, a mainscale teacher with the greatest teaching load will have less than one non-contact period per day. Therefore if more than one free period is scheduled per day it will necessarily increase the number of full days. This point can be overemphasized, however, because the school exists for the benefit of the students and therefore the scheduling should be organized with their interests to the fore rather than those of the teaching staff. However, there is a balance.

AIMS

The school timetable should:

- provide a varied daily experience for all students
- enable the school's setting policy to be implemented in full
- provide a balanced curriculum experience over the timetable cycle
- facilitate a balanced homework timetable
- address the needs of students at different phases of their schooling
- address the workload issues of the teaching staff
- be sufficiently robust that it is capable of being radically adjusted should circumstances require

Comment

The school timetable should be a vehicle that realizes curriculum aims. For our school there is a rigorous setting policy where all students are taught in ability sets for English, mathematics, science, modern foreign languages, technology, history, geography and RE. A central tenet of our policy is that these sets should be independent of one another: i.e. students placed in an ability set for French should have the opportunity to be in any set for mathematics (rather than one subject determining the ability sets of another subject). This cannot happen if subjects are linked in any way. Central to the way in which our school is run is the facilitation of the school's homework policy – here all subjects set homework according to the timetable. Again, this cannot occur if the timetable is such that there is a poor balance across the days of the timetable cycle.

Further, as was mentioned earlier, the timetable is no longer something that is constructed in June and July and remains unaltered over the year. Staff move at various times during the year and many schools will find themselves in a position where their staffing varies; hence the need for a flexible timetable that can be reorganized without too much difficulty.

IMPLEMENTATION

There are a number of elements to school timetable construction that need to be in place before the detailed scheduling can take place:

1. sixth-form timetable blocks. These are constructed by the Assistant Head (sixth form) in consultation with the Deputy Headteacher
2. some sixth-form timetable blocks may have to be blocked together
3. the year 11 optional subjects are carried forward from year 10
4. the year 10 optional subjects blocks are constructed by the Deputy Headteacher in February
5. the staffing spreadsheet – this is a key document drawn up by the Headteacher. At each point where successive spreadsheets are constructed and processed there needs to be a clear statement of what is fixed and what is negotiable. The Deputy Headteacher will provide a written record in the form of minutes to act as a check for this process
6. details on staff deployment from heads of subject

Comment

This implementation model reflects our school's systems but it seeks to illustrate the information that is required before the timetable can be constructed. There has to be clarity about the classes and the curriculum need and the staffing deployment. Often teachers are willing to teach a second subject; in some cases it reflects a change in career (sometimes PE teachers will, as they get older, want to move into classroom-based subjects and gradually reduce their 'outside' time) and this is something that, in our case, is discussed with the headteacher and implemented through the timetable construction. The stages to timetable construction are summarized in Table 5.3.

The construction of the timetable is the responsibility of the Deputy Headteacher.

There are a number of personnel who can assist with the construction process:

- Registrar – inputting the timetable blocks and allocating them to particular days of the cycle. Inputting to the teacher database
- Curriculum Manager – inputting the curriculum plan, ensuring all set lists for 7–11 are accurate. Producing copies of the timetable for students for the last day of term preceding the new academic year

Stage	Details	Outcomes
Construction of timetable blocks for ks4 and sixth form	The timetable for the upper school can be constructed in draft form at this stage. This means that the provisional blocking for all of ks4 and sixth form is done – but without the details of staffing. This stage is crucial because it emphasizes the priority to ks4 blocking for core subjects	Draft timetable without staffing
Construction of timetable blocks for years 7, 8, 9 – core subjects	The core subjects are all block setted. In this context core subjects are En, Ma, Sc, MFL. All year groups will follow the 3 + 3 model for the core subjects. Any variation to this will be determined by the Headteacher after discussion with the Deputy Head	Core blocking for ks3 in place. It is anticipated that in 2002 that the core blocking will be 3+3 for year 9, 3+2 for year 8 and 3+3 for year 7. The least able will be dispersed in 7N and so the provision of lessons for progress tests will be focused. The model 3+2 for year 8 will cause unevenness in the model
Draft construction of the timetable		
Staffing	Staff will be allocated to classes on the basis of the draft timetable	
Publication	The full timetable will be published in advance to the Headteacher. The staffing spreadsheet will be adjusted and the Headteacher will decide whether the changes are acceptable	

Table 5.3 *Stages to timetable construction*

- Assistant Head (sixth form) – creating sixth-form timetable – from staffing allocations, producing sixth-form homework timetable, checking the balance of sixth-form lessons, ensuring sixth-form group lists are accurate

Comment

The school will have its own systems and people responsible for producing various elements of the timetable constructions. This is important because the process of timetable construction is very complex and complicated and therefore the wider the responsibility the better. In many cases much of the data has to be input manually and there is always the possibility of errors – having a range of checking systems helps to minimize this. We heard of a school that distributed timetables one week before the end of term; a boy who had been studying resistant materials throughout year 10 had food technology on his timetable. He didn't say anything to his teachers!

PRIORITIZING THE TIMETABLE

Timetable construction demands some prioritization in order that the aims are fulfilled and the needs of the entire organization are realized. Some of the priorities are detailed below and they have to be determined by the Headteacher:

- at ks3 students have 24 core-subject lessons. It is recommended that there be two core-subject lessons per day for 6 days and 3 core-subject lessons per day for 4 days. This is to balance the core/non-core subjects. At ks4 there are 22 lessons for core subjects. This means 2 core-subject lessons for 8 days and 3 core-subject lessons for 3 days
- lessons should be balanced across the cycle – this means that where there are six lessons there will be 3 +3, if there are five lessons there will be 3+2 or 2+3 with no more than 3 core-subject lessons
- part-time staff on less than 0.6 will be entitled to 1 day off per week. This will be blocked out. No more than one part-time teacher can be on day off on each day. Where the number of part-time staff exceeds 5, then this will be adjusted
- no subject will be timetabled for more than one lesson per day. The exception to this is science where at ks4 there are 9 lessons and optional subjects add extra 5 lessons

- PSHE will not be timetabled for lesson 5 for any year group
- HoDs of core subjects should have one free lesson per day
- MPG staff should have no more than one free lesson per day
- MPG should have no more than 3 consecutive full days
- at ks3 core subjects should be timetabled for lessons 1, 2 or 3 only

During the timetable process the Deputy Head will report to the Headteacher weekly in June and daily in July. The purpose of this meeting is to appraise the Headteacher on what has been done and the impact of this on the school timetable. Written records will be kept by the Deputy Headteacher of these meetings.

Any requests from the teaching staff and HoDs will be copied to the Headteacher.

Comment

The dominant feature of this section is the need for prioritization and flexibility. This is one reason why the timetable should not, in our view, be constructed by the headteacher. We think most who have experience of timetable construction would admit that it is a stressful period and it is easy to become totally immersed in the process and become defensive about the decisions that have been taken. There is a need for some detachment, a distance from the process and the mechanisms of timetable construction where someone else decides on the basis of choices. There are some things that cannot be changed without other priorities being demoted.

Summary

The curriculum is a tactic and not an end in itself. It serves to realize the aims of the school in that, in itself, it is one of the ways in which the whole school experience – for students and teachers – is managed. The curriculum is not a euphemism for the timetable – it is wider than that. It is possible to construct an organization where curriculum is managed autonomously from the rest of the school – we know of a deputy head who has responsibility for the appointment of all teachers on the main scale. Such situations are rare and represent a very unhealthy approach to staff management and curriculum leadership – what is more important to the enactment of the aims and values of the school than the appointment of the staff who will be part of the daily experience of every child in the school? The timetable is the facilitation of the curriculum philosophy and aims. Indeed everything about the taught-time length of the school day, duration of lessons and so on is the realization of its aims. So crucial is this to the management and morale of the school that it is injudicious to overcentralize its execution. This is school leadership at its most poignant and at its most disciplined.

School development planning

All of the decisions, all the mechanics of the school curriculum are in many ways just the nuts and bolts of what makes a school work. We need a taught day to be defined in order to manage the staff and indeed the services that we have to plan within the school and beyond. Readers may have sampled the vision 'Tomorrow's School' of West Burnham and Bowring-Carr where the school is organized entirely around students' individual learning plans with a range of tutors and learning managers supporting the individual. Reading this vision we are able to see the problems and the compromises that mass schooling requires – but there we are.

One of the legal requirements of all schools is that there should be a development plan. We favour a two-year development plan because one year isn't long enough to plan, develop, implement, monitor and review initiatives and five years (especially given the turbulent nature of both recruitment and national initiatives) just seems too long. One of the problems with a five-year development plan is that in some ways it looks so far forward that it is possible to neglect the here-and-now. Two years is appropriate because it allows for review halfway through and a refinement of objectives and tactics.

It is a somewhat hackneyed phrase, but ownership of the school development plan (or improvement plan, or whatever the title) is absolutely essential. This ownership is essential not only for the governors, the leadership team but the whole staff body – and not just the teachers. School development and improvement is as simple and as complex as that.

Most schools are not starting from a zero base – there is a history of what has gone before. For some the start of planning is post-Ofsted. Our school development planning started with the teaching staff working in cross-department groups thinking about the key aims and objectives for the school. This suited our school at the particular point in its history. Asking the staff to think about the issues – raising attainment, the school and the community, improving staff and student services – led to a brainstorm of ideas on the key objectives. We did this as a staff meeting with staff reporting back to a plenary. By taking all of these ideas, using the key phrases that emerged, the leadership team melded the outcomes into a series of objectives that addressed the key priorities. Our process was to set down a pro forma for the school development plan. The plan was under specific headings:

Aims

These were listed as above, the foremost being 'Raising Attainment'. Associated with this key aim was a set of performance indicators. These included the GCSE targets, key stage 3 targets, and also recruitment targets, and targets for public examinations broken down by gender. We had three aims – fewer aims enables the staff to focus on what is important and what is the focus of effort and planning.

Objectives

These are the objectives that realize the aims. For example with the aim of raising achievement, a key objective was to produce schemes of work. Of course this objective would not be an aim because it is one of the ways in which the aim is realized.

Outcomes

The outcomes for the objectives were noted with a timescale. We insist on precision here – it needs to be March 2005 – not 'ongoing'. The problem with 'ongoing' is that it is very difficult to monitor someone's work on this basis.

Timescale

When is the development going to be done and when will the outcomes be completed? It's very easy to accept 'ongoing' – but this is lazy planning and is often the way to ensure that the plan isn't done. Who can challenge 'ongoing'?

Budget

There needs to be a clear link between development planning and the budget to evaluate the plan and assess the value for money that the developments have been. If team leaders have to cost out the development and justify it in, in this case, curriculum terms, then this makes it easy to spot the faddy interests and track implementation in budget terms.

Responsible

Who is going to do the work? We insist on just one person – at the school development planning level, this is normally one member of the leadership team. At department level it is the head of department.

Accountable to

In most cases this is to the headteacher and where appropriate the governors.

We spend a lot of time on this stage. We refine the phrasing of the plan very carefully because at one level, that is all the plan is, it is the embodiment of what the school seeks to achieve, it is what will direct staff activity, but it is a formal record of this, a working document and so needs the care that a document of such multifarious uses should have. Governor involvement is, in our case, something that is woven into the process. The elements of the plan are developed through the various committees and so by the time the plan goes to the full governors for consideration it is a work to which staff and governors have committed a great deal of time and thought. An example of our development plan is included as an appendix to this chapter.

We organize our school development plan to address the school aims and the next stage is to work with heads of department to produce department development plans. We provide them with the format – which is broadly the same as the school development plan format. In some cases the department plan is a personalization of the school plan but as time goes on it does tend to reflect the state of each department. A department that has worked hard on assessment for a number of years will have a different response to objectives relating to assessment than one where little or no work has been done. A commitment to coaching heads of subject through the development planning process is essential at this stage. The outcome is a series of department plans that flow from the whole school plan. Budget sums can be allocated on the basis of these plans and therefore there is a clear link between school development planning, department planning and spending. When the evaluation element of the planning cycle comes around the link between planning and spending is clearer and easier to evaluate.

As part of our planning cycle we prepare an interim and fuller evaluation for the governors on the plan. This is undertaken by the leadership team with evidence drawn from the various areas of the school. The importance of the interim evaluation (and indeed the full evaluation) cannot be overstated. Undertaking an evaluation, halfway through the plan, enables the team to reflect on what has been done, identify the successes and consider how the plan can be refined to address those weaker areas. The plan can then be refined to match the evaluation. A full evaluation is just that. It is summative in that it provides evidence at the qualitative and quantitative levels for the plan and therefore forms the basis for the new plan. It is vital to have these stage points because without them some issues would be endless. Schemes of work are, in our view, never complete – there are always changes to programmes of study, new ways of doing things, new resources and ideas. But to have schemes of work on the development plan, when they have reached an acceptable level, is to set out a plan that can never be completed. Not much fun!

Evaluating the plan

First, evaluating a plan that has been in operation throughout the school for a year (or two) takes a long time. We present our evaluation to the governors – this is an important end point because it is an imperative to evaluate the plan and it provides the governors with the information they need to do their job. The evaluation starts with each member of the leadership team stating to what extent the outcomes have been realized. The next stage is to gather evidence to support the hypothesis. If, for example, our objective was to raise the quality of teaching – with an outcome that 100 per cent of lessons observed were satisfactory or better and 60 per cent were very good or excellent – then in order to evaluate this we need the evidence from lesson observations that have been carried out over the period of review. In some cases undertaking the evaluation identifies a data gap – doing an interim evaluation provides an opportunity to address this gap. Once there is the data – in this case quantitative but in other cases qualitative – then the hypothesis becomes an evidenced-based analysis of the outcomes. Where there is a budget supporting the objective then this can indicate the value for money that the investment has provided. Shortfalls in the outcomes are identified and can form the basis for the forming of new objectives. Collating all of the responses, checking them out with the various personnel involved in the implementation of the plan takes time and the results will need a bit of tidying up to make a presentable document. However, carried out to this level, the result will be a valued document that will celebrate the achievements and acknowledge those development areas.

All this planning is worth little, however, if attention is not paid to the implementation of the plan and the directing, tutoring, supporting and delegating model of performance management, described in Chapter 7.

SCHOOL IMPROVEMENT PLAN 2004–06

AIM: ENSURING THAT ALL STUDENTS MAKE PROGRESS AND DO WELL

PRIMARY OBJECTIVE	SECONDARY OBJECTIVE
1.1 Improve the quality of department leadership	1.1.1 Develop the principle of the Head of Department as the lead practitioner
	1.1.2 Develop department strategies for target setting at key stage 3, 4 and sixth form
	1.1.3 Developing the teaching and learning policy with thematic monitoring
	1.1.4 Develop the curriculum funding process to make it more straightforward
1.2 Improve the quality of curriculum planning	1.2.1 Complete the 'lesson-by-lesson' programmes of study for key stage 3
	1.2.2 Complete the 'lesson-by-lesson' programmes of study for key stage 4
	1.2.3 Create a curriculum map that shows the development of knowledge and skills over the key stage
1.3 Improve the quality of assessment for learning	1.3.1 Develop rich questioning as a whole school and department strategy
	1.3.2 Develop peer assessment as a whole school and department strategy
	1.3.3 Develop self-assessment as a school and department strategy
1.4 Personalize the learning experience for each student	1.4.1 Create a robust system for targeted pupil intervention to address learning needs
	1.4.2 Develop Leadership Team interviews with students to form an integrated experience
	1.4.3 Involve students in learning policy
1.5 The self-evaluating school	1.5.1 Provide each teacher with an entitlement to at least one lesson observation per term
	1.5.2 Peer observation – provide each teacher with an entitlement to undertake one lesson observation per term
	1.5.3 Heads of Department to produce department self-evaluation reports using the S4 format
	1.5.4 Develop the QA system to address the new Ofsted framework

OUTCOME	TIME SCALE	BUDGET SOURCE	RESP	ACC TO
Increased involvement by HoDs in network groups (leading), delivery of demonstration lessons, proactive strategic management of the department, publication of articles for journals, involvement in national groups and initiatives	January 2006	INSET	SMT	AJP
Departments propose targets in advance of September meeting demonstrating challenge and progression	September 2004 (core departments) September 2005 (all departments)	Staffing	SMT	AJP
Departments to use monitoring opportunities to develop shared approaches to aspects of teaching such as questioning, AfL etc.	September 2004 (programme established), reviewed in July 2005	Staffing	SMT	AJP
Clear link between development requests and grants. Simplified process for HoDs to account for funds	July 2004	Staffing	SMT	AJP
All departments to have programme of study for key stage 3 planned on a 'lesson-by-lesson' approach	September 2004	Staffing	HoDs	SMT
All departments to have programme of study for key stage 4 planned on a 'lesson-by-lesson' approach	September 2005	Staffing	HoDs	SMT
Curriculum map for each key stage in department portfolio and on the school website	Key stage 3 – October 2004 Key stage 4 – October 2005	Staffing	HoDs	SMT
Each department to have a policy that sets out the type of questions it uses, justifies its approach and how it monitors and evaluates the policy	January 2005 (reported in the Department self-evaluation)	Staffing	SMT	AJP
Each department to have a policy that sets out the peer assessment approach, justifies its approach and how it monitors and evaluates the policy	July 2005	Staffing	SMT	AJP
Each department to have a policy that sets out the self-assessment approach, justifies its approach and how it monitors and evaluates the policy	January 2006	Staffing	SMT	AJP
Y10 pupils requiring intervention will have been identified and action taken	July 2004	Staffing	RHC	AJP
Students will be interviewed each year by a member of the leadership team, the outcomes recorded on MIDAS	First round of all interviews by July 2004	Staffing	RHC	AJP
Through school council students will address learning issues to inform staff	December 2004	Staffing	RHC	AJP
Increased awareness of impact of teaching and learning policy and lesson observation criteria	Calendar of observations produced termly	Staffing	SMT	AJP
Increased awareness of impact of teaching and learning policy and lesson observation criteria	Calendar of observations produced termly	Staffing	SMT	AJP
S4 is produced in anticipation of Ofsted and this will enable HoDs to prepare for Ofsted. Training carried out during June/July 2004	Reports produced in this format in January 2005	Staffing	SMT	AJP
Create new documents and processes	July 2004	Staffing	SMT	AJP

Suggestions for further reading

Matthew, R. and Tong, S. (1981) *The Role of the Deputy Head in the Comprehensive School*. London: Ward Lock Educational.

Tranter, S. (2002) *Diary of a Deputy*. London: Routledge Falmer.

Begley, P. and Leonard, P. (eds) (1999) *The Values of Educational Administration*. London: Falmer Press.

West Burnham, J. and Bowring-Carr, J. (1997) *Effective Learning in Schools*. London: Pearson.

CHAPTER 6

We can't leave it up to them
On creating a climate and culture for learning, and what to do when it goes wrong

One of the things that makes working in a school so different from any other occupation is the propensity for children to find almost anything else to do rather than learn. While it is undoubtedly the case that nearly every one of those children, left to their own devices, would spend a good proportion of every day engaged in some kind of learning (possibly about science, or reading, perhaps taking part in sporting activities of one sort or another), it is perhaps unlikely that they would organize themselves into groups of 20–30 and decide to spend their time studying the various subjects of the curriculum in chunks of around one hour each for five hours of every day. School, its curriculum and the structure and organization we put into them are very false constructs and so, alongside all of this, we cannot really expect all our students to be waiting for the next pearl of wisdom to be dispensed from their teachers, upon whom they gaze in awe and wonder. No, we have schools, the curriculum and the structure we do and as a result we have to put some effort into ensuring that all children learn effectively – we cannot leave it up to them.

In Chapter 1 of this book we discussed the notion of distributed leadership, of creating the climate in the school where all staff know the part they have to play in achieving the goals of the school and how, if leadership is genuinely distributed, the school learns to function without constant direction from the head. Because people understand and believe in the vision for the school, they work towards it for themselves, not for anyone else. This is the key to successfully creating a climate for learning in the school too. The culture must be developed through the systems and structure and through the interpersonal relationships between teachers and their pupils and between pupils and their peers where it is more difficult for pupils not to achieve than it is for them to achieve.

Now it is easy enough to talk of creating a climate and culture within a school, and it is certainly something that most of us know when we see it or experience it. But what happens if the culture is incorrect? – and this, after all, is the issue that confronts many of us upon taking up a headship. So much of the rest of school leadership is about the technical matters of how things should be done, but the climate for working and learning within the school is the rub. This is what school leadership is all about. Fundamentally the creation of the correct climate is about vision, and the ability to actualize that vision in the daily life of the school. We have dealt in Chapter 1 with the creation of the values and aims of the school. This is a critical activity as it is through the resulting statement that the school culture can begin to be created.

At this point it is worth refreshing on our school aims from Chapter 1, and then we will go on to explore the actions we take to achieve the climate implied by these aims.

> Our high expectations of achievement and behaviour; of openness, honesty, trust and mutual respect, lead to the well-ordered and purposeful environment that are the prerequisites for effective learning.
>
> We encourage our students to work hard and to be enthusiastic in all they do. We want them to attain the highest standards of which they are capable so that they can face the challenging world ahead with confidence and assurance. We value right attitudes and strength of character and by encouraging these in our students we will help them become good citizens in their future walks of life.
>
> We aim to ensure our students:
>
> - are happy and safe within a rich learning environment
> - succeed and achieve their full potential academically, socially, physically and personally
> - have the skills, knowledge and understanding to take their place as mature adults in society
> - value education as a lifelong experience that will continue into the world of work and of leisure
> - develop a sense of citizenship and responsibility to the community and to society as a whole

The most basic requirement for a school must be an expectation that children behave in a way conducive to achievement. Because of the essentially false nature of what we expect of children at school then, no matter who the children are and what type of school it is, there will always be a propensity for them to misbehave. And it is for this reason that we must give consideration to creating an environment where children find it easier to behave well than badly. How do we go about achieving this?

Clear and consistent expectations

Most children want to do what is expected of them. For 95 per cent of young people, 95 per cent of the time, it is enough to make clear what is expected and they will do it. Clarity and consistency are all important in ensuring a well-ordered learning environment. Where there is a lack of clarity then this means that no one really understands the expectations of them. A very simple example is that of school uniform. Now it is very tempting, to try to avoid difficulties with school uniform by acquiescing to what are, on the face of it, reasonable arguments put forward by pupils, and, frequently, by their parents. However, this leads very rapidly to a lack of clarity which makes it almost impossible to know what the rules are on uniform at all. This was the case at one school where the school uniform stated that there was to be no jewellery and that boys should wear a white shirt and a school tie. On looking around the school there was no evidence that there was any prohibition on jewellery, indeed members of staff were unaware that this was part of the uniform code. The boys' uniform, far from being a white shirt and school tie had become a white (or black) polo shirt, no tie and black (or grey) school sweatshirt. It appears that at some time in the past the issue of wearing a tie under a sweatshirt had been raised, the point being made was that as a tie could not be seen under the sweatshirt then why wear the tie. On the face of it entirely reasonable – the rule was adjusted to become a tie should be worn when a sweatshirt isn't worn. This is a contingent rule and lacks clarity as what is someone to do if they take their sweatshirt off but don't have a tie? The end result was that the school tie, over the space of a few years, was no longer worn by anyone at all.

Consistency is just as important as clarity. Most schools have a rule that pupils should not wear outdoor coats in the classroom, yet walking around many schools how many pupils might one see wearing their coats. How does this happen? The rule is clear, but is not enforced. The issue here is consistency of expectations. If a pupil goes to one teacher and argues that they should keep their coat on and wins, this encourages them to try it on with their next teacher. The result is conflict and difficulty. If the expectation is applied consistently and unequivocally across the school then every pupil will know there is no point in arguing and won't try. Consistency of expectations is the most important way that teachers can support one another in maintaining good order in their classrooms.

There are a range of ways of making your expectations clear, and all should be used.

1 The principal way of making expectations clear is through the 'school rules'. These should be clear, unequivocal, as simple as possible and phrased in a positive way. The last point is important as it gives clear messages about what IS expected from pupils rather than what is NOT expected of pupils. A very simple example, and one close to the hearts of many of those in school leadership is that of litter. How much better it is to say 'Litter should be put in the bins provided' rather than 'Pupils must not drop litter'. This may seem a minor point, but it illustrates a point about the importance of the use of language in setting out expectations. Negative language gives pupils a negative behaviour target and furthermore, implies that the generality of pupils behave in an anti-social way and have to be urged not to.

Our school rules, or as we prefer to phrase it, our expectations, have come from a discussion with pupils and staff about what we must expect from all pupils in order that school is a productive place to learn. It is important that they should be general and that there should not be many of them. In one school we know of the list of prohibited activities seems to be endless and specified in minute detail along with the exact consequences for every breach of this extensive code, to the extent that one of the listed offences is 'breaking wind' (it is a boys' school), punishable by an after-school detention! This is unnecessary and quite counter-productive. Far better to have a simple set of easily understood expectations that can be displayed in every classroom. We have developed four baseline expectations – these are:

a) you should arrive on time and be equipped for the lesson

b) you should listen to your teacher and follow
    instructions
c) you should complete the work set to the best of you
    ability and allow others to do the same
d) you should show respect towards other students – keep
    your hands and feet to yourself

Of course there are more school rules than this. There is
the school uniform, homework expectations, instructions
not to bring valuables to school and so on. All the day-to-
day minutiae of school life. It is inappropriate to have all
this listed in every classroom, but nevertheless important
that pupils know the rules. For this purpose we have a
pupil yearbook which is a handbook of everything pupils
and their parents need to know about how the school
functions. This is not just a list of rules, it also contains
information about the curriculum pupils will study, about
the arrangements for contacting the school, coursework
calendar, homework timetable and much more. Of course
much of what is contained by way of school rules is
common sense. But it is really important than even the
most common-sense matters are recorded in this way to
prevent any challenge that a child didn't know something
or other was wrong. But again the imperative should be to
phrase these positively and to be as generally applicable as
possible. Is it necessary, for example, to specify that pupils
should not bring knives to school; if such prohibitions are
listed, then it becomes easy for pupils to argue that the list
is clearly meant to be comprehensive and so anything not
listed is, by this logic, permitted. We do not, for example,
have a rule that says pupils may not bring crocodiles to
school, rather we rely upon a general comment that the
school upholds the law of the land, consequently bringing
a knife or for that matter a crocodile to school is
automatically prohibited. Coupled with the yearbook is a
requirement for form tutors to go through all of these
expectations at the beginning of the year, with guidance on
how they should do this and the points they need to
emphasize.

2   Form tutors have a key role in ensuring pupils are clear
    about expectations. They are the teachers who children
    will usually see first in the morning and who have a

responsibility to ensure that such matters as uniform are correct and homework diaries have been filled in and signed. In a secondary school it is the norm that most teachers have a tutor group. It is also the norm that some teachers enjoy this work and that other teachers don't! Naturally enough this can be a breeding ground for inconsistency of expectations. You need to be able to rely upon these frontline staff doing their jobs properly. They must be monitored. We use a variety of methods to carry out this monitoring. Fig 6.1 shows an example of a homework planner monitoring sheet. These are filled in by every tutor and are monitored by the leadership team every month. The merit of this is that it does not require any real effort by tutors to fill in, for the most part just a tick is required to confirm that the issue has been checked. Of course, that a teacher ticks the box doesn't necessarily mean they have checked and confirmed, but if they haven't, then ticking the box would be an untruth, something most would not wish to do.

3   Assemblies are a vitally important point in the school week for corporate communication. Assembly should be used relentlessly to focus upon the school aims and the expectations that you have of your pupil population. Finding different ways of saying essentially the same thing each time can prove challenging, but it is a challenge worth rising to. Assembly provides an opportunity not only for clarity of expectations but for promoting consistency too. It is important to remember that the audience for assembly is not just the pupils, but also all of the form tutors. We organize assembly as a very formal event. School uniform is expected to be perfect, as well as the heads of year (we present assemblies to double year groups), there are also two members of the leadership team who form a stage party. At the beginning of each term we organize a whole school assembly in the sports hall. This is an excellent opportunity for corporate celebration where the entire school population hear the messages that are being given. The headteacher leads the assembly at the beginning of the academic year, the subject of the assembly is always the same – the successes of the last year and the challenges that lie ahead. We see this as a critical moment in the life

Homework Planner Monitoring Sheet September 2003																
Group: **Tutor:**	**Week 1** **Date:**				**Week 2** **Date:**				**Week 3** **Date:**				**Week 4** **Date:**			
	1	2	3	4	1	2	3	4	1	2	3	4	1	2	3	4

1 Satisfactory
2 Parental signature missing
3 Number of homeworks set this week
4 Homework not set by teacher

Please return to your Head of Year at the end of the month

Figure 6.1 *shows an example of a homework planner monitoring sheet. These are filled in by every tutor and are monitored by the leadership team every month*

of the school where our successes can be celebrated and the vision for the future of the school can be shared with the whole school.

4   Signage around the school. One school we know of put these signs in all the pupil toilets:

**Anyone caught vandalising these toilets
will be excluded from school**

Now what we wondered was the author of this sign expecting to achieve? Clearly they were hoping to put off any would-be vandals from carrying out their evil deeds. But what was the actual effect. It seems more likely that this sign would give the message to all of the pupils in the school that they are expected to vandalize the toilets and that it is only under threat of punishment that they won't. Of course it is highly unlikely that any of the expected target group would modify their behaviour for fear of being excluded, rather it would confirm them in their belief that this is the sort of normal behaviour expected of anyone at the school. There are a whole range of similar (though usually not quite so severe) examples on the walls of many schools. Have a look around your school, how often are there signs that say 'No entry for pupils', 'No pupils allowed unless supervised', 'Don't drop litter' and so on.

In all of these cases there are much better, more subtle, ways of conveying the same ideas in a positive and constructive way. In the case of the toilets, surely it is better to spend time and money ensuring that the facilities are of a high standard and emphasize how important it is to the school that this is the case. This is a much more powerful way of positively creating pressure on those who would abuse their environment.

5   One of the most powerful methods of ensuring that expectations are clear is by having staff model the expected behaviour. Our key value is mutual respect. The most important way to transmit this to pupils is through treating them with respect. This is something that the leadership team emphasize to staff whenever possible. It is too easy for teachers to get angry with pupils and to start berating them, shouting at them, being highly verbally hostile.

All behaviours to which any teacher on the receiving end would take the greatest exception. It is our view that all staff should deal with pupils in the way they would choose to be dealt with by others. This means there should be no shouting, no humiliation and no sarcasm. Readers may believe this all to be hopelessly trendy. We would disagree. Modelling appropriate behaviour to pupils is essential in educating them about how to behave and, more pragmatically, in seizing the moral high ground in any interaction. How powerful is it to say when dealing with poor behaviour of a young person 'Would I ever treat you like that?' All staff should behave in a way that they can ask that question confident in the answer any pupil would give. The response you may get from some of your shouters is 'Well, I'd be more than happy to behave like this is if I could expect the same from my pupils!' Apart from the clear circularity of this argument the most powerful response is that the teacher is the paid professional whereas pupils are adolescent children here to be educated.

6   Wrapping all of this up, how do we reinforce the clarity of our expectations? Well, as indicated above, the approach in one school was to have an extensive and detailed list of school rules and the punishments to be meted out should the rules be broken. While we believe it is undoubtedly the case that pupils need to understand the consequences when they do not meet expectations, we can't help feeling that constructing matters in such a way is perhaps rather a negative way of going about it. We believe most strongly in positive encouragement and rewards when things are done correctly. Anyone who has a dog knows how much more readily they respond to praise and a juicy titbit rather than punishments. People are much the same. Teachers, in particular, should always be on the look out for occasions to praise and reward. There do need to be clear and certain consequences should things go wrong, but the emphasis is always on the positive. Of course some teachers do have some difficulty with praise; perhaps they are a bit too English to be too enthusiastic. The sort of praise that we are looking for is unequivocal. An enthusiastic 'Well done' is worth much more than 'That was quite good'. When a pupil answers a question correctly, acknowledge it with

'Excellent answer', rather than as one teacher we know put it in a very surprised tone of voice 'I didn't think you'd know that'. Watch out for the use of praise in lesson observations and in the interactions you see between teachers and pupils around the school.

An achievement culture

It is a truism to say that the main reason for poor behaviour in classes is lack of challenge and boring teaching. The very first thing that any school should do to create the correct climate for learning is to tackle standards of teaching. Where teaching is not good, standards of attainment and behaviour will be low. The very first point in any behaviour policy should draw attention to the fact that, where teaching is good and pupils are challenged correctly at a level appropriate for them, the scope for poor behaviour and negative attitudes to learning is minimized. But, beyond this or, perhaps more accurately, before this, the culture of the school must be one where achievement is valued. It is a commonplace in staff rooms and governing bodies to hear of the anti-achievement culture prevalent in society, to hear that 'lad' culture is at fault for boys' underachievement. The phrase 'boff' culture is one we are sure will be familiar to many readers, a phrase meaning a culture where pupils apparently do not value achievement. To the extent that any of this exists in your school, clearly the first order of business is to deal with it in order to produce the achievement culture that is necessary for success.

When we consider the supposed anti-achievement culture, what is it we are talking about? Well, it may be the case that a proportion of pupils really does not value education at all, but in our view these cases are very few and far between. We need to hold on to the view that achievement does matter to the very large majority of our pupils, it's just that some of them have a lot of difficulty showing it some of the time! For those who are sceptical about this, we suggest that you spend some time discussing achievement with your year 11 group. Ask them about their hopes for their examinations and what they aspire to in the future. You will find very few who do not want success in some way or another, very few who do not aspire to something beyond school and for whom the standard of their attainment in school is of no consequence. The importance of this is that, to the extent there is an anti-achievement culture in any school, it is our contention that this is only skin-deep. Scratch the surface and you find a group of vulnerable young people who have a whole range of plans and aspirations for their future. The task then is to allow this to be OK. So how to achieve this?

There are a number of steps to creating an achievement culture:

1   Belief – it is absolutely vital that the staff of the school
    believe they can make a difference. Of course this is easy
    to say, but sometimes it can be difficult to achieve. Such
    belief cannot be created overnight, it is a long-term goal
    achieved by incremental change. A range of tactics can be
    brought to bear over a period of time. Managing
    expectations of teachers, particularly in a school that is
    underperforming, is a key task. Every opportunity should
    be taken to discuss attainment levels in terms of baseline
    data. Target setting carried out sensitively and intelligently
    provides an excellent vehicle, this coupled with, over a
    period of time, successful achievement of targets set, will
    bring about the required change. This is dealt with more
    fully in Chapter 8.

2   The messages sent out by teachers in particular are of key
    importance. Any negative comment by a teacher to a class,
    any acknowledgement by a teacher that anyone might think
    that it is not 'cool' to achieve is a step backwards in the
    campaign. For example, a form tutor may have an award for
    a member of the tutor group. Does that tutor call that pupil
    out in front of the class and celebrate the achievement, or
    do they ask the pupil to stay behind and award them
    surreptitiously. If it is the second course, then it is an
    acknowledgement that receiving this sort of praise is
    embarrassing, therefore legitimizing the anti-achievement
    culture. Praise should be public – anyone who says that
    pupils don't like this (most often something said of older
    pupils) is wrong. Some pupils may affect disdain for any
    system of rewards you have devised, but it is our contention
    that such rewards are always well received. We may want to
    consider why there is this affectation. To an extent it is
    human nature not to wish to appear to overjoyed at
    receiving praise – many of us, while liking to receive praise,
    find it vaguely uncomfortable and really don't know how to
    respond. But, perhaps more particularly, the affectation
    results specifically among those who don't receive awards
    and is a cover for the disappointment of not being
    recognized. Of course, there is a simple way around this
    first: ensure that the staff do not conspire with the attitude
    by failing to use the rewards system with older pupils, and

second ensure that rewards are spread around and that a whole range of achievements are recognized. This is not a prescription for devaluing any rewards system you have, rather it is an encouragement to think of achievement in the widest possible sense so that the achievements of the whole range of the pupil population are recognized.

3   Further to the above, a rewards system in the school provides the vehicle for public recognition of achievement. In our school we operate the following rewards:

a)   Merits are awarded to encourage the behaviours that we value; this might be for good homework, or good classwork, or being fully equipped for the lesson, for a naughty child it might be for staying in their seat for the whole lesson, it might be for working quietly, perhaps a merit might be awarded for a particularly good answer in a class discussion, in fact any approved of behaviour. Merit stickers go into homework planners and accumulate towards certificates for 10, 30, 60 and 120 merits. Merits should be given out lavishly, and so the certificate intervals must reflect this expectation. If a pupil needs 30 merits for a gold certificate for example (as opposed to 60 in our system) then teachers will hand them out more sparingly.

b)   Achievement awards are given out in special year-group assemblies on the last day of each term. An achievement award in our school is a certificate given to pupils who are nominated for achievement by three or more of their teachers. Now achievement can obviously be defined in many different ways. We choose to define it in all of these ways for the purposes of achievement awards.

c)   An annual presentation evening. This is a formal event with a guest speaker where GCSE and A level certificates are awarded along with subject prizes for achievement for pupils in other years.

4   We also recognize achievement in our half-termly newsletter and with honour boards where we name the senior prefects.

Although not entirely to do with achievement, we believe that giving pupils responsibilities in school adds to the achievement culture we wish to create and, more particularly, it helps to create a sense of pride in the school which is so much a part of achievement culture. One of our anchor events through the year is our Open Evening. This is a time when pride in the school is very much to the fore, both for staff and pupils. A key part of this event are the students who act as tour guides from year 10, 11 and the sixth form and the pupils from years 7, 8 and 9 who help in departments. Other responsibilities are:

- year 9 pupils act as receptionists. This is on a rota throughout the year. No pupil misses more than one day's lessons, but it gives them a real sense of responsibility as the public face of the school
- pupils helping in the library
- sixth-form students helping with learning support, paired reading and so forth
- pupils acting as tour guides for the many people who need tours of the school
- sixth-form students acting as the school newsletter editorial team, and – most importantly
- the school council

All of these positions of responsibility encourage pupils to feel a pride in their school and to feel that they are an important part of it. In the case of the open evening guides it is noteworthy that it is not only pupils who are most naturally pro-school who come to help, the guides are drawn from across the whole spectrum of pupils in the school.

Above all else, creation of an achievement culture is about having the vision and courage to make it happen. Above we speak of the need for belief – well the most important people to have this belief are the leadership team. The blind faith or, as Tim Brighouse has put it, 'unwarranted optimism' that things will be as you want them to be.

What about when things go wrong?

Things being as they are, no matter how expert your teachers, no matter how well-constructed your rewards system, no matter how clear and consistent all your staff are, there will still be occasions when pupils do not behave as you would wish. This next section is about dealing constructively with poor behaviour of pupils.

There are some underlying principles that must be cleared up about the processes for dealing with poor pupil behaviour. These are largely connected with the management structure discussed in Chapter 3. We strongly believe that effective management of discipline in school is brought about through consistent handling of incidents. This is why our favoured structure gives responsibility for the management of the discipline structure to one person on the leadership team. Different schools adopt different structures, so if you do not choose this recommended approach then you must give careful consideration to how consistency is to be achieved.

Having established the senior staff responsible then there needs to be a clear definition of responsibilities for behaviour incidents within the structure of the school. Dealing with naughty children is one of the things that sets teaching as a profession apart from most others. Teachers who experience poor behaviour feel themselves attacked on a number of levels, they are concerned that their classes are not getting a good deal, they feel personally affronted by the pupil concerned, they may have experienced personal abuse which makes this feeling even stronger, they are concerned about how they might retrieve the situation under circumstances where they have lost face and they frequently feel a whole range of other emotions too, most particularly they may be very angry. Under these circumstances there is a job of work to be done to manage not only the incident itself, but also the feelings of the teacher concerned. Who should take responsibility for it?

Anyone in a senior leadership position will have been confronted by a teacher in just such a state as described above, often they will have the pupil concerned with them having brought them to you for a good telling off. If you have experienced this you will know just how unsatisfactory this method of dealing with matters is. And this goes to the heart of the need for structure in dealing with incidents. Left to their own devices teachers tend to swing from one extreme, marching the pupil to the nearest member of the leadership team for a 'good b*ll*cking', to the other – not dealing with the incident at all and ending up in a terminal spiral of worse and worse behaviour in their classroom. There needs to be clarity about expectations and there also needs to be clarity about what should happen when these expectations are not met. When a pupil misbehaves what should happen?

From observation of practice in a number of schools the default position seems to be that pupil misbehaviour is referred to the pastoral team. Frequently this can take the form of a teacher unloading on the relevant pastoral leader in the staff room just after it has happened. This often seem to us rather like Oscar Wilde's *Picture of Dorian Gray*, as the teacher unloads all their troubles on the pastoral leader, leaving them feeling much better, but leaving the pastoral leader older and greyer. And, of course, the long-term result of this is that issues remain unresolved; poor behaviour simply becomes the expectation with the safety valve of a good moan in the staffroom allowing the escape. It is impossible to believe that any vision for education would include this as a positive outcome. There is no inevitability that pupils behave badly; this is not something that should be put up with. But without structure there can be no solution.

Primary responsibility for behaviour management in any class rests with the teacher. They should ensure that the needs of their pupils are at the heart of the lesson-planning process. Lesson planning in the context of a difficult class means not only ensuring appropriate learning outcomes and activities, but also predicting difficulties that may give rise to behaviour problems and planning to avoid them. Where teachers are finding this difficult they must be supported and helped with their planning. The first line of responsibility for this rests within the department. Where things go wrong, similarly the teacher should be the first one to take action, whatever this action may be. Where they need support, then the person to whom they should turn in the first instance is the head of department. If the head of department needs support then the next point of contact should be with their line manager, who in our suggested structure is the curriculum line manager on the leadership team.

This system should take care of the large majority of potential difficulties, as indicated above; most children will behave themselves given the correct environment. Of course there are some pupils who find the stresses and strains of a mainstream educational environment very difficult to deal with and, as a consequence, present difficulties to most people who come into contact with them. Under these circumstances a second referral route is required; this now becomes the responsibility of the pastoral leader. So we have a referral structure as shown in figure 6.2.

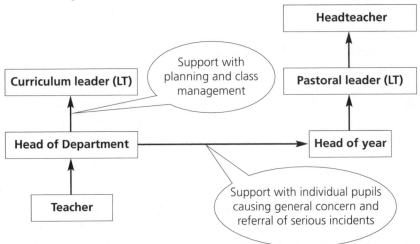

Figure 6.2 *A suggested referral structure*

This structure is important because it drives the responsibility for action to the place closest to the difficulty. It is flexible enough to respond to a variety of different types of issue that crop up and means that there is a clear route for escalation. A particular feature of the structure illustrated is the funnelling effect it has. The curriculum leader in this structure only has to deal with issues raised by the heads of department, but more importantly the pastoral leader only deals with issues referred through the heads of year and the headteacher only deals with issues referred through the pastoral leader. This funnelling is important as it reduces the number of directions of referral and means that no person in the chain becomes bogged down by receiving referrals from multiple angles. In particular, the position of the headteacher is reserved only for dealing with incidents of the most serious nature as the pastoral leader acts as gatekeeper at this critical point. One of the biggest errors headteachers make is to become too involved too soon in disciplinary incidents. The head's position in the discipline structure is critical, and should be preserved. Never has the phrase 'familiarity breeds contempt' had more meaning than at the junction between the head and naughty pupils. Any young person who reaches the attention of the head must know that this means things have become very serious indeed for them. This detachment serves another purpose, where the head has not involved him or herself in matters earlier on it provides an appearance of impartiality to both the pupil and their parents, when things get difficult then this apparent impartiality can be of great benefit indeed.

Recording

Coupled with this, and particularly important for pupils causing ongoing concern or for incidents of a particularly serious nature, is the record-keeping system that goes with referral. Although there is a great deal of importance attached to reducing bureaucracy in schools as a result of the National Workforce Reform Agreement, thorough recording of incidents cannot be underestimated in its strategic importance in creating the correct climate in the school and should never be short-cut. The key features of an incident report form are that:

- it is flexible and easy to use
- it is *circulated* to appropriate members of the staff, not *copied*. This is important as when incident forms are copied it leaves the recipient of one of the multiple copies unsure whether action has been taken, what that action was, and

whether further action is required. By circulating the form, then the incident can be dealt with in a sequential manner

- there is a summary space. This should provide a very brief and easily accessible comment as to the nature and severity of the incident, e.g. 'fighting', 'refusal to cooperate', etc. This is also the comment that is recorded on the central database (of which more later)
- it has a large gap for detail. When dealing with an incident a head of department, head of year, or member of the leadership team will need as much detail as possible in order to follow the matter up. It is important that teachers understand the importance of providing a detailed account. This can also sometimes provide a cathartic opportunity for unloading the problem (more constructively than on colleagues in the staffroom)
- it has a space for action taken. This is most important as it shows that the matter has been dealt with and can also indicate whether or not more action is needed

Although the form we use looks very simple, it has been developed over a number of years and does perform its function very well indeed. The functions are twofold, first to provide a referral record so the member of staff receiving the referral knows the detail of the incident in sufficient depth to take action, secondly, and perhaps more importantly, it provides a lasting record of the incidents a pupil has been involved in during their career in the school. While this is of no great significance to the very large majority of pupils, for those who create significant, ongoing and general difficulties in the school it is invaluable. Action taken must always be informed by the nature of the incident itself and the record of the pupil concerned. A point that needs to be made to teachers who prefer not to fill in referral forms is that if there is no form the incident effectively did not happen!

Managing the data produced by incident reports is of the greatest importance and it is for this reason that it is appropriate to allocate administration resources to creating a database of behaviour incidents. There are many systems available for such recording, but whichever system you choose you need to be able to record the pupil's name, the incident (and probably an incident code for analysis purposes), the date and time, the members of staff involved and the action taken. An individual's behaviour record can then be retrieved when necessary, for example as a preparation for a meeting with the pupil and their parents. Giving the family a few minutes to review the behaviour record provides a good preparation for the meeting, especially when parents are inclined to be somewhat over-protective and belligerent. The behaviour database should also allow the analysis of types of behaviour incident recorded, analysis by year group, by tutor group, by gender and by individual pupil. This then provides a much more effective management tool for monitoring behaviour than some of the more commonly used methods such as number of detentions or number of exclusions, and is suitable for using as a performance indicator in your school development plan (see Chapter 5).

Consequences

Something we all have to confront is the consequences (or sanctions, or punishments) that are available to us when we are faced with serious incidents of misbehaviour. This is important, as there must be a graded response that accords an appropriate consequence to each incident of poor behaviour. Getting this right is of critical importance in building relationships with parents, especially when it is borne in mind that for many young people, the reason why they misbehave at school is because of weaknesses in parenting at home – weaknesses that can manifest themselves in your office as parental over-protectiveness of their children. Furthermore the whole area of school punishments is surrounded by a great deal of law – though perhaps not quite as much as some would have us believe. It is certainly well worth gaining an understanding of the legal framework for school sanctions. A very good reference work is Croner's *Headteachers' Guide to the Law*.

Beyond the normal sanctions imposed by individual teachers we have developed the following range, in order of severity:

- school lunchtime detention (supervised by all promoted staff on a rota)
- school detention (supervised as above and taking place for one hour after school each week)
- internal suspension. This is probably the most hated sanction by pupils, here they are placed with a member of staff and set work for the whole day. The suspension includes morning break and lunchtime
- for specific offences, principally vandalism, we have community service. This will be for a number of hours on consecutive afternoons after school where a pupil will be set work by the site team. In one specific example, where a pupil damaged the minibus, he was set the task of cleaning the minibus each week for half a term

- restorative justice. Not strictly speaking a sanction, rather the follow-up to one. This is an occasion where an offender meets their victim and apologizes for their offence. Particularly useful where nuisance to neighbours is concerned, or where the offence is directed towards another pupil
- fixed-term and permanent exclusion. Both of these will be dealt with more fully in the next section

Whatever range of sanctions you use, for them to be effective they must be fully communicated with home (indeed in most cases this is a requirement). This means that any school sanction (as opposed to those set by individual teachers) should be accompanied by a letter home explaining the sanction and the reason for it in detail, i.e. the misbehaviour should be fully described for parents including full quotes of any abusive language that has provoked the sanction. Simply writing to parents to say an after-school detention has been given for bad language, or misbehaviour or disobedience will not be enough to satisfy many parents of the justness of the punishment and, if this is the case, even if the parents don't challenge the sanction, the all-important level of trust in the school will almost certainly be damaged.

Using exclusion

The very hardest end of the sanctions that can be applied is exclusion from school. An exclusion can be for a fixed term of 1–45 days in any one academic year, or it can be permanent. The use of exclusion is heavily constrained by legislation, and it is legislation that you do need to know about. The original legislation is described in DfES circular 10/99 but this was updated in 2003 to include the many updates to the legislation that had transpired in the interim, as well as to include new additions.

As headteacher you need to be completely clear on your position on the use of exclusion and, perhaps more importantly still, the governors need to be completely clear about it too. As indicated above you do need to familiarize yourself with the legislation but some of the key points are listed in Table 6.1.

For the most part the table overleaf is a very brief list of some of the legalities surrounding exclusion. Beyond this, of course, there is what you actually do to make it an effective sanction. The importance of exclusion is not so much that it is unpleasant for the child – quite frankly, it isn't all that unpleasant for many children who are excluded. The point really is that it is a formal, official sanction recorded with a letter to the education authority, to the governors and placed on the

Exclusion is permitted:	• in response to serious breaches of a school's discipline policy, and • if allowing the pupil to remain in school would seriously harm the education or welfare of the pupil or others in the school
Exclusion is not permitted for:	• minor incidents such as failure to do homework or to bring dinner money • poor academic performance • lateness or truancy • pregnancy • breaching school uniform policy including hairstyle or wearing jewellery[1] • punishing pupils for the behaviour of the parents, for example, by extending a fixed-period exclusion until the parents agree to attend a meeting[2]
Can permanent exclusion be used for one-off offences?	Not usually but the following are exceptions: • serious actual or threatened violence against another pupil or a member of staff • sexual abuse or assault • supplying an illegal drug • carrying an offensive weapon
How long should (can) a fixed-term exclusion be?	Up to 45 days in any one year. But you should always consider very carefully what is to be achieved by lengthy fixed-term exclusions. It is probably best to operate a kind of tariff system so that you have a consistent approach to similar offences Special arrangements have to be made for fixed-term exclusions totalling more than 5 and more than 15 days in any one term, and if the exclusion would result in the pupil missing a public examination
Do the parents have a right to appeal?	• If the exclusion is for 5 days or less in a term, then parents can make representations to the governors who must convene a meeting of their disciplinary committee to hear them. However, the committee cannot direct reinstatement of the pupil and cannot have the exclusion removed from the pupil's record.

- If the exclusion is for between 6 and 15 days in a term, then governors must hold a disciplinary committee meeting between the 6th and 50th school day after being notified of the exclusion. The outcome can be that the exclusion is overturned, but obviously the pupil cannot be reinstated as they will already be back at school.
- If the exclusion is for more than 15 days in a term or is permanent, then the governors' disciplinary committee must hold a meeting before the 15th school day of the exclusion to consider the headteacher's use of the sanction and to decide whether or not to direct reinstatement of the pupil.
- If the exclusion is permanent and the governors uphold the headteacher's decision, then parents have the right of appeal to an independent appeal panel convened by the education authority.

What about the excluded pupil's continuing education?	For fixed-term exclusions of more than 1 day the headteacher must ensure work is set for the pupil. It is our view that the expectation should be clear that additional work will be set upon the return of the work previously set, for marking.
	Where the exclusion is for a fixed term of more than 15 days, then the headteacher, in consultation with the LEA, should make arrangements for the pupil's continuing education.

1 Although where such conduct could be construed as deliberate and persistent defiance of the school's behaviour code then exclusion may be used.
2 This is particularly problematic, as any school discipline system requires parental support. Holding such meetings at the end of an exclusion would be considered good and essential practice by most schools.

Table 6.1 *Exclusions summary*

pupil's file. Its effectiveness rests upon any of this mattering to the child or their parents. Fortunately, of course, for most children and their parents they do care about all this deeply. But it is important to capitalize upon the formality through the procedures you adopt surrounding the exclusion – this means in the lead up to the exclusion and in the aftermath before the pupil returns to school.

Carrying out an exclusion
The investigation
Before excluding a child it is very important to establish that the pupil actually did what they are alleged to have done. For many incidents there will be no dispute. Typically, if the offence is abusive behaviour towards a member of staff, for example, then it will have happened in front of many witnesses and the pupil will not try to pretend it didn't happen, though they will undoubtedly try to minimize the significance of what they have done; this may take the form of pretending they were talking to someone else, or perhaps that they were misheard. It is very tempting to be taken in by this kind of obfuscation; it is equally important to ensure that the pupil acknowledges completely what they have done before proceeding, as this is an important part of the learning process (after all the purpose of an exclusion is for the pupil to learn not to do it again), and it will also make the meeting with the child's parents much easier, although it is very important not to give any impression that a pupil has been pressurized into 'confessing'. At this point there are differing views about asking the pupil to write it all down. Critics of this approach say that it is unnecessarily legalistic, on the other hand taking witness statements and offering a pupil the opportunity to record their account of events provides lasting evidence and is certainly desirable for offences of a more serious nature that may, for example, lead to a permanent exclusion.

Matters are more complicated when it is not an 'open and shut case'. Where, for example, there has been a theft, or perhaps some serious vandalism, someone may have set off the fire alarm, or perhaps someone has set fire to paper towels in the toilets! Here there will need to be an element of sleuthing. The offence must be investigated, feelers put out (someone always knows who did it) and the culprit found. Under these circumstances it is most important to find the culprit, it shouldn't matter how much time and effort goes into such investigations, if the culprit is found and dealt with, then this secures the view of the pupils in general that people don't get away with things, that where there are serious incidents those responsible are found and dealt with. Having found out who did it (on whatever basis), then it is, naturally enough, most helpful if there is a confession. But it is important for the pupil to understand that this isn't a requirement before you take action. Indeed the requirement in law is that:

> If satisfied that, on the balance of probabilities, the pupil did what he or she is alleged to have done; the head teacher may exclude the pupil. (DfES, 2003)

Of course this is quite a difficult test to consider. It certainly means more than you just suspect the pupil committed the offence, but it is a weaker test than 'beyond reasonable doubt', as in criminal law. What might this mean in practice? – a good example might be where two pupils allege a third committed some offence, but the third one denies it. This is probably not beyond reasonable doubt, but unless you have good reason to suppose the witnesses are lying (and, we have to accept, it can often be difficult to find genuinely disinterested parties in a school) then, on the balance of probabilities you may well feel justified in excluding. Many parents of pupils excluded under such circumstances may find your action difficult to accept, but this should not dissuade you from taking action that you believe is correct.

You will see that the investigation as described above is an important part of the process. It is important to make a seemingly obvious point, before carrying out the exclusion, the pupil must be asked to give their account of events. Even when it seems the most obvious and clear-cut case imaginable they must be given this opportunity. This does seem obvious, but there have been occasions where exclusions have come unstuck for the want of this simple step. It might be that the offence comes to light at the end of the school day, after the pupil has gone home. It might be that the pupil is absent from school on the following day (not infrequently the case, perhaps a desire to avoid facing the music?) when the investigation is carried out. Under both of these circumstances it can seem to be an attractive proposition to exclude the pupil in absentia. Under no circumstances should this happen, you must delay the exclusion until the next day when the pupil does have the opportunity to present their defence. Admittedly this is inconvenient because you may well have to look after the pupil in some kind of isolation arrangement for the day. Unfortunately this is unavoidable. There are three reasons for making this case so strongly (apart from it being a clear requirement of the law). First, if it is a lengthy or permanent exclusion then it risks being overturned either by governors, or certainly by any independent appeal panel that hears the case. Secondly, pragmatically, it is very difficult to handle the post-exclusion meeting, if the pupil has their first opportunity to argue their case once the exclusion has happened and, under these circumstances, is likely to be very strongly supported by their parents. Thirdly, it is against natural justice. This would be no way to treat anyone and should not form a part of the processes of a value-driven, moral organization.

Carrying out the exclusion

It is important that the parent of the child is informed once the decision to exclude has been made. Ideally this should be by telephone (though it is probably unwise to leave such messages on answering machines). If this proves impossible, then the pupil should be given a copy of the exclusion letter to take home. In this letter you should ask the parent to telephone to confirm receipt. There are various things that should go into the letter – sample letters can be found in the guidance on exclusions (DfES, 2003), but most importantly there should be a full description of the incident and, if appropriate, you should make it clear that the pupil has admitted to what they have done.

In deciding how long the exclusion should be, there are three main factors that should be borne in mind:

1   The seriousness of the offence – it is usual to give a longer exclusion for more serious offences, though clearly there is a limit to this bearing in mind that the pupil will have to return to school and that the longer an exclusion is the more difficult it is for them to return.
2   The pupil's previous record – it is likely that if the pupil is a repeat offender for the same type of offence you will decide upon a longer exclusion subject to the same consideration about lengthy fixed-term exclusions above.
3   The use to be made of the time while the pupil is excluded – if you are seriously considering permanent exclusion, longer fixed-term exclusion (up to, say, 15 days) can be used to explore the possibility of alternatives to permanent exclusion, though to a large extent the scope for such alternatives will be limited by your LEA.

The post-exclusion meeting

Before the pupil returns to school there should be a post-exclusion meeting. It is imperative that both the pupil and their parents attend this meeting and that it is used as an opportunity to enlist the support of the parents in gaining the compliance of their child. From the school side the attendance at the meeting depends upon where the pupil is in their disciplinary record and the seriousness of the offence. Accepting that exclusions are only ever issued for serious offences, then the lower level offences can be dealt with by the member of the leadership team with this responsibility. If the offence is more serious or the general record of the pupil would warrant it, then the head should take the meeting accompanied by the deputy or assistant head. Where permanent exclusion is being considered then we believe it is good practice to invite a member of the governing body to the meeting. In this case, if the fixed-term exclusion has been issued as 'so many days in the first instance', then at the end of the meeting everyone other than the governor representative and the head should adjourn so that these two remaining members of the meeting can consider their 'verdict'. This is useful for a number of reasons.

- it allows the head the opportunity to discuss the case with someone who has an outside view of the school
- it gives the parents and the pupil a sense that 'due process' is being followed and that whatever the outcome it is not vindictiveness on the head's part
- should the outcome be permanent exclusion then the governors' disciplinary committee know that the decision has been arrived at with the assistance of one of their number and that if they overturn the decision they are overturning the decision of a governor as well as the head

Whatever stage the pupil is at the meeting should follow the same agenda:

1 a description of the events leading up to the exclusion and the reason for it
2 an opportunity for the pupil to give their account and raise any questions they have
3 an opportunity for the parents to do the same
4 any specific points the school members of the meeting want to raise about the incident
5 a consideration of the wider disciplinary record of the pupil (it is very helpful if parents and their child have had the opportunity to study the conduct log before the meeting)
6 an opportunity for parents and their child to say anything they wish about this wider record
7 steps to be taken to avoid a repetition of the behaviour that led to this exclusion and any help the pupil can be given to bring their behaviour into line

8   a final opportunity for anyone to make any concluding remarks

Having concluded the meeting then whoever led the meeting should write a letter to summarize the outcome. This will include any actions agreed to by the school and the date of any review meeting agreed.

The outcome of the meeting should include some agreement on steps that all parties will take to improve the situation in future, in particular the pupil will be expected to commit to no repetition (and give some indication that they are sincere) and there should be some action on behalf of the school to support the pupil in their efforts to improve their behaviour. It is very important that the school does have a range of actions it can take to help pupils. We have a commitment to educate pupils about their behaviour and these actions are a more focused way of doing this; we should be proactive in our attempts to prevent exclusions, and, pragmatically, if you ever wish to exclude a pupil permanently it will be very difficult to make it stick if there is little or no evidence that the school has taken any action to help the pupil to improve their behaviour. This is the topic of the final section of this chapter.

Permanent exclusion

A brief word about the use of permanent exclusion. There are strong views on this subject, frequently those who do not work in schools (LEA officers, the special needs or children's services department in your LEA, governors), will be quick to judge that a permanent exclusion has been issued hastily, that the school has not done enough to improve the pupil's behaviour and so on. Whereas headteachers generally feel that this is very much a last resort, a decision arrived at after everything else has been tried.

It is important to understand the different perspectives of those who have an interest in any case of permanent exclusion, as this will affect your approach to the various legalities that must be surmounted in order successfully to exclude a pupil permanently.

Before going on to the process it is worth giving some consideration to where you stand on the issue. Some headteachers regard permanent exclusion as a personal failure. The view is that no one benefits, least of all the child concerned when a child is permanently excluded. The consequence of this view is that these headteachers will do almost anything to avoid a permanent exclusion. The steps that are sometimes taken are:

1   organizing home tuition at the school's expense, an action that is difficult to justify if the cost is more than that received for the pupil including any statement-related funding

2   an individual programme for the pupil. This might be arranged where the pupil has a statement and really needs a placement in a special school. Of course this simply prolongs the difficulty and avoids the need for the LEA to take any proper action

3   an extended work experience placement. Sometimes this might be (illegally) a full-time placement. Probably justifiable if the pupil is approaching statutory school leaving age, but sometimes put in place when the pupil is near the beginning of year 10 – under these circumstances it is doomed to fail as such a programme is unsustainable in the long term

4   perpetually returning the pupil to classes and simply putting up with their misconduct. This is probably the most popular exclusion avoidance technique

All of the above are legitimate approaches, in the sense that they are legal. Another approach which we believe to be not uncommon yet no less illegal and unacceptable is to advise the parent to find another school for their child as they will be permanently excluded otherwise and this won't look good on their record. We believe this to be a completely outrageous approach for two reasons:

1   The school that receives the pupil does so without any knowledge of the pupil and without the assistance of that pupil having a permanent exclusion on their record. It also avoids the necessity for the excluding school having a deduction from their budget to transfer to the receiving school (the balance of the AWPU for the pupil is transferred on exclusion).

2   Parents have the right to a review of the exclusion by the governing body and subsequently the right to appeal to an independent panel if their child is excluded. Of course if they remove their child voluntarily rather than have them excluded, then effectively the exclusion has happened and however dubious the grounds for it, the parent has given up any rights.

None of these difficulties arise if the view is that permanent exclusion is an appropriate response to very serious one-off incidents, or long-term highly problematic behaviour. The view above, that no one benefits from a permanent exclusion, in our view, is transparently ludicrous. The use of permanent exclusion fulfils a number of beneficial purposes:

1   It removes a very troublesome pupil from the school (not one of the greatest benefits as the result of permanent exclusion from other schools is that your school will probably receive some of them).

2   It can act as a catalyst for some deeply troubled youngsters to get the education they deserve in proper special school setting (though, admittedly, this is somewhat rare).

3   It sends an important message to the whole school population about lines which may not be crossed; there is a clear ultimate sanction.

4   Some of our most anti-social young people conduct their lives as though they are completely untouchable. Their experience of dealing with their parents, their school to date, the police and indeed every other authority can give them the view that their behaviour is someone else's problem. Where they misbehave, their parents are called in, there are educational psychologists and counsellors who are asked to work with them, there may be case conferences and multi-agency meetings of sometimes up to 8 or 10 people, all of whom, from the child's perspective, seem to be taking their misbehaviour much more seriously than they do themselves. In such cases a permanent exclusion which removes them from the school they like and from their friends, may be the first time they have ever had to face a serious consequence as a result of their actions. Of course many people may disagree with this proposition, but to us this is an important principle in our use of permanent exclusion.

When to exclude permanently

There is no simple answer to this; it depends entirely upon your own judgement. There may be a serious one-off incident; an example might be a very severe beating of one pupil by another resulting in the serious injury of the victim. But more likely it will be a response to a consistent sequence of poor behaviour usually resulting in a succession of fixed-term exclusions. At each post-exclusion meeting the pupil will make various commitments to their future improved behaviour. The school will offer various measures of support with this. At some point along this road you will take the view that no more can be tolerated, progress is not being made and the child should be permanently excluded.

There can be confusion in colleagues' minds over the steps towards this end point. It is not unusual after a post-exclusion meeting, where the pupil has made such commitments, for him or her to misbehave almost straightaway. This will sometimes result in (usually) the head of year reporting the incident in the expectation that the pupil will instantly be permanently excluded. Of course this is reaction predicated on the notion that it is reasonable to expect this pupil on the edge of permanent exclusion to be suddenly transformed into a model pupil – clearly unrealistic. Each incident should be treated on its own merits and treated in the same way as it always has been. If the appropriate response is a detention, then this remains the appropriate response, if it is internal suspension, then likewise. It is only if the offence is one that would normally result in a fixed-term exclusion that it would be appropriate to permanently exclude, and then only if it is more of the same sort of behaviour. The point here to remember is that an exclusion can be of two types, fixed-term, or permanent. In other words they are two facets of the same consequence and should only be used for individual offences that meet the criteria for exclusion.

Managing the process

You will probably have decided to exclude a pupil permanently after issuing a fixed-term exclusion in the first instance (this is clearly the expectation in law as headteachers are advised never to exclude permanently in the 'heat of the moment'). You will have held a meeting to consider your response, and we would suggest you enlist the support of a governor for this (as described above). Plenty of time should be given to this meeting, allowing the whole issue to be fully explored. Your governor representative can often be very useful in asking questions from another viewpoint. We think this involvement gives parents more confidence in the process. After everything has been said, everyone other than the head and the governor withdraws from the meeting. In essence you have to make the decision either to exclude permanently or re-admit. In law it is clearly the head's decision alone to exclude permanently. This does not mean you should not take careful note of the views of your governor representative as this makes the decision much more inclusive of governor views and this will stand you in very good stead when it comes to the governors' disciplinary committee review of your decision.

Assuming you go ahead and permanently exclude then you will need to arrange a governors' disciplinary committee meeting within 15 school days of the exclusion. Whether to arrange this sooner rather than later is a tactical decision, but sooner is good as it means the process of finding the pupil another school can move on more rapidly than would otherwise be possible.

Preparing for the committee meeting is important. The most important thing to understand is that the committee does not usually need to be convinced that the pupil concerned is very naughty. Rather they need to be persuaded that permanent exclusion was the correct response to this pupil's record of poor behaviour. The most important aspect of persuading them of this is to show the record of intervention and support that you have put in place. Of course, the other very important thing is to show the committee that you have acted in accordance with the law, and in particular that the pupil has done what is alleged. Generally, when you have got it right, the parents will leave with their permanently excluded child thanking you for all you have done.

Avoiding exclusion

Above we have listed some of the more dubious steps some schools take to avoid exclusion. That we have listed these does not mean that we do not believe that schools should not be committed to avoiding exclusion, but our emphasis is upon adjusting behaviour to avoid the necessity to exclude rather than just finding alternatives to the act of exclusion.

There are a range of activities that a school can offer in order to support a pupil who wishes to improve their behaviour. Generally a good way to proceed is, as a result of, for example, a post-exclusion meeting, to arrange a meeting for the pupil and their parents with your Learning (or Behaviour) Support Department. This provides an opportunity for an analysis of the pupil's difficulties to be carried out. One must be wary here of being presented with solutions which are appealing on the face of it, but are unsustainable in the long term. For example, it might seem perfectly fine for a pupil in year 8 to come out of, say, French as they find it difficult and this precipitates behaviour difficulties, but what are you to do with them in the long term? This is a very costly solution and, furthermore, it is one that takes the responsibility for their behaviour away from the child.

The focus should be upon providing a structure where the pupil can function effectively while fulfilling all their commitments to their curriculum; after all you are running a mainstream school, not a special school. What might this structure include? Some examples might be:

- change tutor group to break up a negative friendship group
- arrange for the pupil to meet a teaching assistant or sixth-form student at the beginning of the day to ensure they have their correct equipment, books, timetable and uniform for the day ahead. This will avoid the trigger points of lateness, uniform disputes or the disruption caused at the beginning of a lesson while the pupil searches for a pen, or whatever
- tactical grouping, placing the pupil out of set, again to avoid combustible combinations of pupils
- counselling – mixed views on this one, but we believe it does have a palliative effect
- one of the most powerful tactics is the daily target sheet. Here the pupil and HoY/tutor negotiate a series of simply achievable targets. These targets are presented on a sheet for the teacher at the beginning of the lesson, at the end the teacher grades the pupil and adds a comment if appropriate, the pupil also has the opportunity to self-assess. The sheet is then presented to the parent that evening. This provides an ongoing record and motivation to succeed. Sometimes colleagues can find this difficult as, despite poor behaviour in other respects, the pupil may have still met their targets and received a top grade for doing so. While we understand this difficulty, it is an important part of the process for pupils to have their targets broken down into sufficiently achievable steps so that they can experience success. An example of our daily target sheet is included as an appendix at the end of this chapter
- making a referral to your local Pupil Referral Unit (PRU). The purpose of this would be for the pupil to spend some time off-site at the PRU undergoing a programme that should help them to control their behaviour much better. Different LEAs operate these differently and how easy it is to make use of the PRU will depend in large part upon the operating procedure, the match of places to demand and the physical location of the PRU in relation to your school. You must also decide whether or not placing your badly behaved pupil in the company of all the other most badly behaved pupils in the county for about 6 weeks on a re-integration programme is really going to have the beneficial effect you desire – but it is certainly one of the options you have at your disposal

Behaviour Support Service

Preferable to the PRU is to set up your own onsite referral unit. We have what we call our Behaviour Support Service. This service mirrors the aims of the PRU. It provides re-integration programmes for pupils in school on a flexible basis, where up to six pupils at any one time can work either for long periods of the day over the short term, or, in certain special cases, for longer-term withdrawal for short periods of time in the week. It is staffed by a teacher who manages and leads the service (we have been fortunate to recruit a former PRU headteacher); we also have a TA and a counsellor.

Although such a service represents a considerable investment for the school, we believe it is justified as it means we can plan provision more effectively for those with behaviour difficulties, it also means that we can extract from class pupils who are causing difficulty for worthwhile intervention and at the same time relieve the pupil's teacher and classmates of their disruption.

Such a service can manage behaviour-support plans for a very large number of pupils beyond those that it teaches directly (taking up one of the six work spaces). In addition the service staff can provide useful advice on behaviour management in general and for particular pupils. A particularly effective intervention was pupil pursuit of some particularly challenging pupils, the result of which was feedback to some teachers regarding the effective practice seen in other classes with the same pupils.

Of course, at the end of all this positive intervention the pupil may well not improve. After all, the main thing in any of this is that the pupil must want to improve their behaviour as it is only they who can make the change and some just simply don't want to. If this is the case the pupil may end up being permanently excluded anyway. Pragmatically you will know that you have done all that can reasonably be expected of you to prevent this outcome – thus the exclusion should stand through governors' review and, should there be an appeal, it should stand through that too.

Conclusion

The crux of the matter when creating an achievement culture and a well-disciplined learning environment is to be completely clear about your vision for the school. You must, above all else, know what you want it to be like and be certain that you can achieve this. Culture is about the way people act and the words people use. They will take their lead from the headteacher and the leadership team. It is vital that you and your team live the vision.

In creating your culture you must always be aware of what you say and how you say it. Words are your most powerful tool and have the greatest impact. Your vision will be about positive outcomes and so you must make your language positive, you must be upbeat, but also you must be able to empathize when others find it difficult. Empathy, but not sympathy. Any exchange that you have must be about reinforcing the culture and meaning of your school

Part of living the vision is the absolute knowledge that there are solutions to the problems you face. Schools, being human organizations, are messy places. Things are often far from simple and there are many occasions when events will conspire to obscure the clarity of your vision. You must develop a sixth sense to feel the onset of this descending fog. Re-focus and maintain your clear sense of direction. The solutions you are looking for may not be quick, or simple, but that they are there is, and must remain, beyond dispute. If things are not the way you wish them to be, then no one else is going to change it if you don't and so first and foremost this is the responsibility of leadership.

We have mentioned on a number of occasions throughout this chapter that schools are value-driven organizations, and this is at the heart of the sometimes very difficult judgements you have to make. Let your aims and values be your compass and you will not go far wrong.

We have mentioned pragmatism on a number of occasions in this chapter too. Pragmatically, you must know the law on pupil-discipline matters in school. If you do not, then it will be your enemy; if you do, then it is undoubtedly your friend.

Bibliography

DfES (2003) *Improving behaviour and attendance: guidance on exclusion from schools and Pupil Referral Units.* London: DfES.

DAILY TARGET SHEET

Name: _____   Tutor Group: _____   Date: _____

Agreed Targets:

1. _____   2. _____

3. _____   4. _____

Students should:	Teachers should:	Parents should:
1. Collect this sheet from their tutor or head of year each day.	1. Receive the target sheet at the beginning of the lesson.	1. Receive the target sheet when their child arrives home each day.
2. Hand the sheet to each teacher at the beginning of each lesson.	2. Assess the extent to which the student has achieved their targets.	2. Read through the sheet and raise any questions they have with their child.
3. Collect the sheet from their teacher at the end of the lesson.	3. Write a comment in the comment box if desired.	3. Sign the sheet to show that it has been received.
4. Fill in their own assessment.		4. Add a comment in the comment box if they wish.
5. Add their own comment in the comment box if they wish.		
6. Take the sheet home for signing.		
7. Return the sheet to their tutor or head of year the next morning and collect a new sheet.		

Please use the following grades:
A – Met all targets all the time. **B** – Met all targets for most of the time **C** – Targets not met.

Lesson	Teacher grade	Self Grade	Comment	Initials
1			Subject:	
2			Subject:	
3			Subject:	
4			Subject:	
5			Subject:	

Parent Signature: _____   Date: _____

Parent comment (optional)

CHAPTER 7

Getting the herd moving roughly west
On performance management and
securing school improvement

Creating the environment where pupils are safe and happy and achieve their full potential depends on a huge range of factors. The locus of control for these starts with the employment of teachers and other staff. Traditionally, the staff has meant the teachers, but more broadly it is the entire staff of the school – the site manager, the catering staff, the person who answers the telephone and the people who clean the school when everyone else is gone. There have been many studies and homilies on the tenets of leadership and the principles of work (ranging from Sartre and Nietzsche to Ozga and Lawn), but in seeking to expound ideas on motivation and the management of performance it is important to understand the very human dimension of the will and how that is affected by the leadership paradigm of the organization.

At one level, the experience of leadership and management is one that is the superiority of emotion over those that must obey. The school leader is one who exercises the principles of command – whether this is of others or of oneself. But the will – the will to power, the will of power – and these are aspects of one another – always encounter circumstances. The reason for this is that we are rarely conscious of the extent to which we are mechanistically determined or programmed by external factors. If we add in the highly unionized aspect of schools – teaching is not absolutely a 'closed shop', but there are few teachers who do not belong to a teaching union or other organization – then we have the basis for a relationship that can tend to the paternalistic and atavistic.

It would be false to claim that this is the case in most schools, we would suggest. The motivation for teaching is often a desire to share the subject – particularly in the case of secondary school teachers. Wanting others to learn, wanting to tell others about what is known are often reasons cited by teachers for their chosen profession. However, while the reason for being a teacher may be located in the relationship with children or the mission to teach – at its basis the relationship with the school leader is contractual and is bound within a legal framework. To use this as the foundation of any performance-management system, which we propose, is perhaps to run the risk of making it appear a mechanistic process that denies teacher motivation, but more of this later.

Fundamentally the paradigm for performance management is a strong leadership and management. It is one that asserts that every encounter with a person for whom one has line responsibility is a performance-management encounter. How this works is explained in the next section.

Structural

The structure is one where the leadership team report directly to the headteacher. The deputy head leads the heads of departments; the assistant head line-manages heads of year. Other aspects of the school are line-managed by other members of the leadership group as set out in Table 3.1 (p. 50–51). There are some difficulties with this structure. The principle is that each aspect of the school is managed, at some level, by a member of the leadership group. All members of the leadership group report to the headteacher. The benefit of this system is that there is clarity to all about where the responsibilities lie – heads of year know that they are line-managed by the assistant head with that responsibility. For the headteacher it means that any discussion about the curriculum is with one person – that one person is charged with implementing the outcomes and there is a consistency of approach that is efficient and coherent. It means that such a high level of lineation, or segregation of task can mean that people feel disempowered from curriculum or pupil or premises (or whatever) issues – but the economy of effort that results frees others to have space to consider wider issues. It seems to us that in the busy and sometimes hectic life of a school the more people that are involved in a process the less chance it has of working and the more complex the task becomes – time is spent on coordinating that could be more usefully spent on the task itself. This view is not quite so functionalist as it perhaps appears on first reading. It is our view that there are better ways for people to work together, the construct of the team can be achieved through deeper shared experiences than necessarily are realized by multiple layers at the lateral level.

Of course, education and schooling do not compartmentalize themselves into neat boxes and there are always grey areas where pupil welfare decisions have curriculum consequences and vice versa. Also, learning is not separated and marked out by bells and lesson changeover. Being at school is a continuous experience – being in a maths lesson and being in a biology lesson are, for 14 year olds, part of what it means to be at school. The lesson construct (30 children, one teacher, four-sided room, whiteboard, books, writing, homework) – the subject difference and the learning experience are what set them apart.

The overall framework therefore for performance management is one that is a dynamic process – all encounters are performance-management encounters – and this extends to memos, brief meetings, casual chats as well as the formal lesson observations, regular review meetings and annual review of performance.

The school leadership team leads this process by example. In this case the headteacher has a weekly meeting with each of the leadership group. Then the members of the leadership group have regular meetings with their team members who in turn have regular meetings with their team. This is a structure that pervades the entire organization and leads to a strongly focused and dynamic leadership style that aligns itself with the aims and values of the organization.

But setting up such a process isn't enough to make it work; it has to have a framework in which it can develop – the meetings themselves will not necessarily happen simply because the headteacher has said that they must. The process needs to be underpinned by a specific and general agenda that results in outcomes that can be monitored.

First the conduct and business of the regular meetings. The conduct of these meetings is designed so that the relationship between the team leader and the team member will develop. When we meet new team members for the first time the agenda is very much one that we, as the team leader will create, and we provide this agenda in advance of the meeting. A meeting with a new head of department might look like this:

1   appraisal of the department
2   appraisal of the issues in the subject – nationally, locally
     and at the school
3   proposed agenda

The important thing about such a meeting is that it is the head of department who does most of the talking – by inviting them to talk about their department the team leader establishes the locus of responsibility for that member of staff. In the resulting discussion the team leader and head of department will identify priorities for the next period of time and as such the discussion will focus on the strategy for these actions. The outcomes are recorded as minutes of the meeting (or action points or whatever) and arrangements for a subsequent meeting are made. The next time the two people meet the starting point is the agreed outcomes from the previous meeting – and so the process continues. Once development plans are set down, of course the agenda will be very much about the implementation of these. The impact of such a system can be considerable because, at one level, having regular meetings is almost enough to make things happen. This is because having a regular meeting creates an imperative to action – if only to avoid the embarrassment of having to say that you haven't done what you said you would do. Most people, we think, will try to avoid this!

Consequently, if the head of department (to continue this example) is going to progress the work they have agreed to do then they will need to engage the members of their team. Indeed this is a matter that may need to be discussed; in order to manage the work of the team the head of department will necessarily have to meet with members and the process is replicated.

This is performance management and its strength is that it is located firmly in the work of individual teachers – it is supportive, can be challenging, but its function is to strongly manage the work and workload.

Links with pay, targets, threshold applications and more

The current system for teacher's pay works in the following way. Generally teachers joining the profession are placed on point 1 of the teacher's pay scale. Teachers will progress on this scale, incrementally, until they reach point 6. (Teachers who join the profession, as mature entrants will have their experience recognized in their salaries (normally one point for every three years' relevant experience)). Teachers should receive an annual statement from the governors (although, in practice, it will be the headteacher who arranges for this) that states their salary and how it is made up. In addition to the basic salary there are responsibility points (there are five that can be awarded), points for recruitment and retention plus teachers working in certain areas (inner London) who receive additional salary.

A teacher does not have to receive incremental increases and indeed can have their salary raised by up to two incremental points. Once a teacher has reached point 6 of the scale they can apply to 'cross the threshold' to access the upper pay spine. There are five additional points available on this spine that are awarded every two years. Thus it could take a teacher 16 years to reach the top of the scale. Salary review for post-threshold teachers is for sustained high performance and there is a lack of clarity on what exactly that means. Broadly, it is up to the head to make recommendations to the governors' remuneration committee, and governors decide whether to award these increases.

Preparing an application to move to the upper pay spine is a lengthy process. The teacher has to demonstrate that they have updated their subject knowledge, that pupils make good progress in their classes and that they are effective professional teachers. Progression on the upper pay spine depends on sustained performance against the same criteria.

The criteria are as follows:

Professional review

1 Knowledge and Understanding
2.1 Teaching and Assessment – planning lessons
2.2 Teaching and Assessment – classroom management
2.3 Teaching and Assessment – monitoring progress
3 Pupil progress
4.1 Wider professional effectiveness – personal development
4.2 Wider professional development – school development
5 Professional characteristics

Given that teachers have to provide evidence under these headings for both threshold applications and post-threshold review, we have taken the decision that performance reviews should be carried out using these headings. Thus each teacher (including those on the leadership group) has an annual performance review that comprises the following elements:

1 Review of the previous year. In this area a judgement is made against the previous year's objectives
2 Lesson observation – at least one lesson observation is required for the annual performance review
3 Review of performance using the above headings
4 Targets for the following year (one of which must relate to pupil progress)

Now the headteacher's targets are set by the governors' committee that undertakes the headteacher's performance review and the objectives for the leadership group should flow from these. In order for the head to achieve their targets, of course the leadership group must achieve theirs. In order for the leadership group to achieve theirs then the targets they set for their team members should reflect these and so on. The following example illustrates how the pupil targets can be disseminated across the school.

Example

The headteacher has a school target of 65 per cent 5 A*-C at GCSE. In order to achieve this, the deputy head, who line-manages heads of departments and is responsible for the curriculum is given this as the pupil progress target also.

Of course this case study is illustrative of the A*-C target only. It does not address the effect that the focus on the A*-C stage may have on the work of the school as a whole. It may mean, for example, that the best teachers are deployed to teach (in the case below) sets 3 and 4, leaving sets 5 and 6 to either the inexperienced or less proficient teachers.

Table 7.1 shows how the target for the whole school is made up from the performance of each department. The table below shows how the target is made up in a particular department. Each department has individual targets that have been created using cognitive ability test data, examination results and key stage 3 results. This gives the mathematics department a target of 71 per cent. This breaks down into the various classes in mathematics that will have targets as follows:

Set	% A*–C	% A*–G
1	100%	100%
2	100%	100%
3	84%	100%
4	53%	100%
5	0%	100%
6	0%	100%
All	71%	100%

Reproduce this across each subject and the following emerges:

1   Each department has a target that contributes to the whole-school target – this department target can be used as the head of department's pupil-progress target.

	Maths	English Language	English Literature	Art	Science	Science	Biology	Chemistry	Physics	All Science	History	Geog	German	French	Bus St	Drama	Music	Social Science	RM	Tex
A	3	4	2	11	2	2	3	2	3		3	0	2	2	0	0	1	1	0	0
A/B	6	3	5	0	0	0	3	3	2		4	6	1	1	0	1	2	0	0	0
B	8	13	14	10	8	8	0	1	2		3	5	0	7	3	6	0	3	1	0
B/C	16	16	16	3	10	10	6	7	6		12	6	4	8	9	1	5	7	2	1
C	63	67	66	20	35	35	15	14	14		24	38	8	34	31	3	0	11	10	8
C/D	3	4	5	5	5	5	0	0	0		0	5	3	2	5	8	5	0	0	8
D	3	10	10	7	11	11	1	1	1		2	7	1	4	2	3	1	0	13	5
D/E	9	5	4	0	18	18	1	0	1		5	1	0	5	6	1	0	1	0	2
E	9	4	4	0	7	7	0	1	0		4	4	0	3	8	0	0	4	1	1
E/F	3	1	1	0	2	2	0	0	0		3	1	0	0	2	0	0	0	0	0
F	4	7	7	1	4	4	0	0	0		0	2	0	0	0	0	0	0	0	0
F/G	5	0	0	0	3	3	0	0	0		0	0	0	0	1	0	0	0	0	0
G	3	1	1	0	1	1	0	0	0		0	0	0	0	0	0	0	0	0	0
A*-C	96	103	103	44	55	55	27	27	27	191	46	55	15	52	43	11	8	22	13	9
%	71%	76%	76%	77%	52%	52%	93%	93%	93%	64%	77%	73%	79%	79%	64%	48%	57%	81%	48%	36%

Table 7.1 *Individual subject targets contribute to the whole school target*

2 Department targets are made up of class targets that can be used to set pupil-progress targets for individual teachers. Those who are on the periphery of D and C can be targeted accordingly. Similarly for set 1 a target of A*/A can be used instead.

3 By putting all of these together for all subjects, we can see which children are at risk of missing the 5A*-C target and focus attention accordingly.

4 The headteacher's target is rooted in the work of the senior team, who in turn root their work in the heads of subject, who in turn root their work in that of their staff.

Targets for those who do not teach GCSE classes are more problematic. However, a similar process for key stage 3 results and AS and A2 results is possible. Of course such a system relies on a data-rich environment and schools find themselves at different levels in this regard. Schools may test pupils with the NFER cognitive ability tests (CATs) and use these to set targets for a cohort and groups in the way outlined above. A similar methodology is possible with YELLIS. ALIS and indeed with no external data save that of key stage 2 and key stage 3 test results – of course, these are statutory and must be passed to a receiving school. Put simply, a target-setting system has to be one that the staff are able to use, can access the outcomes and are able to sign up to the targets that are suggested. A system that has no external reference points is liable to deflation or indeed inflation; we need the moderating effect that external data offers. But schools have developed sophisticated systems using reading tests and other measures that form the basis for any assessment of pupils' potential.

Returning to the performance review itself; the criteria for this review process are those of the threshold standards and if the performance of the individual has been managed over the year then any resulting statement should be an amalgam of the previous meetings. A performance-review session is not the time to say things that are new – it is the time to review, summarize and evaluate performance.

As indicated above the leadership team's objectives flow from the headteacher and so on. In order for this process to be managed then there needs to be a calendar of events thus:

Group	Reviewed by	Completed by
Headteacher	Governors	October
Leadership group	Headteacher	December

Heads of department	Deputy head	February
Heads of year	Assistant heads	February
Department staff	Head of department	March
Administrative and other staff	Assistant heads and other staff	March

The timetable for each school will depend on the precise nature of each person's responsibilities and how many staff are to be appraised by each team leader. The performance review documents (that include the lesson observation, the review of the previous objectives, the performance review and the targets for the following year) are then passed to the headteacher who can check them off and identify any that are missing by the deadline set down. Broadly speaking a system that sets down deadlines for the process has a greater chance of success than one that omits these important features. The annual review is not really enough though to maintain an effective brief of the performance of the team. Our system is one where each teacher is entitled to 30 minutes' development time each half term. Setting up such as system, again, is not enough to ensure that it is enacted – but by asking people when they are holding these meetings (or retrospectively when they have been held) is a simple way to check; it is rare for people to lie and say that meetings have happened when they haven't.

Setting down a performance-management system that gives people deadlines to meet and documents that need to be completed will not in itself yield results. There needs to be some kind of system to monitor this process. One way to do this is for a list of all staff to be made, with the line manager and the date by which the review needs to be completed. A cover sheet for the performance-management review that includes name of the person, the line manager, and date of review will be usefully augmented by tick boxes that show that the pack includes a lesson observation, a review of the previous year's objectives and the objectives for the following year which will enable the clerical check to be made. Thus when the pack – the cover sheet, lesson observation and review of the previous year's objectives and the objectives for the following year – are passed to the headteacher these can be checked off on the list. Using a cover sheet means that this can be undertaken by the headteacher's PA (as confidentiality will not be breached) – and reminders can be sent out as the deadline passes!

Managing the senior team

One of the most problematic areas for a headteacher is where one (or more!) of the leadership group is underperforming. In order to enact the agenda the headteacher relies on the ability of the leadership group to mirror the headteacher's leadership style and manage in the way that is required. The relationship between the headteacher and the leadership team is one of the closest in any school; members of the leadership group typically spend more of their time meeting one another and more regularly than any other group in a school.

There is a need for regular meetings of the leadership group – a meeting of between 90 and 120 minutes each week should be sufficient to discuss the business of the school. It is our view that such a meeting should be chaired by the headteacher and take place during the school day. We know of schools where such meetings take place at the end of the day; to do so is anti-managerial. It says that the leadership of the school is insufficiently important to be timetabled during the day; also, meetings after school are fraught – we are not fresh, and of course they run the risk of going on for ages – there isn't the bell for lunchtime (or whatever) to ensure that the meeting is concluded. The chair of the meeting should be the headteacher, in our view, because in this sense the headteacher is the leader of the team, it is the head's responsibility to set the agenda and ensure that the meeting is conducted properly. The conduct of leadership meetings should be one where everyone has an equal stake – within the team there is the hierarchy of head, deputy, assistant heads and possibly bursars, administrative officers and others, but the leadership of the school should be such that all have the opportunity to say their piece (and indeed should be expected to say their piece) but that once decisions are made then the collective decision is the one that prevails.

This 'cabinet' approach to decisions is not without its pitfalls. There are decisions made that the leadership group do not agree upon, the headteacher has imposed his decision on the school and the leadership group may find it difficult to uphold the decision, but it must be done. There are a number of situations where this can occur and these are presented to the reader as possible problems that are worthy of reflection:

1   Two-minutes silence for the anniversary of 11 September 2001. One year after 9/11 there was a call for a national two-minute silence to commemorate the tragedy in New York. To hold such a commemoration would require the suspension of lessons (albeit for a very short time), the

ringing of a bell and the full range of communications with staff and pupils that this was happening. Some of the leadership group did not agree with this commemoration – they thought that it was an acknowledgment of terrorism. One Jewish member of the leadership group wanted the commemoration for Holocaust Day.

2   Watching the World Cup match. Should lessons be suspended to watch an important football match? Several members of the group said no, but three said that they thought it should be permitted.

3   The suspension of a member of staff. The member of staff had committed, in the headteacher's view, an act of gross misconduct and there was, in his opinion, no alternative but to suspend.

The point of presenting these situations is that they can be divisive even if time and effort has gone into a discussion on how the situation will be managed; if there is no consensus then of course it is the headteacher who decides and as such the leadership group need to play their part and ensure that they support the headteacher.

However, such issues are small when compared to the issues of weak performance and competency.

Weak performance is that where the work of the teacher (or indeed the headteacher and any member of staff) is a concern. Weak performance can become a competency issue if it becomes generalized or protracted, or if the particular area of weak performance is so critical to the organization that it seriously affects its smooth running. Underperformance is different – this is where a member of staff has the ability to work to a higher standard but for some reason is not doing so. Incompetence is poor performance. Each of these needs a different approach and so are taken in turn. In practice many will not make the distinction that we are making, but we do so because the response is different.

Underperformance

For the purposes of this discussion underperformance is where a member of staff works to a standard that is below their capability. An example of underperformance is where a normally reliable member of staff is late for work, is not marking books to the required standard, where a piece of work they do is uncharacteristically poor. However, it can also occur where people have the ability to do the job but choose to underperform for a variety of reasons. The following two cases studies are presented.

NICKY

Nicky is a very good teacher, lesson observations have always been Excellent or Very Good and examination results are consistently good or very good. Nicky prepares thoroughly for work, is never absent from school for health reasons and has been working at the school for over twenty years. However, she takes on a year 11 class and encounters significant professional difficulties – there are significant weaknesses in her classroom control, the test results for this class are poor and there are all the signs of under-performance in this teacher. What should be done?

Such a situation is not uncommon because, in Nicky's case, a change in her domestic circumstances meant that she was unable to focus her attention on her work to the same degree, but also when she was interviewed the loss of her father some months earlier had had a profound effect on her emotional strength and consequent ability to deal with the stresses of a difficult class. This case study illustrates and indeed, reminds us, that teachers are human!

Teachers, as indeed all the employees of the school, have domestic lives and are more than the people who we see going along dutifully and conscientiously to their classrooms. There are times when things 'aren't right at home' and these times have a profound effect on the individual's ability to do their job.

The critical issue for Nicky is that she needs support and there needs to be an examination of what has happened to cause this underperformance. The head of department found out that Nicky was experiencing personal difficulties and when confronted with a difficult class had found it impossible to keep going; her normal levels of confidence were affected by the personal issues. A range of support strategies were employed to enable Nicky to manage this class.

JAMES

James is a teacher of average ability. He is well qualified in his subject and is head of department. The department is a mess. There are no schemes of work in the department. The staff are all pursuing their own agendas, the GCSE results have dropped by twenty percentage points in one year but there are other factors including staff absence and some poor behaviour by students. James meets regularly with the deputy head, his line manager. During these meetings James agrees to produce a key stage 3 overview and the programme for producing the schemes of work is agreed. At the next meeting James produces the overview and praise is given and James agrees to start work of the schemes of work. Over the next few weeks and months barely any progress is made. More time is given and yet no work is done.

These two case studies illustrate the issues that arise in under-performance.

1   The teacher has the ability to do the work but for some reason isn't doing it.
2   Underperformance can be a factor that is localized with a particular group for a teacher or a leadership task. Other aspects of the teacher's work can be excellent.

For James the matters were more complicated. He demonstrated an ability to do the job – and it was one that he recognized the need to do and wanted to do but for some reason wasn't doing it. Detailed discussions were held with James over a long period of time.

James's first professional review illustrates some of the merging difficulties:

PROFESSIONAL REVIEW

Strategic direction and development of the subject

James submitted a development plan for the work of the department last year. However, progress with this has been slow. A key outcome from the development plan is the production of schemes of work and very little progress has been made on these. The importance of these documents cannot be overstated and it is imperative that they are completed.

James has been in post for one year and his strength lies in his willingness to shoulder the burden of difficult classes and students to help his other colleagues. With one of the current year 11 classes, James took on several difficult students in an attempt to support a teacher who was having considerable difficulties with a particular class. The effect of this was to add to his own workload. However, progress in the role of the head of department was evident when James had to deal with a challenging interview with this teacher.

The direction of the subject needs careful review and consideration. Students are permitted to disapply from MFL at key stage 4 and this has created three distinct groups that the MFL department has to serve:

- students for whom ks3 is a stopping point
- students for whom ks4 is a stopping point
- students for whom languages may be a course for further and higher education

The department needs to give careful consideration to this. There is a danger that, simply because students can disapply, they should disapply and this must be addressed through a consideration of the aims of languages teaching. In addition, there are very few students who want to study double languages and this must be reviewed.

Teaching and learning

The schemes of work are the key vehicle for setting and maintaining high standards and raising expectations. By attending to these, by setting out learning objectives and teaching strategies then the valuable discussion that James facilitates in the department meetings is recorded and remembered. A key feature of James's leadership style is that of consultation and discussion. Relationships in the department are very friendly but, given that there are only two full-time members of the team (the others are, in some respects part-time), the means will need to be developed to communicate in other ways.

The outcomes from the lesson observation are documented earlier.

James has joined the Learning to Learn Group and is a valued member. In addition he is a member of the Curriculum Planning Group. As part of the work of this group, the decision was taken to increase the amount of 'double languages' time. The effect of this, together with the increase in the school roll makes flexibility in teaching languages more desirable.

James expressed a desire to become more ICT proficient; I suggested that a target of producing one resource per week using the ICT facilities would be appropriate. This might include a clip-art image (to be produced as an OHP) or a series of flash cards or a word-processed worksheet. James will keep a copy of each of these as evidence of progress in this area.

Leading and managing staff

James spent some time establishing the job description for the second in languages. This was an important step. However, over the next year it will be important to review the key tasks of the post holder in the light of the professional review. In addition, the part-time members of the department have contributions to make and it is important that these are documented as part of the department's handbook in a planned manner, rather than an over-reliance on 'goodwill'.

James has recently commenced a middle management course and it is hoped that this will help him to develop better management skills. A key issue is assessment – as the department moves to a setted situation throughout the school, it will become increasingly important to be confident in asserting the department views and rationale for its actions. There has been little evidence of testing across sets to measure progress over time. This is a key task.

Clearly from this professional review, this was a teacher who was struggling in his professional role. Note that praise was given for progress made and there are indications that the teacher has the ability to undertake the management and leadership responsibilities. An important next step, following this review was to agree targets for the following year.

The targets for the year were agreed as follows:

- to complete the department development plan
- to review the aims of the department – one outcome will be an aims statement in the department's handbook
- to achieve a GCSE A*-C rate of 50 per cent (French) and 90 per cent (German)
- to ensure that the schemes of work, in particular, are completed
- to develop some proficiency in ICT – target: to produce one resource per week using the ICT facilities

James volunteered to join curriculum groups and went on INSET for heads of department – but all the time the basic work of the head of department in leading the curriculum development was not being done. Each time James met the deputy head, his line manager, no progress was being made. Eventually the case was referred formally to the headteacher.

Weak performance

For the purposes of this discussion a weak performance is one where the member of staff does poor work and there are concerns over the person's ability to do the tasks they have to do. This is very different from underperformance, because the person can be working very hard – often long hours – but the outcomes are poor. The following case study is presented:

LEWIS

Lewis is head of year and has the responsibility for managing the coursework calendar for his year group. After discussions with his line manager, an assistant head, it is agreed that dates for coursework need to be collated and regular checks need to be made on progress and parents contacted if progress is poor. On the face of it, things look fine, but on closer inspection there are memos from staff to which there has been no response, communications with parents that are not followed up. Lewis always looks very busy – has a bulging diary and folder – but he cannot cope with the job that he is trying to do. After several interventions by the assistant head, Lewis is failing to do the basic requirements of the job.

Response

On the face of this case study, Lewis is struggling. The assistant head has met the teacher, agreed a course of action, but there are problems with the implementation. The assistant head needs to find a way of becoming aware of the fact that these memos are unanswered. Lewis needs to find a way of managing his workload. However, when a range of strategies have been tried, then one may have to consider whether Lewis can do the job he is employed to do. Such conduct will have a direct impact on the progress that children make and this level of ineptitude cannot be tolerated.

All of these case studies are common in that the teacher is failing to do their job to the required standard. The headteacher will learn of these issues sooner or later. Hopefully, the head will learn of the problems via the leadership group member who manage the staff (or from a line manager reporting to a member of the leadership group) but the imperative for action is implicit. There are a number of stages that need to be followed through:

1   Informal monitoring. At this stage the line manager simply needs to be holding regular meetings and keeping notes of what is happening (or not happening, as the case may be). The notes can be in the form of action points or diary notes from meetings. The outcome from this stage is one of three possibilities: that there is no problem, that a further period of monitoring is required, or that a period of support is required.

2   At this stage the teacher (or indeed the employee) needs to be informed that there is concern. This can be a meeting with a member of the leadership group and the head of department and the teacher. The informal stage continues, but there is an increased emphasis on the written account of the meetings and outcomes. Again, after this period of support the outcome is one of three possibilities: that there is no problem, that a further period of monitoring is required, or that a period of formal monitoring is required.

3   At this stage the headteacher needs to review the evidence. The concerns need to be discussed with the teacher and steps taken. One outcome is a period of formal monitoring. It is recommended that someone other than the head undertake the monitoring and preparation of the evidence. The evidence (that is the copies of memos and responses, etc.) needs to be assembled in date order – labelled with a summary sheet. The benefits of this approach are that the headteacher comes fresh to the case without having had to do the monitoring or having been involved in any of the meetings. The teacher needs to be given a copy of the dossier – this gives them the opportunity to look at the evidence and prepare a response. The outcome of the meeting between the head and the teacher is one of three possibilities: that there is no problem, that a further period of informal monitoring and support is required, or that a period of formal monitoring is required.

4   Formal monitoring. At this stage there needs to be a precise identification of the problem and a programme of support offered to the teacher. This might include support from the LEA (for example, a subject leader may require help in organizing the department, a teacher may need help in making lessons more exciting and so on). There will be regular meetings between the employee and the line manager with review points. At each review point there

will be targets for the employee to meet and all meetings must be recorded. Each record of the meeting should give the employee the opportunity to refute the record – a useful phrase for each record is to write 'if you disagree with the contents of this memo as a record of our meeting, please let me have your response in writing by . . . ' This gives the employee time to look at what has been written and decide whether to respond. This stage is very difficult for all involved and absolute discretion is key. The employee needs to be told in very plain terms what the issues are. For example, if there is a concern over the quality of teaching, the teacher has to be told the lesson judgement – if it is unsatisfactory they have to be told this and also what they need to do to raise the standard of their teaching, what they need to do to improve. Judging the quality of teaching using the Ofsted criteria can be problematic and the involvement of the LEA subject advisers is recommended. The outcome of the formal monitoring is one of three possibilities: that there is no problem, that a further period of formal monitoring and support is required, or that a formal disciplinary hearing with governor representation is required.

5   The governor's hearing. All the information needs to be presented at such a hearing. The teacher has to be given written notice of the hearing and is entitled to bring a union representative or another teacher to the meeting. A teacher is not permitted to bring a solicitor – unless the union representative is a solicitor. The outcome of the hearing is one of three possibilities: that there is no problem, that a further period of monitoring and support is required with some kind of warning, or notice of dismissal is given.

6   The teacher is allowed to appeal and if an appeal is heard then the governors on the committee must be different from those at the previous hearing. This is the case for all governor hearings. It is important that this is considered when arranging such a hearing so that governors are not 'used up' too quickly.

7   These formal procedures will conclude with either the problem being solved (i.e. the teacher works to the required standard) or dismissal.

These procedures are complicated and it is vital that senior staff consult their personnel departments at LEA or professional association level at each stage. The benefits of seeking the advice and updating the personnel department of the LEA is that they have the expertise about what exactly has to happen at each stage. They will go through the evidence with you. If their advice is followed, should the teacher take recourse to a tribunal or other judicial review, then the headteacher knows that they have the support of the LEA, because it is their advice that has been followed.

Incompetence is different from incapability and misconduct. Incompetence is where there is a weakness and the competency procedure is designed to determine the steps that need to be taken by way of training and meeting targets in order to correct deficiencies. Failure to improve or to meet targets established in this way may then be grounds for disciplinary action. Incapability is where the teacher is not able to do the job – usually because of health reasons – this procedure is often used where a teacher has been absent for a long period of time and the prospect of the person being fit for work is low. Misconduct is where an employee does something wrong – gross misconduct (for example, stealing money, sexual relations with a pupil, compromising examination regulations or an action that breaks down the trust between the teacher and the headteacher (or the headteacher and the governing body)) can result in instant dismissal. The procedures for dealing with misconduct are the disciplinary ones and the response to these will depend entirely on the severity of the misconduct. If the misconduct is of a gross nature then the headteacher (or the chair of governors if the person is the headteacher) may choose to suspend the teacher. Suspension is a neutral act and gives all involved the time and space to consider the situation.

For the leaders of the school dealing with such issues is very unpleasant and absolute discretion is key. However, the staff do need some information; if a colleague is to be suspended then this will have an effect on the staff at large and indeed the whole school community. One way to tackle this is to follow the procedure below:

1   Having sought advice from personnel a decision to suspend is taken. The headteacher needs to see the teacher and tell them that this is the case. The reasons for the suspension should be stated and the consequences of this action outlined. This must also be written down in the form of a letter to the teacher. It is likely that such an action will result in a very upset person and if a friend is available to support the teacher then this is good practice.

2   Brief the senior team – the senior team needs to be told what to say if staff and children ask about the whereabouts of the teacher – referring all enquiries to the headteacher is a good ploy.

3   The staff of the school should be informed. Some kind of written statement from the headteacher is recommended. The staff need to be told what to say if children ask about the whereabouts of their teacher – again, telling staff to refer all enquiries to the headteacher is a good ploy.

Hopefully this sort of action is one that is never required but it is important to be prepared for the possibility.

It is likely that during this time you will be in contact with the professional associations or unions. It is important to appreciate that the officers work on behalf of their members and therefore will act accordingly. However, they will often provide a useful buffer between the school and the member of staff (the phrasing is deliberate because by the time that a member of staff has reached the point where dismissal is an outcome, the teacher will often have distanced themselves or have been distanced from the staff and so the dispute will often polarize itself in this manner). Indeed union officers will often broker discussions between managers and teachers to achieve the best outcome for their members.

Where a teacher has engaged the union or professional officers then every courtesy should be offered to the officer to enable them to do the best job they can for the teacher. It must be remembered that the teacher is still in the subordinate position and therefore the union representation and relationship needs to be viewed in this context. The headteacher and governing body still are the dominant side of the power relationship and it is the teacher who is in danger of at best compromising their career and at worst losing their job. Therefore every professional courtesy should be extended to the officer, to enable them to advise the teacher accordingly.

Relationships with the unions are better if there is regular dialogue and a regular meeting should be arranged between the headteacher and the union representatives on the staff. Asking the union representatives for an agenda in advance is good practice as it enables the headteacher to prepare answers. The outcomes of such meetings should be freely reported to the staff – but this is the responsibility of the union representatives, not the head. Unions may make representation to the governing body – in the same way that any other member of staff or group of staff may do. However, the contact with the union represent-atives is not a communication structure. The structures that the headteacher develops should not be dependent on union representation, nor on this being the dominant discourse; there may be situations where there is no one representing members of a particular union and also not all teachers belong to one.

Staff relations can be fraught at times and the employer/employee relationship is at its most strained when things go wrong. However, it is worth noting that most people are relieved when the headteacher takes action to support a weak colleague. Dealing with wrongful acts is very unpleasant; the response of people when in these situations is one of heightened emotion, but to refrain from action is poor leadership.

Performance management has emerged as one of the dominant themes in education systems today. Great emphasis is placed on the performance of the individual teacher. One of the consequences of this has been a greater use of lesson observation, individual meetings, targets and, indeed, the use of competency procedures. While these can have pejorative tones, the impact of a value-laden system based on principle-centred leadership surely is one that invests heavily in the individual teacher. It is supportive of the individual teacher's work; it seeks to recognize problems, acknowledge progress, but fundamentally starts from the belief that the education of children does matter and that teachers can improve the life chances of children through increased levels of performance.

In a way there is no reassurance for teachers; or indeed their managers. It is about having systems that support all those engaged in education. The principles are fair and the rights of children are paramount and their teachers are important, but there is no compromise on the progress of the school. A high-performance culture requires a complex interaction between collective and individual values and principles. The leaders of schools at senior or middle levels have to manage that tension. But the rewards for their heightened awareness of just what it means to be someone working in a high-performing organization are immense in terms of personal and professional growth and realization.

References

Ozga, J. T. and Lawn, M. (1981) *Teachers' Professionalism and Class*. London: Falmer Press.

Nietzsche, F. (1976) *Beyond Good and Evil*, trans. Kaufmann, W. New York: Penguin.

Sartre, J.-P. (1974) in Stevenson, L. *Seven Theories of Human Nature*. Oxford: Oxford University Press.

CHAPTER 8

Hitting the target
On target setting and monitoring

In Chapter 5 we discussed target setting from the perspective of school development planning. This chapter is very much about how monitoring and target setting becomes part of the daily life of a school; how it moves from being pieces of papers with long lists of figures to something that influences the way in the school functions.

First there is the concept of monitoring in itself. We think that monitoring the work of the school is one of the most important tasks that the leadership team in general and the headteacher in particular undertake. How else can the headteacher be sure that the policies that have been agreed are being implemented? How else can the headteacher provide information to the governing body that will allow them to discharge their duties effectively? But there is no doubt that the concept of monitoring for some teachers is a threatening and stressful business and for some leadership team members a difficulty.

Of course there is also, in any monitoring process, the principle of making judgements. The focus is on creating an environment that promotes continuous examination of professional effectiveness (and, of course, wider school effectiveness) so that specific deliberated improvements can be made. Of course making judgements is something that as teachers we sometimes avoid doing. A profession that spends much of its time making judgements about children (in terms of the quality of their work, assessments, behaviour judgements and so on) is curiously reluctant to make judgements on one another. Is this because teachers are incapable of doing so? We do not think so, but there is a mistaken loyalty and perceived approach to professionalism that will often prevent teachers from doing so. We are wary of making comparisons with other professions but, for example, doctors in superordinate positions make judgements about the efficacy of treatments and quality of a doctor's decisions regularly. Why then should we be averse to making judgements about one another's teaching?

There are a number of possible explanations. First there is the isolated and entirely personal nature of being a teacher. Teachers spend their time, for the most part, on their own with a group of students – to do this daily requires huge amounts of self-confidence. Teachers need to have the confidence to direct the work of others, to gain and secure the attention of a class, to keep order, to deliver the programmes of study – these are essential if the teacher is to be successful. This means that when a teacher's work is criticized they feel it keenly; it goes to the core of what they are as a person. At one level this is understandable but at another is somewhat immature. If a lesson goes badly – and we are sure that all readers will have experienced this at least once! – then we do feel deflated and suffer a loss of confidence. The strength to go back into a class and make it work is something that we all have had to do. Therefore, when making judgements we need to consider the effect of what we say and write will have.

But acknowledging the potential difficulties of making judgements and giving feedback is not enough to junk the whole process. We live in an age where judgements are made on the quality of teaching and will be made. How much better if we make these judgements for ourselves. Also, how can we say that we are a learning organization if we do not acknowledge our own learning needs and recognize our capacity to develop? Put like this it becomes a powerful argument and one that we need to consider carefully – because making judgements is not easy but it represents a mature organization that believes it can improve and get better. It also is an organization that believes that there is a methodology to the teaching process that can be broken down into constituent parts and consequently each element analysed and considered.

We do have to consider whether the frameworks we use for making judgements do in fact raise the standard of teaching. Reading the Ofsted criteria there are statements that describe satisfactory teaching and good teaching and indeed very good teaching. If this were the best that a teacher could achieve then the grade descriptors would in themselves represent a barrier to the quality of teaching. That there is no description of excellent teaching gives scope for the quality of teaching to reach higher levels and therefore the system need not inhibit the quality of teaching.

We make no excuses for monitoring and indeed consider it a professional obligation, but there are various tactics that can be employed to make it a more inclusive process.

Quality of teaching

Improving the quality of teaching starts with an understanding of the Ofsted criteria for lesson judgements. We arrange for all of our heads of subject and the leadership team to be trained to observe and judge lessons using the Ofsted criteria. Of course, there are many ways to assess the quality of teaching (through looking at the number of interactions, quality of questioning, using the ideas of assessment for learning and so on), but eventually the school will be subjected to an Ofsted inspection and the overall judgement will be made on the quality of teaching using the framework and so it makes sense to use this from the beginning – Ofsted criteria can be where it begins not where it ends.

In order for teachers to use the Ofsted criteria successfully there is a training need – this is essential for both understanding of the criteria and making judgements about the quality of teaching of others.

The training for lesson observation has three phases. First the observer needs to know the individual categories for lesson judgements. These are listed in the school's *Handbook* and broadly are:

Teaching

Does the teacher have the necessary knowledge and understanding of the subject and the topic to be taught in order to teach the class? It is not sufficient for an observer to assume that simply because the person is the class teacher that this is the case. (We are sure that all readers will have encountered a teacher who has the knowledge but not the understanding!) There is a requirement to assess ability of the teacher to teach basic skills – this is numeracy and literacy (therefore there should not be basic spelling or numerical errors in the teacher's work). The lesson needs to be planned (and therefore as an observer you need to see a lesson plan and be able to follow the plan as the lesson progresses) and there should be objectives. A teaching objective is how the purpose of the lesson is framed – this might be in terms of what the pupils will be able to do, will know and so on. The methodology for the lesson should be appropriate and effective: i.e. a long-winded and protracted explanation of a simple concept to a class that has understood it quickly is not effective. The lesson needs to be managed in the sense that the children in the group have to be organized – if there is group work then there is a sense that the groupings are managed (i.e. who is in each group, what they have to do, how long they are to work as a group, whether group work is appropriate, how they will feed back to the rest of the class, the amount of time allocated to the task and so on). As the lesson has objectives, how are these to be assessed? Finally, how does homework fit into the programme of study for this class?

Learning

In many ways the teaching is the easy bit to judge. The second section is learning. This section looks at how successful the teacher is in delivering learning. Do the children in the class acquire new knowledge and skills? (Of course if they are not learning anything new then this is not satisfactory – this is a useful point to bear in mind when preparing for Ofsted – if a teacher is tempted to repeat a lesson with a class!) There needs to be evidence of effort – this can be intellectual, creative and or physical effort. Of course, the context for that effort needs to be that of a lesson that is about progressing the pupils' knowledge, skills and attitudes. Children need to be interested in what they are doing and concentrate on the tasks they are given for a period. For learning to be satisfactory they have to understand what they are doing and why they are doing it – and know how their learning fits into the overall programme and, hence, what to do to perform at a higher level.

Attainment

This is difficult to judge as a non-specialist and therefore needs to be addressed with some caution. To assess the level of attainment there are a number of considerations: first the scheme of work for the class – does it have National Curriculum references (or indeed GCSE grade levels or A level references, etc.)? It is possible, by looking at the national curriculum for the subject, to work out what level the class are working at – and if this corresponds to the scheme of work and your expected level at which the group should be working then some assessment can be made. However, it is difficult for the non-specialist in subjects including the performing arts. There are other ways (work scrutiny for example) to assess attainment and some caution is advised in this area.

Behaviour

This is a key area for judgement. The class should be keen, eager and respond well to the teacher. There should be high-quality relationships within the class between the teacher and the children and between the children themselves. Evidence of bullying, sexism and racism should be noted. In this category we are looking for evidence that children are aware for their own behaviour and show respect for themselves, one another and their teacher.

Other evidence

The other evidence category is one where the application of core strategies (literacy, numeracy and ICT) is considered. In addition where there are issues of resourcing (and the use of these resources – are they well used, or wasted?) and the use made of the accommodation. A key resource in a classroom is the support staff and the quality of inclusion is a key judgement for a lesson.

The Ofsted framework judges lessons on a seven-point scale. There is a seven-point scale judgement made for each of the categories, teaching, learning, attainment and behaviour. Lesson judgements are as follows:

1 Excellent
2 Very Good
3 Good
4 Satisfactory
5 Unsatisfactory
6 Poor
7 Very poor

All of the staff who routinely observe lessons have been given the basic training that consists of:

1 reading of the Ofsted framework
2 discussion of the criteria for the judgements (i.e. how to apply the seven-point scale to each of the categories, teaching, learning, attainment and behaviour)
3 lesson observation – we arrange this so that the trainer and the trainee both observe the lesson together
4 discussion of the evidence and the judgement reached (this is to ensure that the judgement the trainee reaches is accurate and the evidence valid)
5 observed feedback – the trainer will observe the trainee feeding back to the teacher
6 writing up the lesson observation

We use a standard pro forma; all lesson observations are carried out and recorded on this pro forma. A copy is given to the observed teacher and a further copy is given to the headteacher for the staff file. If there are difficulties, then these are discussed with the deputy head (who has the responsibility for the quality of teaching) or the headteacher.

It is for the school to judge whether it uses the seven-point scale when judging lessons. Some schools may choose to identify lessons as being:

- less than satisfactory
- satisfactory
- better than satisfactory

There are some advantages to this approach. If an unsatisfactory lesson is observed then this clearly is very different to a poor lesson – but this may be completely uncharacteristic of the teacher and to give a poor judgement may be professionally destructive. Without the necessary training and development there may be a tendency towards grade inflation (i.e. a lesson is given an 'Excellent' when really it is just 'Very Good'). These fairly loose categories avoid potential problems.

Judging a lesson to be unsatisfactory (or worse), clearly will have an outcome. The fact that a teacher has taught an unsatisfactory lesson cannot be ignored by the leadership team because at some level action will need to be taken. Embarking on a programme where all lessons are judged using the Ofsted framework implies a willingness to respond if the need arises (and, given the nature of people, this is more likely than not). The criteria for a 'less than satisfactory' lesson judgement is where any one of the following is observed:

- the teacher's knowledge is not good enough
- a significant minority of pupils are not engaged
- lessons are poorly planned and time is wasted
- weaknesses in class control
- pupils do not know what they are doing
- pupils are not making progress

No discussion of the Ofsted framework would be complete without a consideration of what to do if the lesson is less than satisfactory.

First, the observer needs to be sure that it is less than satisfactory. It is recommended that before such a judgement is delivered to the teacher a discussion takes place with a senior member of staff (in our case the deputy head) to confirm on the basis of the observation that the lesson is less than satisfactory. The observer needs to be very clear about the evidence that is being used to form this judgement and indeed to give some thought to how the teacher will respond.

Secondly, feeding back the judgement to the teacher. Our preference for feedback is to deliver the judgement with the necessary evidence. However, others may wish to seek the opinion and views of the observed teacher. The second option gives the observer the opportunity to gauge the response of the teacher (it may be considered easier to tell a teacher that the lesson is very good when they think it is good – but less so the other way around) but it does offer the opportunity to assess the person's perspective on their lesson. However, all of this delays the moment when you have to say that the lesson was unsatisfactory. This is where the need for some discussion before feedback comes to the fore. It is not easy to tell someone that you judge their lesson to be unsatisfactory (or worse) and you need to be absolutely clear in your evidence and be able to say what the teacher needed to do differently at least to make the lesson satisfactory.

Thirdly, giving the teacher a copy of the lesson observation. Having talked through the lesson and its judgement some arrangement needs to be made to see the teacher again. The observation may prompt the involvement of the head of department, LEA subject adviser or senior member of staff (in our case it is the deputy head). Some arrangement needs to be made where the opportunity for the teacher to improve is given and a further lesson observation carried out. (Hopefully, when the second observation is carried out, the lesson will be at least satisfactory and the teacher will continue to improve). The outcomes of these meetings need to be recorded as they may precipitate competency proceedings and evidence of support needs to be in place. Also, it is unfair to tell a teacher their work (at least this aspect of their work – however brief a snapshot) is unsatisfactory and then not provide the teacher with the means to demonstrate their progress.

The purpose of this training and the policy that it suggests is, of course, to be able to monitor the quality of teaching. For the headteacher, who will see all lesson observation reports, evidence will grow of the state of teaching in the school and all of this can be accumulated as preparation for the S4 and Ofsted reports. It is our experience also that the process of training raises people's perceptions of the quality of teaching and gives them a better understanding of how to assess lessons and improve.

Of course, as part of a teacher's performance review there has to be a lesson observation report. In addition, we ask all our heads of department to write an annual report on the work of their department. This includes a section on the quality of teaching (the department report will be discussed later in this chapter). If heads of subject are to comment on the quality of teaching then, of course, they need evidence. They will need to carry out some lesson observations; the consequence for us is that each teacher is being observed at least three times during the school year. For a school with, say, 75 staff this means over two hundred observations. Clearly this is a very small proportion of the number of lessons delivered but it does give a flavour of the quality of teaching. Using the same framework means that some comparisons between departments, year groups, key stages and so on are possible.

Quality assurance

The headteacher needs to be able to comment on the quality of teaching in the school whether speaking to parents, governors, LEA or Ofsted inspectors. Of course, the headteacher has the overall responsibility for the quality of teaching and learning in the school and to this end we have a quality assurance process. This process is designed to provide the leadership team with the opportunity to examine in depth the work of a curriculum area. We have a rolling programme of quality assurance and the areas we consider are:

Quality of teaching
This is evidenced by lesson observations (each teacher is observed twice during the period).

Quality of learning
This is evidenced by scrutiny of a sample of books across the full age and ability range.

Performance management
How the performance management policies are being implemented.

Financial planning
The head of department produces a financial analysis of the department funds.

Schemes of work
We look in detail at the schemes of work and any other curriculum planning documents.

Leadership and management of the subject
We interview the head of subject to gain an understanding of their vision for the subject and their philosophy and practice of subject leadership.

The result is a report written very much in the style of an Ofsted report under the following headings:

QUALITY ASSURANCE OF ....
20 MAY . . . .

An opening statement saying when it took place and who was involved. (If the department is small, then only a selection of the leadership team are involved in the lesson observations, etc. But we all do the work sampling and scrutiny of schemes of work.)

What sort of department is it?
Some facts and figures about the department – how many teachers, their qualifications, issues from Ofsted, etc.

How high are standards?
About the results in public examinations. Proportions of A*-C, etc. over time. If there are benchmarked data (from the PANDA) available we include these here.

How well are pupils taught?
How many lessons were observed and some summary judgements (facts about percentages that were very good or better and so on). In this section we comment on the methodology that is prevalent in the subject and make judgements on the efficiency of this. We comment on the marking and assessment as evidenced in the work scrutiny. By comparing the marking and assessment policies with the work sample we can evaluate the efficacy of these. This section concludes with a statement of the strengths and areas for improvement in the teaching of the subject.

How good are the curricular and other opportunities offered to pupils?
In this section we comment in detail on the quality of curriculum planning – by key stage. We look through the schemes of work and where possible compare the curriculum plans with the lessons observed. Again, this section concludes with a statement of the strengths and areas for improvement in the teaching of the subject.

How well is the department led or managed?
This section reports on the outcomes of the meeting to discuss leadership and management of the subject, looks at staff development in the department, financial planning and other

matters including records of meetings (whole department meetings) and performance management. The leading member of the Leadership Team carries out an interview with the Head of Department to discuss the vision for the department, the subject, conduct of meetings (using the format of the pro forma). (The section on performance management is led by the head as these documents are confidential.)

Again, the section concludes with a statement on strengths and recommendations for further development

This is the section where we would comment on matters such as ICT development, deployment of staff, use of facilities, etc.

What should the department do to improve further?
This section summarizes the whole process and makes recommendations for the future development.

Strengths and areas for improvement – this section needs careful wording, as it needs to be supportive of the department (as the process is intended), but also developmental. All of the comments on development areas need to be phrased in such a way that they are capable of implementation and can be monitored over a period of time and that the HoD can respond to them in the department self-evaluation in January.

Overall
We give an overall judgement.

Making this process happen

This process is a major undertaking for the leadership team and indeed the department staff. Its primary function is to moderate the work of departments and to provide an opportunity for feedback to departments on the work that they are doing. The result is a report that is written by the leadership team and fed back to the department. The report is copied to the governors as part of its brief to monitor the delivery of the curriculum.

We have a calendar for the quality assurance process and we look at one large and one or two small departments each term. Where the department is a large one (for example English, mathematics, science and so on) then the whole leadership team is involved in the lesson observations; where the department is small – for example music, drama – then two or three members of the leadership team will undertake the lesson observations. We all look at the schemes of work and do the work scrutiny and set aside 30 minutes of the leadership team meeting during the week of the quality assurance for this purpose.

All departments know that this is something that will happen to them; we give them four weeks' notice. The deputy head works out the schedule of lesson observations and so on and publishes this to the leadership team and the department. The schedule sets out what the department needs to provide, in terms of documentation and when the lesson observations and other meetings will take place.

One member of the leadership team is responsible for coordinating the process and writing up the report. We have developed a policy on this process and this is set out below:

QUALITY ASSURANCE AT MATTHEW ARNOLD SCHOOL

Rationale
All departments at Matthew Arnold School undergo the QA during a three-year cycle. Therefore, with the current Ofsted programme departments might expect to undergo the QA at most twice but at least once between full inspections.

Aims
The purpose of the quality assurance process is to:

- monitor the work of departments
- validate and authenticate the department self-evaluations
- develop the work of departments through external verification of standards
- provide the governors with detailed insight into the work of departments
- prepare department teams for Ofsted

Implementation
The Leadership Team carries out the Quality Assurance of departments. The Headteacher is responsible to the governors for the quality assurance process but this is in practice delegated as follows:

- the Deputy Head manages the schedule, prepares the programme and ensures that the quality assurance schedule runs to time
- Leadership Team members, variously, lead on the QA of departments. In this respect they lead on the process, receive

documentary evidence, write the draft and final report and liaise with the department

The process has several phases:

Documentary evidence: as part of the process the department is asked to submit the following documents

- schemes of work for key stages 3 and 4
- evidence of planning for the sixth form
- evidence of individual teacher planning (lesson plans for observed lessons)
- finance records
- records of student assessments
- performance management evidence
- department handbook

1   QA – during the week of the QA the Leadership team observes lessons, reviews documentation, interviews the head of department (and occasionally other postholders)
2   production of the report – the report is drafted for consideration of the Leadership Team and is amended as necessary
3   feedback to the department – once the report is finalized it is fed back to the department by the Headteacher and the member of the Leadership Team responsible for writing the report
4   report to the Pupil Achievement Committee – the report forms a report to the PAC

The report
The report has several sections – the process is designed to mirror the Ofsted report: (This is outlined as above – the pro formas we use are included in Appendix A.)

Overall
Some summarizing statement that celebrates the achievements of the department but encourages further action and development.

Protocols

- any issues about the process should be referred to the Headteacher
- issues to do with the schedule should be referred to the Deputy Headteacher

- issues concerning the conduct of the process should be referred to the member of the Leadership Team responsible
- advice on the format of the report should be sought from the Deputy Headteacher
- all lesson observations should be carried out using the Ofsted framework, and judgements fed back to the teacher within 24 hours. Written feedback should be presented at the time of feedback to the teacher. A copy of the lesson observation should be provided for the teacher, the Leadership Team member responsible for the QA and the Headteacher (for the staff file)
- if colleagues are unavailable to do lesson observations then this must be referred immediately to the Deputy Head who will make alternative arrangements so that the schedule is followed
- any lesson judged to be less than satisfactory should be referred immediately to the Headteacher (so that appropriate action can be taken)
- it is important to note that once the report is finalized it represents the Leadership Team's view and the Leadership Team individually must not suggest any level of dissension from the report
- the Deputy Head is responsible for ensuring that the QA is followed up by the Department

Monitoring and evaluation
The Headteacher and the governors monitor this process.

Moving forward on the quality of teaching

We stated in the introduction to this chapter that the Ofsted criteria as a means of assessing and judging the quality are where it starts not where it ends. However, the strength of these as a leadership and management tool should not be underestimated. There will be times when people are disappointed with the judgement made on their teaching – e.g. if a teacher who has not been exposed to this kind of scrutiny and has always considered himself (and perhaps always been considered by others) an excellent teacher – and this is often the case with older teachers who have no disciplinary problems! – but this understanding of the mechanics of teaching is excellent if seen as a step on the path to improving the quality of teaching and also creating the forum for professional debate on the quality of teaching. Although, as we have said, disappointment and other emotions may accompany the judgements but the Ofsted criteria form the basis for dialogue and at least the teacher can understand why, using the criteria, the judgement is what it is. It provides a way of talking about the teaching that is less personal – and indeed, when teachers are experiencing professional difficulties, provides the means of setting targets to improve.

For the school to progress its teaching quality there needs to be a discussion of what makes for excellent, very good and good (and so on) teaching – as a whole and at department levels.

We think that it is necessary to consider this at department level because there are subject-specific issues (for example, comparing PE with English). There are generic features – such as differentiation, target setting, challenge, effort, concentration and so on, but the means to improve for students are different and require the teacher to have different skills. Of course, the dominant feature is the need for the teacher to have clarity about how to improve in their subject – how can you advise students how to improve if you don't know! This is rather a bald statement, but schools embarking on this path may be surprised to find how little clarity there is on how to improve in a particular subject. Little wonder then that how to improve as a teacher can be so difficult for teachers to decide.

There needs to be a discussion at department level: by looking at each of the pointers in the Ofsted criteria and thinking through what is happening at each point in the teaching process and what represents good practice. The outcome from this is a policy at department level where teachers are clear about what satisfactory teaching in their subject means and what they need to do to make it good and then very good. Much of this will be by exemplar – we think that stating that this is how to be an excellent teacher is very difficult. Excellent doesn't mean perfect but it does mean of the highest standard. In our view to put a standards on excellence would be to create a ceiling for the quality of teaching that would be counter to the belief that despite being excellent it could still improve. As school leaders we have to have the belief that everything we do can be done better.

Of course a focus on the quality of teaching neglects the other side of the desk – the quality of learning.

Looking at the quality of learning, there are a number of methods for evaluating the success of the teaching process.

First, the results in public examinations those students achieve. This is, in our view, the most important thing and there is no compromise in our assertion that the achievements of students are of paramount importance. But they are where the job begins not where it ends. While the performance indicators – key stage 3 and 4 results, AS and A2 grades – are essential, there are other ways in which we can assess the quality of learning that will generate issues for a school.

Secondly, pupils work. As detailed above, the quality assurance process, for us as a leadership team, gives us a means to make judgements about the quality of learning. It is important to note that it gives us an indication of the quality of learning as evidenced by pupils' work. Put simply, if there is good quality work in pupils' books that is assessed with developmental feedback, then pupils will know how to improve and there should therefore be evidence of improvement. If all this is in place, then this is a positive indication of good work going on in the classroom. Conversely, books where there are no notes, there is little evidence of sustained effort, homework is missing (and if it has been set yet not done, has there been a follow-up?), scant or absent marking – these are all indicators of poor and ineffective teaching and little learning taking place.

Rarely, of course, is it as polarized as the above examples suggest. More often it is somewhere between the two and within department teams there can be considerable variation. There should be an agreed policy on assessment at the school level that is underpinned by a department policy that takes account of the particulars of each subject (for example, we would expect a lot of work in a pupils' mathematics book (that showed notes, practice, homework with corrections and comments, etc.) but in music there are other ways in which the effort that pupils apply to their work is demonstrated).

Financial monitoring of subjects – linking to planning

Anecdotally a weakness identified in Ofsted inspections is the link between budgets and curriculum planning. Of course we would not recommend action because of Ofsted – but an explicit link between department planning and the budget seems to be a good thing. We described in Chapter 5 the way in which we can link whole-school planning with department plans. Of course, when doing the whole-school improvement plan we allocate sums to support various objectives; it seems sensible that when departments are preparing their plans that these should contain applications for funds to support their objectives also. Add to this a cycle that includes in-depth evaluation of progress against specific objectives, then it is possible to link budget decisions to curriculum planning. This is a powerful way to evaluate the curriculum, its planning and implementation.

Of course, it is unusual for curriculum applications to add up to less than the total amount available (however, our experience tells us that it is not impossible!) and there needs to be some methodology to assess the strength of one application over another. We have a curriculum group and it is our practice to summarize all of the applications for funds and to consider them together and reach a collective decision.

Of course, the allocation of funding against budget headings is not sufficient in itself to ensure good spending. This is where the system of department self-evaluation comes to the fore. Each year department heads are required to write a self-evaluation report and one section is devoted to financial planning. In this section we expect our department leaders to comment on how much they have received from formula funding, how much from applications and any other sources (some are canny in selling items to students). Against this they look at how much has been spent on books, stationery and photocopying, and comment specifically on how curriculum monies have been used and how successful this has been. It is not just about the money – but looking at things from this perspective does give an indication of how successful the funding allocation and initiative has been.

Department monitoring

In a school, of average size – with say 1000 pupils – there will be some 2000 periods scheduled. So ways need to be found to monitor the quality of teaching and the behaviour and the implementation of policies throughout school. We have described the quality assurance process – this is an in-depth process that spends a week looking at the work of one department. With the best will in the world this can only be the occasional snapshot of work done. As an adjunct to the quality-assurance process we have developed a standards' audit. This is where the leadership team visit every teacher over a short period for 15-20 minutes. The brief is that the visit is unannounced (although we tell the staff that we are doing this over a specific timeframe) and that we are looking at the implementation of a range of school polices:

- punctuality to class
- homework – the homework timetable
- seating plans – we require a seating plan for all classes
- learning outcomes – for each lesson there should be learning outcomes
- uniform – our strict code for uniform should be in place
- premises – the effect of the premises on the learning experience

- student planners – these should be out on the desk for every lesson

It is possible for a staff of 60 with a leadership team of five to visit every lesson for 15-20 minutes (for us this is 3 lessons per hour) in a couple of days (we do it in 2.5 days). The impact is considerable because it really concentrates the efforts of everyone and it gives a clear picture of what teaching and learning is like in the school. Of course, the judgements are not comprehensive – in the sense of Ofsted – but they do give a very good insight into how things are progressing.

This is our policy:

LEADERSHIP TEAM – STANDARDS AUDIT

Preamble
The Leadership Team has decided to introduce a regular standards' audit as part of its quality-assurance procedures.

Aims
The purpose of the standards' audit is to assess the implementation of a range of school policies and procedures. These include:

- baseline expectations
- punctuality
- homework policy
- standards for written work
- uniform

Implementation
Over a period of three days commencing . . . each teacher, including members of the Leadership Team, will be visited once by a member of the Leadership Team. The visit will last for approximately 15 minutes. The visit schedule will not be published.

The member of the Leadership Team will complete a short pro forma (copy enclosed).

The outcome will be a report copied to all staff and the Governors' Pupil-Achievement Committee. No teacher will be named in the report, but best practice will be exemplified. The findings of the report will be shared with staff at the Staff Meeting on . . . Individual data sheets will be copied to the appropriate member of staff. A copy will be filed in the individual confidential staff file. Any queries should be raised, in the first instance, with the member of the Leadership Team visiting the class and secondly with the Deputy Head.

Monitoring
The Headteacher will monitor this process.

The report is composed of three sections based on evidence drawn from the lesson report form:

Standards Audit – the report
Section 1
Data summary
Duration of audit
Number of visits
Reference to appendix with full data analysis

Overall summary
Section 2
Commentary on findings

Section 3
Recommendations and concluding remarks.

The lesson report used in the standards' audit can be found in Appendix B of this chapter.

To carry out such an audit demands excellent organization – the schedule needs to be planned so that there is a balance of classes (over the age and ability range) and that the leadership team regard this of sufficient importance to carry it out. Staff do find these things stressful and a worry and so considerable effort needs to be applied to ensure that they at least understand the criteria for the judgements. With our quality assurance all teachers are entitled to full feedback on their teaching; but with the brief timeframe of the standards' audit it is not feasible. Thus judgements need to be about implementation, not qualitative. The report on the lesson can simply be copied to the teacher, with the option of discussion, but with no expectation on either side.

When we do this standards' audit, the impact is considerable, but it does remind us of some important safety features. First there is the need to give people plenty of notice and let them feel that they have been involved in the process. We tell the staff in September that we will be undertaking the standards' audit, and undertake it in October. This announcement is followed by briefing in heads of department meetings and papers circulated to staff. The audit itself required considerable organization to ensure that all staff are visited by the leadership team over a short period – we always intend to do the standards' audit in one day, but find that – with teaching commitments, availability of part-time staff and so on – we need three days in which to complete the audit.

With an Ofsted inspection looming the standards' audit prepared staff to being observed without notice, but in itself underlined the importance of the policies of seating plans, uniform, punctuality, etc. It demonstrated to the staff that the cumulative effect of all the staff was considerable; if a policy was implemented in full, then this had a dramatic impact on the way in which the school functioned.

However, both the standards' audit and the quality-assurance processes require considerable effort by the leadership team and the staff (although in some ways less by the staff) and there needs to be a real commitment towards these processes. It also is not enough to want these things to happen – they do have to be organized and set up. This is quite a job and needs to be done – and isn't the job of a moment.

Having set all of the targets, the various measures we have discussed are a way of establishing them in daily life. But the standards' audit and the QA procedures are about the quality of teaching. Performance management is, of course, a very useful way of developing and sustaining intelligence on the quality of teaching. Combine this with the standards' audit and quality assurance and this adds up to a rich picture of the quality of teaching in the school.

Of course, monitoring something is not enough to bring about improvement; there needs to be clarity about the difference between satisfactory and good teaching, between good and very good, between very good and excellent. In themselves, unless they are related to an individual's performance as a teacher, measured according to the performance indicators these are of limited impact. Target setting is a way of establishing a focus for the improvement and a means of measuring the impact of the improvements being planned and delivered.

Monitoring as an inclusive process

The striking feature of the policies on standards' audits and quality assurance are that they are both somewhat 'top–down' policies. We make no apologies for this because we believe that they fulfil an essential function and provide us with an insight that benefits all of those who are involved in its implementation and subsequent progress. However, the fact of the 'top–down' nature would make the policies weaker if these were not balanced by other monitoring and evaluation strategies.

First, there is department monitoring. This is the monitoring and evaluation that is carried out and is led by the head of department. This has two phases. The first phase is the meeting in September to review the exam results and consider the targets for the following year. We ask our heads of department to write an analysis of the examination results – this isn't a statistical exercise – we provide the data for them. We ask them to respond to five questions:

1 which students did not meet their targets and why – the point of this question is to provide accountability (in that they have to say what happened – and to say what happened, they have to know what happened!) and also a context for the results
2 which students exceeded their targets? – again, and why? This helps to frame a discussion on whether the targets were sufficiently stretching and acts as a rejoinder to question one
3 performance at A level – student by student
4 strategies employed by the department that were particularly successful
5 barriers to progress for the current cohort

The report that heads of department produce focuses completely and precisely on what their role is as subject leaders. It emphasizes the accountability, their responsibility for the results and provides the basis for quality discussion. As school leaders it gives us a full picture of the work that is being done, provides opportunities to 'name and praise' best practice and act strategically where barriers are consistently identified.

The second phase is the department self-evaluation report. Each January every head of department produces a self-evaluation report. This contains a number of sections:

1 the quality of teaching – the head of department summarizes all of the lesson observations to come up with an overall judgement of the quality of teaching in the department. Of course, it is obvious – or becomes obvious to some – that in order to make this judgement there needs to be some lesson observations carried out to talk

about! One outcome is a list of three targets to improve the quality of teaching

2 the quality of learning – the head of department summarizes the progress made in learning with evidence from work scrutiny

3 financial report – how the money that has been allocated to the department has been spent and the impact that it has had (this was mentioned earlier in the chapter)

4 department improvement plan – how this is progressing

5 Year 11 strategy – the impact of the year 11 strategy. Analysis of mock exam results, coursework progress and so on

6 leadership of a subject team – how the head of department assesses their own impact on the department. In this section we ask heads of department to comment on the provision of INSET and its impact

7 any other issues – this gives the head of department the opportunity to raise any matters

This report is followed up with a meeting with the headteacher and deputy head – the meeting is led by the head of department and forms the basis for a discussion on a range of issues.

Performance management

Of course, each department leader is managed, in our model, by the deputy head. Teachers are line-managed by the head of department. Therefore when performance management reviews are submitted to the headteacher these also give a great deal of information about the way in which the department and the individual teachers are progressing. All told these four elements – quality assurance, standards' audit, department self-evaluation and performance management – give a rich picture of the work of the school and provide the leadership team with much quality information on which to make judgements and base reports to the governors.

Target setting

We discussed in Chapter 3 how the targets could be created from the various data sets. The important thing about target setting is that it really isn't about percentages; it is about individual students achieving results at key stages. It really can only work if these targets become someone's job to realize: the deputy head who is responsible for the quality of teaching and learning, the head of department, the individual classroom teacher. It is a missed opportunity if these targets are not communicated to students and their parents. The targets need to be part of everyday practice – teachers need to be thinking: How can I realize these targets? what do I need to do to make this happen? – instead of some fatalistic notion that whatever will be will be.

If you set the targets in September and fail to mention them again, then of course you won't be surprised if nothing happens. There are various ways in which they can be maintained at the fore.

First, setting review points. Having agreed the targets – in our case in September – then it seems appropriate to have review points at least every two months. These review points need to take the form of some data collection (of test results or some other assessment). Comparing the assessments with the target grades will show up any under-achievement. If it is with individual pupils, then using the head of year and tutor system is an effective way to bring about a discussion with students and parents; if it is with a departments or class, then a discussion with the head of department with a member of the leader-ship team seems to be the obvious next step.

Secondly, making sure that everyone is entered for the exams and has done all the coursework. This seems to us an obvious point, but our experience is that not everyone who starts the course ends up taking the exam! One only has to look at the statistics in performance tables provided by schools to see that there is variation – the core subjects are the most obvious.

One school we looked at had 250 children in year 11 – yet there were 249 entered for maths, 230 for science and 219 for English. If this is happening in the core departments then it is surely happening in others! By ensuring that everyone who can possible get a grade is entered (and the decision on this needs to be a judicious one – we insisted that a child be entered for GCSE geography – a boy who wouldn't pass according to the teacher – but achieved a grade D). Similarly checking on the coursework – one year there were 10 children who had failed to present their coursework for ICT – it turned out that their coursework was sitting on the computer but they had not printed it out and written it up. A few conversations with parents and late-night sessions by the teacher and students resolved this one.

What the examples above say to school leaders is not to take things for granted – do not assume that all that can be done is actually being done.

Thirdly – mentoring. There are some students for whom having some intensive monitoring and discussions will be beneficial. It is our view that, unless care is taken, mentoring systems can involve the teachers in loads of work and the child in very little. This seems perverse and entirely the wrong way around. We think that the children who are identified under this criteria should be selected carefully and the aims of any mentoring programme clearly established. Our system is such that students have a meeting with their parents about the reasons for underperformance. Targets are set that are reviewed monthly using a spot subject report (each teacher writes how the student is getting on). The results of this subject report are summarized (by a member of the admin team) and discussed with the parents and students. The imperative is on the students to set targets and make the improvement; there is discussion on the reasons why there is underperformance but these are seen in the context of barriers to achievement that can be removed.

Fourthly, making assessments relate to performance. Put simply, if we have a job to do and know the standard, are told what we need to do to improve and the steps we need to take – then it is relatively straightforward. As adults we think it is completely reasonable that we should know the criteria on which we are to be judged and the means of demonstrating that we have met the criteria (a good example of this is the application process for Threshold Assessment). Why should it be any different for children? We do not think that it should be and therefore we insist that the criteria for assessment be shared with children and that marking should be referenced to the assessment criteria so that students know what they have to do to improve. The reporting system should have checks to ensure that this is happening, but checking the content of tests is another (by asking for tests with mark schemes is one way of looking at the assessments).

Target setting is not something that happens in September (or whenever) and then is only re-visited when it comes to the perform-ance review. To make it happen it needs to be the subject of regular review points that acknowledge its importance in the whole school improvement strategy.

APPENDIX A

Pro forma used for the Quality-assurance process:
- Analysis of Students' work
- Curricular opportunities
- Effectiveness of the department
- Leadership of the department
- Management of the department

Analysis of Students' work

Criteria

Assess students work thoroughly and constructively • Marking is diagnostic • Students assess their own work • Targets are used to inform progress	
Use assessment to inform planning and target setting to meet the needs of individual student and groups • How do teacher's records fit in with programmes of work? • Consistency of practice across the department	
Students understand how well they are doing and what they need to do to improve • What do students think of their work? • Are students clear about the criteria? • Understand the comment made about their work	
Homework – does homework extend learning? • How well is the homework policy implemented? • Is homework tailored to the needs of students?	
Evidence that students consistently produce work of a good standard	

Overall judgement	Evidence
Very good – students' work is assessed thoroughly; they receive well-focused critiques of their work that help them improve	
Good – marking is diagnostic, helps students improve their work and gives teachers a clearer understanding of students' knowledge	
Satisfactory – work is marked regularly and students are aware of the quality of what they have done	
Unsatisfactory – insufficient use is made of assessment in planning students' work	

Assessment of students' work cannot be satisfactory if:

• Targets set for students are too low, too high or too general
• Marking does little to help students improve
• Recording is unsystematic and not related to progress
• Teachers have too little knowledge of students' progress
• Teachers' approaches are inconsistent

Curricular opportunities

Criteria

The curriculum meets statutory requirement	
Provides well for students with special educational needs	
Has well-developed programmes for students aged 14–19	
Is inclusive by ensuring equality of access and opportunity for all students	
Prepares students for the next stage in their education	
Seeks to develop the curriculum	
Takes account of National strategies	

Overall judgement	Evidence
Very good – imaginative curriculum promotes high achievement. The curriculum is evaluated rigorously and well judged carefully managed innovations help to meet changing requirements	
Good – the curriculum enables all students to achieve well and develop in a rounded way. It is reviewed and regularly updated to take account of new development and to improve its relevance.	
Satisfactory – the curriculum is inclusive and responsive to diversity and soundly planned to make learning worthwhile. It meets the broad statutory requirements.	
Unsatisfactory – the curriculum does not meet broad statutory requirements. The curriculum is regularly evaluated systematically	

The curriculum planning cannot be satisfactory if:
- The programme of study does not meet statutory requirements
- The curriculum is disorganized and lacking coherence
- Routes are unclear
- Planning is unimaginative and has little effect on teaching and learning
- Students are regularly given work that does not match their needs

Effectiveness of the department

Criteria

How effective is the department?	
Changes in the department's performance over time What should the department do to improve?	
The department's actions as a result of previous inspections or QA	
Areas in which the department excels – has a highly effective solution to a particular problem or represents exemplary practice to which other departments might aspire	

Overall judgement	Evidence
Very good – students make very good progress and achievement in the subject is very high throughout the school. Teaching and learning are highly effective and the curriculum meets the needs of all students very well	
Good – almost all student progress very well and the achievement of most is high. Students relate well to one another and respect their teachers, are keen to learn and behave well	
Satisfactory – teaching and learning are at least satisfactory across the age and ability range. The department is competently led and managed	
Unsatisfactory – marked weakness. Significant minority do not make progress. Some teaching (up to 10%) is unsatisfactory	

The department cannot be satisfactory if:

• It has problems of behaviour that have not been tackled
• Leadership is slow to identify and act on weaknesses
• Widespread underachievement
• The department is static and shows little capacity to improve

Leadership of the department

Criteria

Leadership shows clear vision, a sense of purpose and high aspirations for the school with a relevant focus on student achievement	
Strategic planning reflects and promotes the school's ambitions and goals	
Leader inspires, motivates and influences staff and students	
Leader creates an effective team	
There is knowledgeable and innovative leadership of the subject	
The leader is committed to running an equitable and inclusive department Leader is a good role model for students and teachers	

Overall judgement	Evidence
Very good – leadership is dedicated to ensuring the highest possible standards and achievement in all of the department's work. It is reflective, self-critical and innovative	
Good – leadership is principled, well-established and dynamic. There is a drive for improvement and a sense of direction. Staff share a common purpose. Relationships are cordial and characterized by mutual respect	
Satisfactory – firm, competent and committed. Clear lines of responsibility.	
Unsatisfactory – has little effect. Lacks confidence or drive	

Leadership cannot be satisfactory if:
- Pays insufficient attention to teaching and learning and standards
- It is complacent, insecure or insular
- So participative that it lacks decisiveness, or is autocratic and insensitive
- It does not face up to the challenges it confronts
- Performance lags behind that of other similar departments

Management of the department

Criteria

Criteria	
Manager undertakes rigorous self-evaluation and uses the findings effectively	
Manager monitors performance effectively, reviews patterns and takes appropriate action	
Performance management of staff is thorough and effective in bringing about improvement	
A commitment to staff development is reflected in effective induction and professional development strategies and where appropriate contribution to ITT	
Recruitment, retention, deployment and workload of teachers is well managed and support staff are well employed to make teachers' work more effective	
Approaches to financial and resource management help the department to achieve its priorities	
Principles of best value are central to the department's management and use of resources	

Overall judgement	Evidence
Very good – HoD is committed to enabling the department to fulfil its vision and strategic objectives. Developing skills of staff is a high priority	
Good – department is organized efficiently and managed reflectively, informed by good management practice elsewhere. Essential functions are carried out well	
Satisfactory – department runs smoothly. Procedures are clear and generally followed. There is an up-to-date plan that outlines priorities for development	
Unsatisfactory – disorganized, quirky or inexperienced with the result that the department works inefficiently	

Management cannot be satisfactory if:
- It is so regimented that it inhibits the work of staff
- Staff are unsure of their responsibilities
- Policies are not applied systematically
- Performance management is not linked to improvements
- Staff development is based on responding to a menu of opportunities rather than being linked to an assessment of need

Standards' audit lesson report

	Grade	Comments (where appropriate)
Date		Time
Teacher		Class
Leadership team member		
Punctuality		
Register		
Seating plan in operation		
Uniform correct		
Student planners on desks		
Equipment on desks		
Premises		
Homework		
Learning outcomes		
Barriers to progress		
Students eager to learn?		

Comments:

Grades for judgements
1 Satisfactory or better
2 Less than satisfactory

CHAPTER 9

What's so special about this school?
On publicity, marketing
and customer care

The notion of marketing the school arouses strong reactions from some. It can be somewhat controversial to start talking of the work of the school as a 'product' that needs marketing to 'customers' or 'clients'. To some this indicates a commercial set of values that do not sit well with the purity of the education process. And of course there is a point here. After all, whichever way you look at it, finding the 'customer' is not a simple matter in the process of education. The economic utilitarian viewpoint is that the customer is the country (or the employers within it) and the product is educated potential workers. It is interesting that the vogue language for performance tables seems to reinforce this particular viewpoint, the emerging orthodoxy of performance is about 'value added', a clear analogy with a manufacturing process that takes in raw materials (children) and then adds value by creating a new product from these raw materials (educated workforce) rather in the manner of a shoe factory taking in leather and turning it into shoes thus adding value to the raw material. Perhaps unsurprisingly this analysis is unpopular with most who work in schools!

More acceptably the customers of schools are the children and their parents and the product is the service provided by the school. This is still problematic for some who dislike the notion of schools as a business – however, we believe given that secondary schools have multi-million pound budgets and are employers of perhaps 100 people (many more in very large schools), then to try to run this organization other than on very businesslike lines is courting disaster.

Do I need to market my school?

It may be that you take what might be considered as the principled view that 'We do what we think is best for our students and it is up to parents and children to decide whether this is what they want' – in other words the customers can either like it or lump it! If you are in the position of being the only school serving a relatively isolated community (and there are many such schools around the country), then given the fact that your customers have no other choice of school your view may well be reinforced. It has to be noted that it is much more difficult to take such a 'principled' view if you are operating in a highly competitive area. Under these circumstances market forces can take an unpleasant toll on the school where the population turn against it, so, pragmatically, school leaders have to be concerned with how they position their school in the market in order that they may attract children and remain buoyant.

But it is our contention that these positions present a false dichotomy. Surely any school leader will want their customers to think well of the school? It must be the case that from a good reputation flows confidence in what the school has to offer and good reputations and confidence largely stem from good communication between school and customers. This is what we see marketing as being all about. It is communication of a strong message about what the school is, what it stands for and how it is serving the interests of the community it serves. Taking the notion above where parents and children have no choice about their school, surely under these circumstances it is even more important to market the school, as at least where parents have a choice they can exercise that choice and take their children to another school if they are unhappy. If they are in the only school available then unhappy parents and their children become reluctant conscripts, with all the difficulties that will flow from that.

So, in summary, whether your school is always the first choice in the area, or the last choice, whether there is lots of competition around you, or none, you should market your school well. Marketing is about telling people about the good job you do, but most importantly it is about ensuring you do a good job in the first place.

Publicity and marketing

At this point it is worth making a distinction between publicity and marketing. We see marketing as the process of providing a very good service and ensuring all steps are taken to demonstrate this is what we do. Marketing is about being responsive to customers and also proactive in considering their needs. It is about showing the best face of the school to visitors, it is about ensuring congruence between the different elements of the 'front of the house'. For example, ensuring that the aims and values are evident in the publications from the school and in the words and actions of those who work within it. On the other hand, publicity is much more simple. Publicity is simply ensuring people know who you are and how to get in touch. Publicity is about getting people to think about your school, in terms of recruiting pupils for example, publicity is about getting people to visit the school, marketing is about ensuring that they want to 'buy' the product they see when they get there. Publicity on its own is worth nothing. There is no point in having a really successful publicity campaign that encourages hundreds of families to come to your open evening (a marketing event), if when they get there they don't like what they see. Ensuring that they do like what they see is where marketing comes in.

How to publicize your school
The extent to which publicity for the school is necessary depends to a large extent on the environment in which you are operating. If there are few choices of school in the area, then publicity is less important because parents will naturally think of your school when it comes to making their selection. However, for most of us we have at least to give consideration to the public profile of the school in the community at large. There are a variety of different ways of publicizing the school, some of which have a real cross-over into marketing, some of which don't.

For most schools the annual open evening is the key marketing event of the year. Publicity for this event is of key importance as parents need to know that it is happening. Not only do they need to know that it is happening, but they need to know why they should attend: what makes this school special. If a family lives a way outside the catchment area then why should they contemplate the journey and the expense for their child?

Of course, within your traditional feeder schools it is a straightforward matter to publicize the event. It is accepted practice to write to the parents of year 6 pupils with an invitation to the school for the open evening. We go a step further by distributing our prospectus along with this information. The headteacher delivers the prospectuses to the primary schools to emphasize the importance of the distribution of the prospectuses. This is one of the important times in which the head's position can be used to provide emphasis to elements of the publicity and marketing campaign. The other steps we take are:

- place poster advertisements in the feeder schools to capture the interest of parents of other year groups
- place poster advertisements in newsagents and on parish noticeboards in areas bordering the catchment area
- we have placed an advertisement in the local newspaper for a number of years. We have traditionally gone for a small text-heavy advertisement in the interests of economy; more recently (as it seemed that the advertisement had no impact whatsoever) we decided to go for a half-page colour advertisement. This is expensive but we believe created an impact encouraging many more parents from outside our catchment area to come to the open evening
- we have an annual community lecture series and the leaflets for this are distributed through the local free press in the run-up to the open evening, thus raising our profile through another means

The main point about all of this is to have an understanding of the desired outcome of the publicity campaign and ensure that the areas of the intended market are covered. In our case we can easily cover those parents who will naturally choose our school, but there are not enough children in these schools to fill a year group. It is important therefore that we are able to attract pupils from further afield – hence the importance of newspaper and poster advertisements. Of course, and to reiterate the point from a previous section, however successful the publicity campaign is in getting parents to the school event, this will founder if the event itself and, indeed more broadly, if the school does not match the publicity.

Working with the media

An important and usually free outlet to publicize your school is the local media – the local paper, radio and TV. There are three elements to coverage in the media, firstly there is the proactive kind, when you produce a press release about something exciting you are doing. Secondly there are the occasions when the press desire a comment from a headteacher about some current story – so, for example, if there is a concern about school budgets the press will usually ring around a number of schools for comment. Thirdly, there are the occasions where your school is in the press for a reason you wouldn't particularly choose, an example of this in 2003 was the war protests in which many school students took part. Here the heads of schools where students took time out to demonstrate would have been contacted by the press for their comment.

Proactive coverage
This is relatively straightforward but time-consuming. How much energy you devote to such coverage will depend upon how important you think it is to get the school in the local papers. It is probably a good idea to appoint a press officer for the school. This may be a relatively junior member of staff who will have responsibility for producing the newsletter, preferably with a team of students, but they can also have responsibility for contacting the local media or producing press releases for events that they think may be of interest. Press releases can be produced to a fairly uniform formula. Around 300–500 words, no more than this; it should be structured into 3 or 4 paragraphs providing a very good key in to what the story is and why it is interesting in the first paragraph. There should be quotes from the headteacher and perhaps some others involved (these can be made up without too much difficulty), and there should be facts and figures at the end of the piece. It is a good idea to make contact with a specific individual in the particular media outlet, telephone them to say you have a story, fax or e-mail the press release and then telephone to confirm it has been received and follow it up. For those who wish to take this sort of thing to the next stage then it is possible to engage a public relations company to ensure coverage, especially if you have a need for national coverage or more specialist coverage (for example, if you are trying to raise sponsorship for a specialist school application). Professional help of this sort will be expensive. You will be able to judge whether or not it is worth it.

Requests for general comment
You are under no obligation to provide comment and so you need to consider whether or not it is something that you wish to have a public opinion upon. If, for example, your school has mobile-phone masts (a popular income earner some years ago, but many heads are now suffering from the change in public perception of these installations), then you may not wish to make a contribution to a general story about mobile-phone health risks. On the other hand if it is a matter of commenting upon some public policy, then you may consider it a harmless matter and therefore comment away!

Reactive coverage

If your school is involved with a bad news story the temptation is not to comment. This temptation should be avoided. 'The headteacher was unavailable for comment', or 'We asked the school for a comment but they declined' do not play well in the press at all. Furthermore, it gives the press a free run at the story if you do not comment. A typical example might be that a parent feels your actions were unfair towards their child and, as any loving parent would do, they immediately go to the press about it. When you are contacted you should be prepared to comment, but be circumspect. Decide what your line on the story is and give this in response to questioning. Of course accepting interviews on the radio and television is much more problematic. Be aware of the propensity for editing and taking your words out of context – far more damaging in these media than in the press – be clear about your line, what point you are intending to make, and make these points irrespective of the question.

The prospectus

It is a legal document but more than this it is probably the key document for both publicity and marketing and is consequently worth some considerable thought. The contents of the school prospectus are defined by law. There are a whole range of items that you must include – for a full list you should consult *Croner's Guide* or the relevant DfES circular. Of course, that you must include certain things does not mean that there are things you may not include. A good example of this would be the examination results, while these have to be presented in a particular form there is nothing to prevent you putting in statements that put your own gloss on the results!

Creating your prospectus is an important job as you will wish to make the most of it. A good place to start would be to gather up a number of examples from other schools. There are many ways of sourcing examples – sending off for details for senior staff posts often yields a good crop – and of course there are the offerings from the other local schools. Having a good look at the range of offerings available will give you an idea of the sort of things you want to do, and equally importantly the sort of things you'd like to avoid.

Some things to consider

The cheap and cheerful approach is the entirely home-grown and home-produced prospectus. This will typically be designed by someone on the staff who can 'do' desktop publishing. It will generally be mono-chrome and photocopied. It will also generally be much too long, giving vast amounts of unneeded information. It will be very difficult to keep up-to-date because of its length and consequently will usually give the impression of having evolved, slowly and inefficiently over a number of years. Where there are photographs they will be of poor quality because photographs don't photocopy so well. Generally this sort of prospectus gives the impression that the school does not care much about the image it presents and can be quite off-putting to parents – at best a prospectus such as this does no harm, it certainly does nothing to encourage people to put their faith in the school.

The next step up from the completely home-produced example is the professionally printed but home-designed product. Frequently, as is the way with schools, it is assumed that anyone can design a publication such as this and that, after all, we do have an English department and an art department, these people have heaps of expertise in this sort of thing. This approach can work reasonably well. Having the prospectus professionally printed means that basically it will look good. Given the cost of commercial printing it might well be shorter in length and better as a consequence. The difficulty is that teachers generally do not have the experience or time to make a good job of designing an important document such as this.

The third approach, and the one that we would recommend is to use a professional graphic designer to create the prospectus. The designer will help you decide on the brief for the work and will provide you with design ideas based upon your brief. It is important to understand that the more specific you can be with the brief the better; it is a good idea to know the kind of look you are after and the kinds of finishes and effects you would like. Although a designer will come up with something without a tight specification, it is unlikely that you will like it very much. As the prospectus is designed to last longer than one year there will be a need for supplements, because the up-to-date examination results need to be included each year. As you will have this supplement anyway and as the prospectus is going to be quite expensive, you should decide very carefully what goes in the glossy part and how much you can reasonably leave to go into this supplement. A point to note here is that your glossy prospectus will need a pocket to put these supplements in, and also that this pocket is going to need to be big enough to take standard sizes of paper, meaning that the prospectus itself will need to be a little larger than a standard-size document, but don't make it so large that it won't fit into a standard-size envelope.

In terms of content, our approach is to include in the glossy part everything that relates to the values that we want to get across to our potential customers, while all the mundane stuff (uniform guidance, transport arrangements, etc.) and all the stuff that will change each year (exam results as already noted, holiday dates and so on) are put in the supplements, and further to this, all the policies that are required (special educational needs, substance abuse, act of collective worship, etc.) are listed as policies that can be requested from the school thus removing the need for a considerable amount of the bulk of some prospectuses we have seen.

Having decided upon the approach you desire for the production, further thought must be put into considering the content of the prospectus. This content is the text, but also the photographs. The text is very important, altogether you should be aiming for no more than about 2000 words of text. This should describe and exemplify the aims and values of the school. Certainly it should include a straightforward statement of aims right at the front of the prospectus, there should be a foreword from the head and preferably a photograph of him or her as this will help your potential customers identify with someone when they visit the school and meet the head. The rest of the text needs to cover such matters as the curriculum, the approach to school discipline, the different teaching methods children will encounter and anything particular you want to describe – for example the sixth form or anything specific related to the school's specialist status if it is a specialist school.

Photographs are very important. It is particularly effective to devote whole pages to photomontage with no text at all. Remember it is quite likely that some recipients of the prospectus will never read it, relying instead upon what they glean from flicking through. Even where people do read the prospectus it is the visual impression that will last rather than the text. Therefore it is important that the photographs tell the story you want told. It is tempting to fill the whole thing with exciting activities, year 9 mountaineering, the school production, the orchestra, the sixth-form visit to Prague and so forth. Undoubtedly these images will be engaging and interesting, but what impression does a predominance of this sort of image make? Perhaps the intended one, or perhaps it gives the impression that all the school is interested in is having a jolly time? There is a place for these images in balance, but the pictures should tell the story of the school. Are there any facilities you are particularly proud of? What is it that children spend their time doing? There should be photographs showing the range of curriculum activity, normal classroom work, science, technology, PE, drama as well as anything showing unique aspects of school life. Very attractive children should be used with care – one prospectus we saw had a full-page photograph of a fabulously glamorous girl from year 10 or 11. She was certainly very attractive, but this was perhaps the wrong message to send from the school, there was something a bit tacky about it in fact!

Perhaps all this business sounds very expensive – professional design, professional photography, full colour brochure and so on. It will certainly set you back several thousand pounds for two years' supply, but set this against the cost of advertising for a teacher or a member of the support staff. We have been paying over £1000 in 2003 for an advert in the local press. Perhaps, set against this, a prospectus that the school can be proud of and which presents the school as a professional and thorough organization to the outside world will reap its rewards.

The open evening

It is perhaps surprising how important this event is. One might suppose, given all the information that there is about schools these days, with Ofsted inspection reports, league tables and of course the all-important playground grapevine at the primary schools, that the open evening might diminish in significance, being dismissed as a marketing puff by potential customers (parents and their children). There is some truth in all of these points, but somehow they seem to add up to a situation where the open evening is even more important.

Before going any further, we need to consider the purpose of the open evening. Many of us will recall having open days when we were at school. The main purpose of this was to open up the school to the parents of children at the school to show what is going on. This is, of course, a worthy activity and one which many will want to engage in, but these days, the open evening is principally a marketing activity. It is the time when the school puts on its best bib and tucker and shows itself off to the parents who are choosing a school. It is really important not to get these two potential functions confused. It is our view that it is not possible to reconcile the open evening for existing parents of the school with that for prospective parents. Trying to hit both of these target groups will inevitably mean that you miss both. Open evening should be squarely aimed at the potential new intake and everything should be done to ensure it is as effective as possible in meeting these ends.

Preparation

Preparation is really important. Typically open evening is held in the second quarter of the autumn term. This means that along with getting the school year underway the preparations for open evening must also take place. It is well worth flagging this up to heads of department at the end of the summer term – they will need to be gathering materials for display and considering how best they are going to show off their departments. It is a good idea for the leadership team line manager of the heads of department to schedule a discussion on this point during July with each head of department individually. If you have a technician who organizes display work (which under workforce reform you should), then heads of department need to be aware that they must be sufficiently organized to allow the technician to schedule all the work that needs doing so that it can all be done.

The site must be spick and span too – use the summer holidays for intense maintenance of any areas that need to be brought up to scratch. An expensive, but in our view essential measure, is to have all the windows cleaned inside and out – this really lifts the appearance of the building, especially as it is so rare to see public buildings with clean windows. Keep a particular eye out for graffiti, some of the classroom furniture may have some on it and, if you can't afford replacements, then the tables should be covered for the evening with display board backing. Junk is something that teachers become blind to in their classrooms (indeed this is something that afflicts many of us in our homes too!). Ask teachers to clear out any junk and arrange for it to be collected by the caretakers. Then organize the leadership team to carry out a site inspection two weeks before the open evening, divide up the building between the team and have them list any site issues or junk that they see. This can be fed back through whoever is coordinating the open evening for resolution, then do the same thing again a few days before open evening to ensure that all matters raised have been dealt with.

Of course, the summer holidays is often a time when building projects or refurbishments take place, it is also often the time when ICT systems are upgraded. These are real bear traps for the open evening. You must be on maximum alert to harass contractors to ensure everything is done to complete the work by open evening. There was one occasion when we had an ICT contractor in until 11.30 pm the day before open evening ensuring that the system was working for the next day – because of course, a whole row of blank monitors looks very silly come the event itself.

On the evening
How are parents going to find their way around on the evening? There are a number of different approaches: some schools give the parents a programme and a map and leave them to find their own way around,

sometimes members of staff will take parents for a tour, sometimes sixth-form students are hand-picked to guide groups – our preferred solution is to use students from years 10, 11 and the sixth form, we have as many as possible (around 250 is usually enough) and they take a family each for a full tour. This gives an excellent impression of the school, frequently the warmest praise received for the evening is for the guides. Many departments will try to collar the older students for their displays and demonstrations. It is our view that the students best suited to this aspect of the evening are the younger ones in years 7, 8 and 9; these are students who are closer to the age of the children who are visiting and will be showing things more closely associated with what those children will be doing when they arrive in the school in year 7. Of course, all the students involved must be fully briefed on what is expected of them – school uniform must be immaculate, if they are in the sixth form and don't wear school uniform then something appropriately smart must be insisted upon. We make them feel special by having name badges made with their names on (not just 'Guide') and by giving them a flower to wear as a buttonhole (this is their 'guide' badge). Each guide should have a tour route, it is a good idea to have several different routes (printed on different coloured paper) to avoid bottlenecks.

Thought should be given to how parents will be greeted, and where they are likely to arrive on site. All possible arrival points should be covered by members of staff (preferably leadership team) who can direct parents to the main greeting area. Here it is nice if the head, deputy (or deputies) and any other spare leadership team members can greet parents, give them a programme and prospectus (if they haven't already received one) and be allocated a tour guide from the waiting reservoir of guides (who will need to have someone with them to organize them and to keep them from becoming overexcited).

The formal presentation

If you are the headteacher of the school, it may offend your sense of teamwork to acknowledge just how important the head's address to parents is as the centrepiece of the evening. Whether you like it or not, this is essential, and it is essential to get it right. Of course the way you go about this will depend very much on the aims and values of the school. If you want to demonstrate that this is a very relaxed, laid-back school, then a relatively casual 'chat' type approach would be suitable without lots of formality. At the other end of things if you want to give the impression of Tradition (with a capital T) then you may wish to present yourself in academic dress and lecture the audience on how lucky they will be to get a place in this school (an approach favoured by some grammar schools we know of!). Our approach is to have four speakers, the head, the deputy head, a sixth-form student and one from year 8. We have a formal approach to the evening, with the stage party seated behind a table with flowers on either wing of the stage and the speaker talking from a lectern. We have found amplification to be useful as in a full hall the number of people there can absorb a lot of sound, making the younger speakers especially difficult to hear. Each speaker has a different function. The head's speech is about the aims and values of the school, and how the school demonstrates these aims and values. This is also an opportunity to make any comments about future plans for the buildings, or indeed for the school. The deputy head's speech focuses, for example, upon how we go about ensuring each child achieves their potential – in this example they will speak of the assessment procedures. The year 8 student will talk about settling in to their new school and how much fun it is, but also how hard they have to work. The sixth-form student will be able to relate the bigger perspective of someone who is nearing the end of their time at the school (and of course who has experienced a large amount of academic success in the process). Preparation for this event is all, rehearsals are essential, not only rehearsals for the students who are taking part, but also for the head and deputy. Now this is something that anyone who has not done this before will find very difficult, people will often say they are 'better off the cuff'. Whatever the protestations, rehearsal is an absolutely essential part of the process, the stage speeches will not work without it! The whole thing should last no more than 30 minutes, with the head's speech taking no more than half of this time.

After the formal presentation then the leadership team should be available to answer questions; the head at this point should beware of being monopolized by one parent – if it looks like this is happening, then the leadership team should be briefed to interrupt and take over.

Afterwards
At the end of the evening the leadership team and preferably the head should go around the school making sure that parents are on their way out of the building (there is no need to let the event over-run), it is important here that the opportunity is taken to thank the staff for all their work and make sure they know that you think the evening a great success (if this is what you think). When it is success-ful the school staff will be on a high and will very much welcome your appreciation.

Parent tours

At the outset of this section we described how the open evening is a setpiece event and that everyone knows that this is a key marketing event. Of course parents will want to know that what you say about the school is evident on a day-to-day basis. The only way that they can satisfy themselves of this is by visiting in a normal session. You may choose to arrange a number of open mornings when parents can book in for a tour. This is fine, but risks the same accusation of being a setpiece as the open evening itself. The truth is that it is very difficult to arrange something as a setpiece when the school is in session, so you may well end up with the worst of both worlds, people believing it to be set-up, so if anything does go wrong (member of staff having a 'paddy' with a class for example), then it looks even worse.

Better in our view to go for an open arrangement where parents can arrange a tour any morning to suit them. We organize ours before morning break (for obvious reasons), parents are greeted by the head preferably, or another available member of the leadership team and then taken for a tour with a sixth-form student (if you have a sixth form, otherwise arrange a rota of other students who may be taken out of a lesson for the purpose). This is recommended because your students are your greatest ambassadors and will undoubtedly impress any visitors. At the end of the tour the parents then have the opportunity to meet with the head (or deputy if the head is unavailable), at which time they can ask any questions they may have.

We believe this to be a very important part of our marketing procedures because it sends out a numbers of powerful signals:

1   we are confident in our school, you can come any time and be shown around anywhere, there are no no-go areas
2   what you see is what you get – you've heard about the school at open evening and here you see it as it was described
3   we are student-centred, you can have a student tour guide and ask them whatever you want
4   the head makes time for parents and is happy to take any questions on any subject

And of course the parents who make the effort to come for tours are those, in the main, it is worth putting the effort into attracting!

Over a period of four years the number of parent tours that we have conducted rose from 18, to 25, to 38, to 65. The very large majority of these tours are by parents outside the catchment area who are making a decision about travelling their child a good distance to the school. This becomes very time-intensive, but it is well worthwhile as it indicates to parents the importance they hold for the school.

Customer care

It is said, perhaps apocryphally, that according to research by British Airways every satisfied customer tells, on average, seven people of their good experience whereas every dissatisfied customer tells 19 others. Whether strictly true or not it is beyond doubt that our everyday experience is that bad news travels faster than good. What is also beyond doubt is that schools are highly susceptible to gossip in the community. How often do we hear that this or that school is a good one, or a bad one. On what evidence are these reputations built or lost? In marketing terms the most powerful of all publicity is that of word-of-mouth. As school leaders we need to know that the reputations of our schools are as important as they are fragile. And it is upon the extent to which we look after our customers that our reputations will be built.

So far we have used the business notions of 'market', 'customer' and so forth in a relatively unabashed way. It is worth revisiting this for a moment as it is only by understanding how parents and children are our customers that we can genuinely work on our customer care. If we are not to think of these stakeholders as our customers then where does this leave us? I suspect that rather in the manner of the traditional image of doctors discussing the patient in whispers at the end of the hospital bed, those who reject the notion of customer prefer the notion of the professional who knows best. To caricature it for a moment: 'We are the school and we know about education, we know about what is best for children and parents had better keep their noses out'. Of course, a more recent perversion of this is the rejection of parents who take an interest in their child's education as in some way middle-class busybodies – a label when applied by teachers to others that strikes us as a most astonishing example of hypocrisy, given that most teachers are middle-class (by definition almost) and most have a very healthy interest in their children's education.

To us, viewing parents and their children as the customers of the school places them where they should be, at the centre of the process. We are proud to consider that we provide a service to the community and where a service is provided it is incumbent upon us as leaders to ensure the service is of the highest possible standard and that we are able to communicate with our customers about our service and be responsive to their needs. Now there are some things that being responsive means and some things it doesn't mean. Responsiveness is simple things like ensuring the phone is answered promptly by the receptionist, ensuring letters and e-mails are answered, ensuring that changes that affect the lives of pupils (timetable changes and so forth) are communicated well in advance and where there are staffing changes that these are explained to parents, that concerns are taken seriously and in particular that any allegations regarding bullying are treated seriously and quickly (this will have fuller treatment later). Being responsive does not mean rolling over in the face of any criticism, it does not mean letting the customer always have their way (in this sense the customer is not always right), it does not mean sacrificing principles in the face of sometimes quite extreme hostility from parents. A very good example of the last point is school uniform. Most secondary schools have a school uniform, there are a number of reasons for this, but in the context of this chapter it certainly does provide a good impression of the school. But only if it is worn correctly. On occasion parents can be quite hostile towards the school in its insistence that their children wear correct school uniform. Responsiveness to customers in this case does not mean allowing children to get away with it – this is not being responsive, it is being weak. Responsiveness here means taking the time and trouble to work with the parent to help them understand why it is important and to provide solutions to the difficulties they may face in, for example, providing the uniform. The key is to listen and respond, to communicate well, to acknowledge clearly if you have got it wrong and issue an apology if appropriate, but to hold the line, ensuring the reasons for your apparent intransigence are fully explained.

A brief note about bullying

The most damaging thing that can happen to the reputation of a school in our view is that it acquires a reputation for bullying. Anyone who is in the position of taking over a school that has been in some difficulties will almost certainly have come across parents who are reluctant to choose the school because they have heard there is a lot of bullying going on there. This strikes at the heart of what the school is about, i.e. first and foremost somewhere that provides a safe and happy environment for learning.

It is very much in the common experience of adults that they understand that children can be unpleasant to one another – indeed they have all been children themselves and will undoubtedly have experienced this to a greater or lesser extent themselves. The issue here is not to try and convince people that there is no bullying in the school – this lacks credibility (we would not for example recommend the approach of one school we know where the head, when questioned about this turned to his deputy and said, affecting a slightly baffled air, 'Do we have bullying here?') No, the point here is not whether or not there is bullying in the school but what the school does about it. The responsive approach when there is a complaint about bullying is to deal with it as the highest priority and contact the parent as soon as possible to say what has been done and that the matter is resolved. In this way the potential bad news story of a bullying issue can be turned to the school's advantage because the story becomes not that the child was bullied, but that the school dealt with it very effectively and rapidly. It is from this sort of action that a school's reputation is enhanced.

As an aside, bullying has turned into an intractable problem in the national consciousness; it seems that the population at large believes there is nothing that can be done about it. We reject this notion completely. Bullies make a choice to behave in the way they do, the weight of the school discipline system needs to be applied to them to ensure they stop making that choice. We reject completely the notion of 'places of safety', bullying councils, no blame approaches. Where there is bullying going on then it can and must stop immediately. In the end the most powerful message to give to prospective parents is that, although you know that children can be unpleasant to one another, whenever you know about it, it stops. You must be able to reassure parents that telling won't make it worse, secure in the knowledge that your systems and procedures mean that you can and do stop bullying should it arise.

Administration systems

Perhaps more prosaically the backbone of customer care must be the administration systems. Whatever issues are raised with the school they are likely to begin and end with members of your admin team. First contact is likely to be by telephone or by post, both of which are handled by administrators and the matter is likely to be concluded with a letter home, also produced by administrators. The record of the event will be filed, by administrators. Therefore, however effectively the matter is dealt with by others, the whole thing can founder as a result of weak admin systems.

Now there are a variety of quality standards that the school can implement – we promise to respond to matters raised within 24 hours and resolve the matter within the week, this may suit you or it may not. However, it is important that the whole organization understands the commitment. Members of staff who are somewhat further from the front line with parents can, on occasion, be a little less than focused on customer-care issues than those who are likely to carry the can for ineffective action, specifically the leadership team and within this group, the head! How often are you told that phone calls have been made but not answered for example? These are priority matters for customer care, parents will become frustrated and angry very rapidly if they do not feel they are being taken seriously, and not responding to phone calls or letters rapidly creates this impression. The following are some things to think about:

- ensure that you have coverage of reception for reasonable hours – perhaps 8 am to 4.30 pm
- ensure that reception is always staffed throughout the day
- if there is an answering machine or voicemail then it should have a current message on it. If for example, unusually, the answering machine is switched on during the day it should not have a message saying that reception is staffed between 8 and 4.30, when clearly it is not
- use a telephone-message logging system, this can be something sophisticated on a network workstation, or it can be just a duplicate book at every telephone where people can ring in to the school. This system should be used rigorously so enabling claimed phone calls to be tracked (it is not unheard-of for parents to claim to have phoned when they haven't, it is nice to know if this is the case)
- incoming post should be date-stamped so that there is a record of when it was received
- if the head receives a letter that is passed on for action, make sure that the letter is acknowledged as soon as possible, preferably upon receipt, saying who is dealing with the matter. Ask for a copy of the response before it is sent out
- surprisingly, not all colleagues can be relied upon to write letters that are particularly literate, or indeed that express views congruent with the aims and values of the school. Have a system for checking letters either by the head, or by other leadership team members before they go out
- ensure that all correspondence with a family is recorded in the pupil's file, if heads of year or the learning support department want to keep copies then they can (having been reminded of security and data protection) but the originals should all go in the central file

- ensure that absent parents get a copy of all correspondence, this is their right and entitlement unless there is a court order preventing this
- finally, ensure that every opportunity is taken to discuss the importance of presenting a professional 'front of house' with all concerned, but in particular, heads of year and the admin team

Quality of service

Finally, and briefly, marketing is about presenting what you do to the outside world. But it rests, fundamentally, upon what you do being something that people will want to know about. Without a good quality 'product', all the marketing in the world won't be able to make the difference. You can get a long way by telling everyone that your school is excellent, or very good or however you choose to describe it. It is possible to convince many people for a short time just by telling them often enough. But marketing is fundamentally about the quality of the service you provide, and hence it is about the contents of all the preceding chapters in this book. If you get all of the other stuff right then, for the most part the school will sell itself. If insufficient attention is paid to it then, in the end, no one will be interested.

Epilogue

The village master taught his little school;
A man severe he was, and stern to view,
I knew him well and every truant knew;
Well had the boding tremblers learned to trace
The day's disasters in his morning face;
Full well they laughed with counterfeited glee,
At all his jokes, for many a joke had he;
Full well the busy whisper circling round,
Conveyed the dismal tidings when he frowned;
Yet he was kind, or if severe in aught,
The love he bore to learning was in fault;
The village all declared how much he knew;
'Twas certain he could write, and cipher too;

Oliver Goldsmith (1730–74), The Deserted Village

Few would argue that education has become of increasing importance both politically and socially over the recent years. The plethora of initiatives designed to raise the standards achieved by the nation's children are testament to the imperative of the task that teachers and indeed society faces.

If ever people were in doubt on the importance of schooling, then scanning the press will underline this point. Each year the *Sunday Times* produces a guide for parents on the best schools. In 2003 the supplement was entitled *The Sunday Times: Parent Power* with a subtitle of 'How to choose the best education for your child'. It is no longer about what is given must be received, it is instead about how parents exercise their choice to ensure that the best quality education is received by their child. The position adopted by the *Sunday Times* is that more information equals more choice. It developed its own methodology to 'reveal' how many pupils get the top A* and A grades at GCSE, identifying the schools achieving the very best results at 16. There are tips for parents to help to get a place for their child at a school of their choice.

Litigation has been a growth area for lawyers with a specialism in educational law. The emergence of the General Teaching Council where teachers can be 'struck off', together with stories of embezzlement, fraudulent practice, misuse of exam papers and so on have added to the stories of the law relating to teachers. Parents have been sent to prison for failing to send their children to school, teachers have been convicted of failing to look after children on trips with sufficient care. Add these up and we have a very different school scene from the one where the teacher, and the especially the headteacher was a revered and respected person in the country village.

Paints a grim picture? Surely not. Our contention in this book is that there are some things that schools must do, but there are far more things that schools should do and still more that they could do. Creating a culture where the discretionary part is the dominant feature of the schools business is surely the way forward. In some ways identifying what has to be done is the easy bit (although getting it done can be somewhat more problematic on occasions) but creating and sustaining the environment where the discretionary part is the dominant feature is the journey that the preceding chapters has sought to demonstrate.

In Chapter 1 we started off asserting that for us running a school is the best job there is. To judge from the public face of school leadership it would appear that heads are pawns in the game of education. They are set targets by – well practically everyone – there is a constant stream of bureaucracy landing almost daily on the desks of heads from local and national government, there is apparently increasing indiscipline within schools and decreasing parental support – and whatever powers heads did have to deal with these are being gradually removed. Heads have to manage everything with no money, are generally held responsible for all the ills of society and preside over declining standards as evidenced by improving or worsening results. On the face of it there doesn't seem to be much going for the job of secondary headteacher. We hope that our discussion of the issues that we determine have shown that, if anything, we are the chess masters and those who seek to determine the game are in fact the pawns – it is schools that determine their futures not the so-called political masters.

We went on to say that there are many people who make up the school community – the stakeholders as they are often called – the children, parents, governors and the local community. These are relationships that can validate so much of the work of the leadership team and as such can be intensely rewarding and positive. So while for much of the time many headteachers find themselves spending huge amounts of time looking after their governors, it is our contention that this time is worthwhile, because a governing body working well and taking part in the work of the school genuinely can add value. Spending time sorting out the difficulties that children face – sometimes of their own making – is the fabric of the school. Working closely with teachers in meetings gobbles up time, and time is one of our most valuable resources and its use must be prioritized in the same way as, in fact even more carefully than, any other resource. Time is a tricky chap; it evaporates if you let it.

The crux of the matter when creating an achievement culture and a well-disciplined learning environment is to be completely clear about your vision for the school. You must, above all else, know what you want it to be like and be certain that you can achieve this. Culture is about the way people act and the words people use. They will take their lead from the headteacher and the leadership team. It is vital that you and your team live the vision.

It is still very much the case that in creating your culture you must always be aware of what you say and how you say it. Words are your most powerful tool and have the greatest impact. Your vision will be about positive outcomes and so you must make your language positive, you must be upbeat, but also you must be able to empathize when others find it difficult. Empathy, but not sympathy. Any exchange that you have must be about reinforcing the culture and meaning of your school.

Part of living the vision is the absolute knowledge that there are solutions to the problems you face. Schools, being human organizations, are messy places. Things are often far from simple and there are many occasions when events will conspire to obscure the clarity of your vision. You must develop a sixth sense to feel the onset of this descending fog. Re-focus and maintain your clear sense of direction. The solutions you are looking for may not be quick, or simple, but that they are there is, and must remain, beyond dispute. If things are not the way you wish them to be, then no one else is going to change them if you don't and so first and foremost this is the responsibility of leadership.

Schools are part of the society they serve – as such they are integral – they shape society and are shaped by society. There is an interdependence of the culture of a school with the dominant discourse of the local community. Where the school is a strength, the local community is strengthened by its presence – where it is weak the community structure is dealt a blow. The imperative this creates for school leaders is considerable but it is something that defines the importance of education. The outcome of a person's education lives with them for the rest of their lives – the outcomes of a teacher's experience lives with them for the rest of their lives. But as school leaders we can make that difference. We can set the compass – we can do the things that are set out in this book to create a cultural hegemony that will enable us to make the space do what we must do, but also lead us towards realizing the 'would, should, could' that defines and sets apart our place in education history.

Where to next perhaps? The late nineties were dominated by a system that was highly directive. Responsibility was located in the corridors of the DfES and accountability in the offices of schools. Now, the level of micro-management needed to hold this all together was unsustainable and undesirable – it needed to be transitional so that it could move from the transactional to the transformational. How could this be achieved and sustained? – well, perhaps the only way to make this a plausible and sustainable way of doing things was to adopt an entirely new mantra for the leadership of our schools.

First, the emphasis is on decentralization. For leaders this means an earned autonomy. It means that if you run a highly efficient and effective school then you can strike out. It means also that if you are strong, know your school and its context, you can determine the agenda of your school and move onward with this to the fore. Good examples are to specialize and such initiatives as Leading Edge and Beacon. Specialism offers schools opportunities to develop their own distinctive curriculum; schools are no longer bound by a rigid curriculum that insists on a modern foreign language and a technology subject being studied throughout key stage 4. There is the opportunity to create a distinctive curriculum choice. Of course this new dimension provides schools with the opportunity for a new wave of marketing; it is important that the specialism that is chosen is reflected in the cultural ethos of the school. We might argue that this opportunity for decentralization is predicated by a need to submit a lengthy application to the DfES – and, of course, applying for the opportunity to create a distinctive curriculum is part of the bargain that is struck. It is, however, the case that if government is going to take risks with the quality of children's education then safeguards must be in place. However, much of the opportunity for this decentralization is bought at the price of applications, reviews and submissions – but the question arises: what impact does this have on the staff of the school? Is it the case that what is decentralized for the leadership team is in fact a new level of directive leadership for the departments and individual teachers? If this is the case, then it is a missed opportunity; it fails to acknowledge that successful schools are culturally bound places; there is a dominant culture that is enabling in that it creates a climate for risk taking and the capacity for growth. This requires a new definition of what it is to be a school leader.

Secondly, it is distributed. Again, if you lead an organization where the leadership is distributed then you are in a position of strength.

What does a school where the leadership is distributed look like? First, it is a school where roles and responsibilities are clearly defined – there is absolute clarity on who is responsible for what. This isn't about a hierarchically defined process where decisions have to be passed up a chain and then are communicated from one to another – it is about saying that one person performing a particular role is responsible for a particular function – and this is not only defined in utilitarian terms – it might be the welfare of a group of pupils. Secondly, this clearly defined responsibility is balanced by increasingly high levels of accountability. Not only is this accountability defined in terms of the function but also in terms of the behaviours of the organization. Put simply, each person in a leadership role is accountable for their behaviour and the performance of the team they manage. If we start from a position that all members of the school are in a leadership role then it therefore follows that all are accountable; we want this high level of accountability so this is predicated by distributed leadership. Perhaps we need to think for a moment about what this means for the headteacher.

Does distributing the leadership of the school make the headteacher a less powerful figure? Not at all. In our view it makes the headteacher a more powerful figure – the power and authority of the office is necessary and sufficient to carry out the job as it stands. However, in order to build an organization, the power and authority must be shared within and across the organization – indeed if it all depends on the headteacher there is no organization. A school that is dependent so entirely on the headteacher is one that cannot function when the person isn't there (and by the person we might mean literally the person who does the job – i.e. Mr Smith, Mrs Jones – but also the person who occupies the office); it is a group of people who flounder otherwise – that in our view is not an organization at all. It is necessary to pause for a moment to think about this notion of distributed leadership; as leaders we have to be careful that we know what it is and just as importantly know what it is not. We know of a school that prides itself on the quality of its leadership – the leadership team are keen to express their faith in the distributed leadership model they share. They illustrated this to us by telling us about their budget-setting process; there is an amount of money that is allocated to departments via a formula (this is pretty standard – there is a standard amount per pupil taught and weighted by the number of lessons and the costs of teaching the subject – it being more expensive to teach science than say, history), the rest being allocated via curriculum applications (or bids in their parlance) – the leadership team assess the quality of each bid and allocate funds accordingly. Sounds good. Further, when heads of department want to spend the money they are allocated they fill out an order form that is authorized by the deputy head – to check that they are spending the money as agreed. This is the point at which any notion of a distributed leadership model falls down – surely if there is shared leadership and executive authority, such people can be trusted to spend the money as agreed but be held accountable for it in some kind of monitoring and evaluation process that underpins the ways in which the school evaluates its work? This is the crazy situation of pre-LMS days explained in Chapter 4 where all spending decisions were made and carried out and actioned by someone else – it is restrictive practice but on a different scale.

To make this new paradigm we come to the third element. The approach is highly disciplined. We ask the question – how do we trust people? Is the organization characterized by trust? What does trust mean? Literally trust is about doing what you say and saying what you do. But trust is built up and sustained through quality working relationships. It is about thinking to yourself – having had that conversation with that person that I know that this is the way they act. It is about responding positively when you find out that your hopes were well founded and taking action when they weren't. Quality working relationships do begin with clearly defined responsibilities and also with an acceptance that you have to trust people because you can't do it all yourself. People are responsible for their behaviour and accountable for those areas that have been defined for them – but also we have a responsibility to the profession to develop the capacity for leadership in our staff. To do this means a high level of discipline at all layers of the organization. There must be clarity about the teaching process, clarity about what a performance review is, clarity about what it means to lead an area, clarity about the vision. The vision has to be shared if it is to be realized; it cannot be random, instead it should be articulated – and often. Reminders of the vision – whether manifested in mission statements or other means – are only powerful forces to change people's perceptions of themselves if they are underpinned and constantly refreshed and renewed by the culture of the organization. For us this is manifested clearly in our approach to programmes of study – each department has a programme of study that has lesson-by-lesson plans, each with a set of learning outcomes. This means that there is clarity about what is to be taught; there is advice on how it is to be taught and a process by which students and their teachers can evaluate progress through assessment. Is this highly directive? – we don't think so – we think it is disciplined; it is about having a minimum quality standard that frees teachers to think about the how rather than about the what. It is an acknowledgment of the cyclical nature of the curriculum – that it is easier to update something than re-create it each year, that where teachers work on curriculum planning in a collaborative manner, the sum of the parts is greater than the whole.

In this book we have devoted our attention to the principles and values that underpin the way in which we run our school and how to run a school successfully – as we do. There has been very little on such matters as schemes of work, policies on teaching and learning and . . . we are sure that the reader will have some others that he feels have not been tackled in sufficient depth. All of this has been deliberate. The most important work that goes on in any school is what happens in every classroom. How it happens is as much about why it happens and as much about the impact it has.

We visited a school recently where the timetable is published in March of the preceding academic year. As a school that publishes it during July we asked how they did this. We were told that the timetable 'rolls over' – the curriculum is set, children make choices within tightly defined parameters, staffing levels are pretty stable and therefore if any changes need to be made they are minor – or where they are more seismic then the necessary compromises are a con- sequence of the predetermined structure. It seemed to us that the administration and organization was the driver for the curriculum rather than in our model where the needs of the students were the driver for the curriculum. We have moved to a position where students have their own copy of the timetable in advance of the end of term – nothing remarkable here – but the following event explains something about why this is important. We had agreed a deadline for set changes – this was to be a week before the end of term – this was so we could do a full timetable print-out for students during the last week. Various events conspired and the head of one department had done a deal with the registrar and submitted them on the penultimate day of term. The registrar's view was that printing out the timetables was a job that could wait for the holidays, the children would lose them anyway. They may lose them – but would we take that view with teachers? – of course not. We would all assert that if teachers are going to prepare for lessons then they need to know! Why is it different for children?

We think that these events really cut to the heart of what it means to run a school successfully. Everyone matters. No one person is worth more than any other. No one person has more rights than any other. If it isn't right for a child to shout at a teacher, it isn't right for a teacher to shout at a child. If it isn't right for a child to swear at a teacher, it isn't right for a teacher to swear at a child.

The debate on teaching and learning is an ever-present one – it is very much about realizing the potential of students. The principles we have discussed – about the way in which we lead the school – start from the position that we are the compass bearers – we set the direction – but that the vision is one that is shaped by the organization as it moves forward. Premises and the budget are very important elements of the whole-school experience for a school leader – and they should be. How can we expect children to behave as considerate, respectful young people with a heightened awareness of their shared community, if the facilities we provide for them are dirty, antiquated and unpleasant? A wealthy country with high standards of living should have high expectations of the quality of education that is provided; and this is not only about what happens in the classroom but also the corridors, eating areas, toilets and on the bus to and from school. This means however, that school leaders have to think in new ways – the most important work is teaching and learning – and a model that is highly personalized. Personalized learning is about the teacher knowing exactly what each child can do and having a teaching programme that addresses what they need to do. Moreover, it is about the child knowing what they can do, what they need to do to improve and being guided to do it. For a child to be able to have the three elements in their personalized learning programme demands clarity of process and expectation. It is also highly inclusive of the child; it implies a different relationship with the child in the class – he or she is not a passive recipient of the teacher's knowledge, more an active participant in the pursuit of learning.

Taking it all – leadership, working with governors, sorting the money out, scheduling the curriculum, developing the work of the school, creating a learning climate and a place where staff want to and can work – is a tall order for a small group of people responsible for a large organization. Doing all this can be a challenge. When it works it is the best thing ever – but commitment to the vision is important. Is it doable? – yes it is. It is about working together so that the big things get sorted and the small aspects are not forgotten. All this is in pursuit of the greatest prize in education – the realization of the potential of the community we serve.

Index